Making the Local News

Local journalism in context

Edited by
Bob Franklin and David Murphy

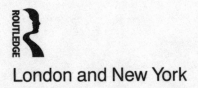

London and New York

First published 1998
by Routledge
11 New Fetter Lane, London EC4P 4EE

Simultaneously published in the USA and Canada
by Routledge
29 West 35th Street, New York, NY 10001

Typeset in Garamond by RefineCatch Limited, Bungay, Suffolk
Printed and bound in Great Britain by Clays Ltd, St Ives PLC

British Library Cataloguing in Publication Data
A catalogue record for this book is available from the British Library

Library of Congress Cataloguing in Publication Data
Making the local news: local journalism in context/
[edited by] Bob Franklin and David Murphy.
Includes bibliographical references and index.
1. Journalism – Great Britain – History.   2. Journalism, Regional –
Great Britain.   3. Local mass media – Great Britain.
I. Franklin, Bob.   II. Murphy, David.
PN5124.L65M36   1998
072 – dc21   97–32618

ISBN 0–415–16802–3 (hbk)
ISBN 0–415–16803–1 (pbk)

Contents

Tables

Contributors

Richard Beamish is Head of Development, Education and Training at the Newspaper Society.

Peter Cole is Professor of Journalism at the University of Central Lancashire. He was founding editor of the *Sunday Correspondent* and deputy editor of the *Guardian*.

Andrew Crisell lectures on media and communication at the University of Sunderland. He is the author of *Understanding Radio* (1986) and *An Introductory History of Broadcasting* (1997), both of which are published by Routledge.

Rachel Eyre is a research student at the Centre for Mass Communications Research, University of Leicester. She has a research interest in the local media and is currently examining media coverage of women in the 1997 general election.

Bob Franklin is Reader in Media and Communications at the University of Sheffield. His publications include *Newszak and News Media* (1997), *Packaging Politics* (1994) and, with David Murphy, *What News? The Market, Politics and the Local Press* (1991).

Gregor Gall is a lecturer in industrial relations at the University of Stirling.

Brent Garner is the Central Division Director of the Central Office of Information's Regional Network. He has worked previously as a journalist and at the Open University.

Mike Glover is Editor of the Westmorland Gazette. He was previously Editor-in-Chief of Newsquest York, which publishes the *Evening Press*, York, the *Yorkshire Gazette and Herald* and the *York Star* series. He formerly edited *Yorkshire on Sunday* and the Bradford *Telegraph and Argus*.

Tony Harcup is a freelance journalist based in Yorkshire. He writes on media, cultural and urban issues and is the author of *A Northern Star: Leeds Other Paper and the Alternative Press 1974–1994* (1994). He also works in journalism training.

Shirley Harrison lectures on public relations, the media and local government at Leeds Metropolitan University and the Emergency Planning College, and works independently as a consultant in these fields. She was formerly Head of Public Relations for Sheffield council. Her publications include *Public Relations: An Introduction* (1995).

Andrew Leather is a researcher at the Manchester School of Management at UMIST. He has recently completed his doctorate on local newspaper reporting of economic and business news.

David Murphy worked as a local journalist during the 1960s and was news editor of the *New Manchester Review*. He is Senior Lecturer at the Manchester School of Management at UMIST and has written several books on the local press, including *The Silent Watchdog: The Press in Local Politics* (1974) and *The Stalker Affair and the Press* (1992).

Ralph Negrine is Senior Lecturer at the Centre for Mass Communications Research, University of Leicester. His main areas of research and teaching include political communication and media policy; his book publications include *Politics and the Mass Media* (1994) and *The Communication of Politics* (1996).

Jon Parry is a researcher in the Department of Politics at the University of Sheffield; he is working on models of politicial activism in the Labour and Conservative parties. He is co-author of *Labour and Conservative Party Members: Social Characteristics, Political Attitudes and Activities* (1995).

Rod Pilling began his career on the *Birmingham Evening Mail* in 1972. He is currently Head of the Department of Media and Communications at the Birmingham Institute of Art and Design at the University of Central England in Birmingham.

Robert Pinker is Privacy Commissioner for the Press Complaints Commission.

Karen Ross is Director of Research in the Faculty of Business and Social Studies at Cheltenham and Gloucester College of Higher Education. She has researched and published extensively on 'race' and media policy and is the author of *Black and White Media* (1996).

John Short lectures at Trinity and All Saints College, Leeds. He has worked previously as a journalist and for the Central Office of Information.

Peta Van den Bergh is a freelance journalist, broadcaster, writer and media trainer, with ten years' experience as a full-time trade union official negotiating on behalf of freelances. Recently she has been acting as an 'agony aunt' for freelances, writing a regular fortnightly column in the *Press Gazette*. She wrote and produced the audio cassette histories of the TUC and the Labour Party.

Granville Williams teaches journalism and media policy at the University of Huddersfield, is a member of the National Council of the Campaign for Press and Broadcasting Freedom and edits the CPBF journal *Free Press*. He is the author of *Britain's Media: How they are Related* (1996).

Introduction

Local news in a cold climate

Bob Franklin and David Murphy

Readers will not need to possess the forensic skills of Sherlock Holmes to spot some divergence of views among the contributors to this collection of writings on the local media. This deviation from the Blairite doctrine of rigid uniformity stems from our desire to include the perspectives of academics, critics, public relations specialists, media regulators, government information officers, broadcasters, journalists and editors among whom, as a matter of fact, experiences and perceptions often overlap but do not always coincide. As the biographical vignettes reveal, many of the authors have had careers which combine several of the viewpoints indicated, reinforcing further the pluralism evident throughout the book.

The chapters by ourselves and Andrew Crisell, for instance, indicate that local media are experiencing a bleak present and a worse future. Mike Glover on the other hand suggests that the local press is strong and growing stronger. Ralph Negrine and Rachel Eyre argue that local media will survive so long as they continue to complement each other by providing a combination of national and local news, with leisure and feature articles, while also offering an outlet for local advertising. Rod Pilling adds to the variety by showing that any tendency to compare a grey present with a rosy past is undermined by a careful scrutiny of a journalistic past which derives its hue less from its character than from the bloodshot eyes of oldtimers stooped in nostalgia for printer's ink, hot metal, trips on the office bicycle to meetings with informants and long lunchtimes in the high street pub.

A number of themes arising from various interrelated characteristics must, however, inform any understanding of the local media in their present stage of development. The first is the development of new technology which has substantially changed the face of the local media. From a time in the life of the currently middle-aged when there was only a print-based medium, we have moved via the addition of local radio in the hands of a monopoly and then a duopoly, to the current situation where the range of 'choice' in local media is burgeoning and where local and regional television stand on the brink of massive expansions reflecting the opportunities created by digital and cable technologies. At the same time, changed print technology has revolutionised the production methods, the distribution and the possibilities for innovation in the local and regional press. We explore some of the issues that arise from these developments in the first section of the book.

These technological changes have had particular effects on the economics and range of the local and regional media. Changes in ownership are not simply manifested in a greater concentration and conglomeration, but in a greater fluidity as a continuing condition of the corporate structure of the industry (chapter 6). This is reflected in a constant search for ever cheaper methods of production and ever greater financial returns. The outcome is local media which are increasingly geared to the market with an editorial focus on entertainment, advertising and 'lifestyle' journalism while labour costs are kept to a minimum. This is reflected on the one hand in the training of multiskilled journalists and on the other in the aggressive industrial relations policies of the employees. This enables Gregor Gall (chapter 7) to bemoan the attrition of union bargaining while Mike Glover (chapter 9) is able to celebrate the business success of the local press.

In the context of the advance of the corporate media giants not only has the typically left-wing alternative press succumbed to the market, as Tony Harcup shows (chapter 8); the free newspaper enterprises established by Thatcherite swashbuckling entrepreneurs have also been swallowed by the corporate giants (chapter 10).

Underlying the arguments by the authors in this volume is the perennial tension between the news media as businesses and as institutions of democracy. This is poignantly illustrated by Granville Williams (chapter 4) who shows how the advent of local cable television is pushing newspaper owners, recognising that the local press is in decline, to respond with attempts to 'muscle in' to local broadcasting in order to survive as a newspaper business. And in doing so, they are planning to economise on costs by training the same journalists to provide news materials for a number of different media outlets which will appear to the audience to be in competition with one another; this provides a prima facie case for believing that the logic of the market will lead to the elimination of possibilities for choice and pluralism.

Finally, a number of contributors explore the editorial content of local media and its significance in a changing context. Particular chapters consider local newspapers' coverage of economic and business news (chapter 18), recent general elections (chapter 16) and the way in which 'race' is reported (chapter 17). Rod Pilling (chapter 14) suggests that the force of market imperatives may have had much less effect on local news reporting than many have suggested, while Robert Pinker (chapter 19) argues that local newspapers are insufficiently distinctive from national newspapers – so far as the complaints they generate among readers are concerned – to warrant a separate system of regulation.

In sharp contrast to the view of local newspapers, offered by Robert Park in 1920s' Chicago through to David Morgan and Harvey Cox in the UK in the 1970s, which suggested newspapers occupied a world of enduring stasis, the local media are now characterised by remorseless change.

REFERENCES

Morgan, D. and Cox, H. (1974) *City Politics and the Press*, Cambridge: Cambridge University Press.
Park, R. E. (1929) *The Immigrant Press and Its Control*, New York: Harper.

Part I

Local newspapers and local media

Chapter 1

Changing times: local newspapers, technology and markets

Bob Franklin and David Murphy

Of all the news media that were in existence in the UK in the immediate postwar period, local newspapers seemed the most staid and traditional. Yet in the subsequent half century, the local press has proved to be the most prone to innovation, instability and structural change. This chapter explores these changes and their implications for local newspapers.

STABILITY, COMMUNITY AND THE LOCAL PRESS

Until the early 1970s, the terms 'local media' and 'local newspapers' were co-terminus. Local papers, moreover, were simply updated versions of those that had been founded in an upsurge of business innovation in the latter half of the nineteenth century (Franklin and Murphy, 1991: 55–6; Hayes, 1996). The way in which journalists worked – in terms of the way that they produced news as well as the clear distinction between editorial activity and advertising – had been established since the beginning of the twentieth century as a result of moves by journalists' organisations to establish themselves as a professional group with skills and responsibilities which were part of the democratic civic process. The ownership of local and regional newspapers was the outcome of a process of acquisition of smaller papers by larger ones and by newspaper chains. The emergent pattern was one of consolidation of what was already there in a *de facto* system of local monopolies – definitely not one of innovation. The number of local newspapers was in slow decline. Competition among big city evening papers except at the periphery of their circulation areas ended in 1964 when the *Manchester Evening Chronicle* closed down despite sales of a quarter of a million and ceded the regional monopoly to the *Manchester Evening News*.

The circulation of newspapers sold was also in slow decline, in the face of competition at first with the national press. Up until the interwar period the majority of working-class readers acquired their knowledge of the world as well as local affairs from their local daily newspapers. The content of the local press was also by and large an updated version of what it had been for at least half a century. Local morning and evening papers ran national and international stories predominantly sourced from freelance agencies such as the Press Association. Both daily and weekly papers provided local 'civic' news and features based on information from the local councils, courts, police and fire services and the Coroner's Office (see chapter 9). In this way they established the social and political reality of abstractions associated with the municipality, such as the magistracy, and gave substance to place names such as Bedford, Nottingham or Reading. Other news stories were sourced from local churches, chambers of trade, amateur dramatic societies, schools, Townswomens' Guilds, Rotary Clubs, sports clubs, gardening associations, local businesses and local branches of national businesses. These substantiated in narratives the ideas of the local community and local business. The world portrayed in such papers was a comfortable conservative world of institutional stability, focused on a locality with a population whose inhabitants were identified with their community which generally shared its boundaries with a municipality and a world of local business activity.

Even the technology on which the local newspapers were printed was only an improved version of the hot-metal typesetting and printing processes developed in the nineteenth century; the industrial relations between management and the men (literally) who operated these systems was based on a trade union structure of even greater antiquity. The National Union of Journalists (NUJ), the trade union which negotiated for journalists, was, in many respects, based upon the model of organisation of the skilled manual unions in the printing industry.

Journalists were organised nationally and negotiated pay rates accordingly, with the then national 'Fleet Street' newsrooms on the top scales, while wages on local papers varied according to the size of the population in a circulation area and whether journalists worked on a weekly or daily (morning or evening) local paper. In this sense the job of the journalist was seen as undifferentiated, using the same skills and relying on the same professional ethics regardless of where or on what paper the journalist was employed. It only varied in terms of gradation of pay and status from the local weekly to the Fleet Street newsroom.

This was reflected in the training of journalists (see chapter 5). Most of them were non-graduates who learnt their craft at work, under the auspices of the National Council for the Training of Journalists (NCTJ) – a joint employer–union body. The place in which the training took place was routinely the local press, where youngsters on leaving school first worked as reporters before moving on to the regional evening press and subsequently to Fleet Street. The normal career pattern of the national daily journalists was one which had begun in the local press. The vast majority of journalists were male. Women reporters at that time still existed only in small numbers and were generally allocated 'women's work': articles to do with cookery, clothes and shopping, the editing of children's competition pages.

Much of the vocabulary which is employed in the description of the local press, often by its owners and employers, is steeped in the assumptions of this past. But more radical and extensive changes have taken place in the local press than in any other news media which existed three decades ago. Local newspapers, in terms of their ownership, distribution, productive technology, the employment and training of their journalists and the competitive market in which they are obliged to operate, constitute a set of phenomena which can no longer be explained by reference merely to the 'local'. The local press must be analysed in the setting of national media but increasingly local newspapers must be located in the context of a global media system.

LOCAL NEWSPAPERS: DEVELOPMENTS AND CHANGE

Seven significant and closely connected changes have radically altered the essential character of Britain's local press. The last three decades have witnessed: a continuing decline in the number of local newspaper titles and their circulations; the emergence of free newspapers with their important consequences for the paid-for newspaper market; newspapers' increasing commitments to publishing 'advertorial' (articles which are a hybrid between advertising and editorial) rather than political or other news; managements' eagerness to introduce new production technologies; the casualisation of the profession of journalism manifest in the explosion of freelance working and growing job insecurity for local journalists; the tendency for local newspapers to become tabloid in size and content; and changing patterns of ownership of the local press.

Fewer and fewer people are reading fewer and fewer local newspapers as circulations and numbers of local press titles continue a long-term downward trend (Franklin and Murphy, 1997). Table 1.1 reveals the mixed fortunes enjoyed by the different newspapers which constitute the local press. Regional morning papers have suffered only a modest (6.5 per cent) drop in circulations from 1.24 million in 1981 to 1.16 million daily sales in 1996, while the reduction in evening paper circulations from 5.74 million to 4.2 million has been more dramatic (27 per cent).

Circulations of weekly paid-for papers have plummeted from 9.7 to 6.2 million, a 36 per cent decrease across fifteen years. Numbers of published titles have also declined. Morning papers reduced slightly from 18 to 17, evenings from 79 to 72 but weekly paid-for papers from 915 to 478, a 48 per cent contraction of titles. There are some horror stories when Audit Bureau of Circulation (ABC) figures are compared for the eight years between 1988 and 1996. The *Manchester Evening News* circulation dropped from 276,665 to 183,543 (34 per cent decline); similar figures for the *Swindon Evening Advertiser* are 37,177 to 25,755 (−31 per cent) and for the *Southend Evening Echo* 61,716 to 46,072 (−26 per cent). *Kent Today* suffered a 13 per cent reduction in circulation in a single year (1995–6).

Table 1.1 Local newspapers: declining circulations (in millions) and numbers of published titles, 1981–96

Type	1981	1982	1983	1984	1985	1986	1987	1988	1989	1990	1991	1992	1993	1994	1995	1996	% change
Mornings	1.24	1.29	1.27	1.27	1.27	1.56	1.52	1.51	1.56	1.55	1.26	1.25	1.23	1.24	1.20	1.16	-6.5
	18	18	18	18	18	17	17	17	17	17	17	17	17	17	17	17	-5.6
Evenings	5.74	5.63	5.39	5.38	5.32	5.31	5.22	5.15	5.1	5.01	4.83	4.67	4.54	4.41	4.29	4.19	-27
	79	79	78	74	73	72	72	72	72	73	70	70	70	71	72	72	-8.7
Sundays	0.58	0.54	0.42	0.41	0.41	0.4	0.39	0.46	0.51	0.5	0.51	0.89	1.03	0.98	0.77	0.78	+25.6
	5	5	4	4	4	4	4	6	7	7	7	9	9	10	9	9	+80
Weekly paid-for	9.7	9.9	9.1	8.6	8.2	7.5	7.3	7.6	7.4	6.8	6.7	7.1	7	6.7	6.6	6.22	-35.6
	915	880	812	812	749	696	569	548	492	434	448	473	477	473	473	478	-47.6
Weekly free	15.3	22.6	29.9	31.8	35.5	36.3	37.4	39.3	42	41.3	37.2	34.5	33.1	33.4	31.7	28.02	+83.1
	494	520	653	731	843	882	879	852	821	802	722	691	667	685	713	630	+27.5
Total	32.56	39.96	46.08	47.46	50.70	51.07	51.83	54.02	56.57	55.16	50.50	48.41	46.90	46.73	44.56	40.37	+24.0
	1,511	1,502	1,565	1,639	1,687	1,671	1,541	1,495	1,409	1,333	1,264	1,260	1,240	1,256	1,284	1,206	+20.2

Source: Newspaper Society Database, 1997

The news is not all bad. The Sunday regional/national papers such as *Scotland on Sunday* and *Wales on Sunday* have increased both in terms of numbers of titles (from 5 to 9) and circulations (0.58 to 0.78 million) although in each case it is growth from a very modest base. Free newspapers remain the most vital element in the local press although their growth has been halted from a peak in the late 1980s. But their expansive distribution figures (from 15.3 to 28 million [+83 per cent]) and their increased number of titles (from 494 to 630 [+28 per cent]) account for the overall increase in local newspaper circulations across the period 1981–96; but free newspapers' expansion could not disguise the decline in overall local newspaper titles from 1,511 to 1,206 (−20.2 per cent).

This decline in circulations and titles has had a predictable impact on revenues from copy sales and advertising revenues.

Table 1.2 illustrates that revenues from both advertising and sales have declined for all paid-for regional and local newspapers. Only the expansion of free newspaper advertising revenues, returning in 1996 to their 1989 peak figure of £629 million, has 'bailed out' the aggregate local newspaper revenue totals which show a modest increase from £1,997 million in 1987 to £2,052 million in 1997. Free newspapers of course cannot help to salvage the substantive decline (18 per cent) in revenues from copy sales which fell from £458 to £397 million between 1987 and 1996. Perhaps unsurprisingly, regional newspapers' share of total advertising revenues for all media declined from 25.8 per cent in 1980 to 20.6 per cent in 1996 (*Advertising Statistics Yearbook 1997*).

The second, but undoubtedly the most significant, development in the local press was the emergence of free newspapers or 'free sheets', as they were initially and disparagingly named, during the 1970s and 1980s (see chapter 10). The free newspapers simply extended to its logical conclusion the financing of the local press which was already heavily and increasingly reliant on advertising (see table 1.2). At first the free newspapers seemed to be a marginal irritant to the established order: local entrepreneurs, often estate agents, set up papers largely filled with advertising and simply gave them away to every home in a circulation area. They generally carried little news and editorial was often simply a pot pourri of public relations handouts from local authorities (see chapter 12), the information services of central government (see chapter 13), local businesses (see chapter 18), pressure groups and political parties (see chapter 16). Letters from readers offered a further and significant source of cheap copy. Free newspapers also carried a large amount of 'advertorial' articles. A major problem for this editorial format, however, was that advertisers promptly came to realise that if readers perceived these newspapers as being 'newsless' they diverted them directly from the letterbox to the dustbin.

Consequently, many of the new ventures either failed quickly or were compelled to become more akin to the traditional local newspaper. The usual

Table 1.2 Regional and local newspapers' total net revenues, 1987–96 (constant prices, in £ million)

	1987	1988	1989	1990	1991	1992	1993	1994	1995	1996
Dailies and Sundays										
From advertising	721	799	825	755	656	625	632	667	680	702
From copy sales	391	392	372	374	352	363	365	362	345	335
Total	1,113	1,191	1,198	1,129	1,008	988	997	1,030	1,025	1,037
Paid-for weeklies										
From advertising	328	372	365	329	301	285	290	311	313	324
From copy sales	66	68	63	65	59	58	61	62	63	62
Total	395	440	429	394	360	343	351	373	376	386
All paid-for newspapers										
From advertising	1,049	1,173	1,191	1,084	957	910	922	979	993	1,026
From copy sales	458	460	436	439	411	422	426	424	409	397
Total	1,507	1,631	1,627	1,523	1,368	1,331	1,348	1,403	1,402	1,423
Free weeklies										
From advertising	490	603	629	578	540	545	574	614	622	629
All regional newspapers										
From advertising	1,539	1,774	1,819	1,662	1,497	1,453	1,496	1,592	1,615	1,655
From copy sales	458	460	436	439	411	422	426	424	409	397
Total	1,997	2,234	2,256	2,101	1,908	1,876	1,922	2,017	2,024	2,052

Source: Advertising Statistics Yearbook 1997

process of agglomeration through combinations and takeovers took place, accelerated by the largely defensive response of the existing newspaper combines. These either took over the competitor free newspaper, started up their own or converted their paid-for titles to free papers. And although the emergent product had more editorial content than the first tacky give-aways they replaced, these new papers were more advertising dominated than their traditional predecessors.

But successful free newspapers have dominated the local newspaper market in terms of the number of published titles, and the advertising revenues they generate, since the late 1980s. The growth of free newspapers was breathtaking: from 185 titles in 1975 to almost 900 in 1986. Distribution figures expanded at an equivalent rate from 15 million in 1981 to almost 40 million in 1988. In 1970 advertising revenue was £2 million but by 1981 it had mushroomed to £100 million; by 1987 it was almost £500 million (Press Council, 1987: 328). The phenomenon was widespread throughout Europe. By 1986 an estimated 4,000 free newspapers distributed 200 million copies throughout Europe (Porter, 1986: 7). Traditional newspaper groups were attracted to free newspapers because of the advertising revenues and high profit potential which they promised. By the end of the 1980s, the major traditional newspaper publishing groups had purchased nine of the ten largest free newspaper groups which in aggregate accounted for slightly more than half (20,412,481 copies) the free newspaper production and distribution in the UK (Franklin and Murphy, 1991: 11–12).

The third development in local newspapers is a major consequence of the free newspaper 'revolution'; namely the general move towards the pursuit of advertising and to the use of the editorial pages as a means of attracting advertising (see chapter 18). So far as free newspapers were concerned, this simply reflected the operation of an increasingly competitive market. After all, if the supplier of a product wishes to survive, she or he has to satisfy the demands of customers and, if advertisers are paying the full costs of a newspaper's production, then they *are* the customers. Bowing to these pressures, the content of the local press began to shift from its previous emphasis on the municipal and the political towards the provision of information about consumption. The production of advertorial became more central to the work of the journalist (see chapter 14). This development in free newspapers triggered a similar emphasis on advertising in paid-for newspapers which operated in the same local markets for advertisers; paid-for newpapers' editorial increasingly mimicked free newspapers' stress on advertorial (Smallman, 1996: 11). These trends contrast strikingly with BBC correspondent Fergal Keane's very affectionate and finely crafted recollections of his first job as a journalist on the *Limerick Leader*. In those days, 'working on a good local paper was the best of all beginnings. I covered everything and travelled every mile of the Irish midwest. Halligan [the editor] had a strong social conscience and encouraged his reporters to take the side of the underdogs, even when that threatened the newspaper's lucrative and vital advertising revenue' (Keane, 1996: 21–2). Such observations illustrate the distance which local newpapers themselves have travelled from such editorial commitments.

But the shift in content has also reflected the decline in the power of local government and the reduction in the number of local authorities. The Heath government's local government reorganisation legislation of 1972 abolished many of the town councils which were served by individual local newspapers. The result was that what had formerly been geographical units, with their own political identity based on a municipality, simply became residential areas with shopping centres hollowed of any political significance. This process was exacerbated during the Thatcher years with the transfer of political decisions to quangos and the reduction of democratic representation in the administration of the police and health services. In this way, much of what had been conducted as part of the public sphere and was open to debate became subsumed into an administrative or quasi-market process which, in the case of the NHS for example, was subject to explicit suppression of open information.

This movement away from the democratic editorial function of the local press towards advertising and consumption was closely connected to a fourth significant development: the introduction of new print technology. It was the very cost advantages which the new technology made possible, which were instrumental in creating the new free newspapers in which advertising was so prominent above editorial.

The introduction of new technology came in two quite distinct phases. The first took place in the 1960s when the *Wolverhampton Star* series went over to Web Offset and abandoned the old hot-metal technology which still dominated the newspaper industry. Other local newspaper series such as the *Wigan Guardian* also innovated with colour printing. This was often done in the context of a gradual consolidation of titles around centralised new printing facilities whose use was maximised by printing as many local editions as could be acquired and by doing contract printing work. Gradually national publishing groups would move in and take over such enterprising local chains. Reed Regional newspapers became the owners of the Tillotsons Newspapers of Bolton and United Newspapers took over the Wigan Guardian group during this period. But in many ways it seemed as if the new technology was being introduced into a system of industrial relations which was fundamentally unchanged, and in the context of a long-established ownership pattern which was characterised by gradual consolidation through mergers and takeovers first by regional and then national or multinational groups. For reasons that lie beyond the scope of this text, this process of technological innovation never spread from the local and regional press into the national press in the UK.

The second phase in the introduction of new technology was more radical and more significant. It followed the introduction of new industrial relations legislation by the Thatcher government in the early 1980s, and it involved the use of computerised typesetting technology which made obsolete the skills possessed by the unionised print workers (Gall, 1996). The battle to introduce the new production methods on terms entirely dictated by management and owners took place at Warrington when Eddie Shah moved the entire production process of his local free-sheet Messenger Group from the old printing works at Stockport, twenty-five miles away (Goodhart and Wintour, 1986). The print unions attempted to take industrial action against the move but the new laws against secondary industrial action and against allegedly intimidatory pickets were used with some enthusiasm by the police and the strike was crushed (Goodhart and Wintour, 1986: 12).

This was significant because Shah's methods were subsequently used by Rupert Murdoch at Wapping and the new technology spread rapidly to the whole of the national and local press. This is not to argue that Shah was the prime mover in the process, but his battle at Warrington certainly marked the definitive end of the old technology for the whole of the newspaper and printing industry in the UK. It was also significant because it marked the beginning of a battle against all the unions in the newspaper industry (Gall, 1996: 93).

Many journalists believed that the demise of the power of the print unions such as the Society of Graphical and Allied Trades (SOGAT) would herald a new golden age for the NUJ, since much of the production work was now transferred into 'Black Box' technology with processes such as on-screen layout and subediting which would logically have given work to NUJ members. This was a logic which arose out of the nature of the new technology and the jobs associated with it. But the process of stripping away union power depended on a different logic. First the new labour laws gave the owners the opportunity to cut costs and control processes and to opt increasingly for personal contracts: they had tried out these powers on the print unions and found them advantageous. Second, the increasing commercial pressures on costs arising from the reasons already referred to, and others we will address below, encouraged owners to seek to find ways of producing newspapers with less and less reliance on journalists, while those who remained would be called on to perform more and more tasks; journalists had to become 'multiskilled' renaissance figures (see chapter 14).

This 'employers' offensive' in the late 1980s and early 1990s led to a widespread withdrawal of recognition from the NUJ as a representative body, and the imposition of individual contracts on journalists. The process of union derecognition meant that many journalists lost their traditional rights to collective bargaining and, more significantly, they lost their job security. This has prompted the fifth significant development for local newspapers; the growing trend towards the casualisation of journalism as permanent staff posts have been replaced by freelances, part-timers and journalists on short-term contracts. One study talks of 'regular casuals' employed for up to three days a week (Tunstall, 1995: 55).

The 1990s have certainly witnessed a rapid expansion in freelance journalism (see chapter 15). It used to be commonplace for journalists to choose freelance work because it offered a greater degree of freedom than a staff journalist's post; now redundancy is the motive for freelance work in one out of three cases (National Union of Journalists, 1994: 12). By 1994, approximately one-third (11,000) journalists were freelance while a further 15 per cent were employed on short-term or part-time contracts (ibid.: 7). Wages for freelance work are poor. It is piece work, with journalists being paid for each line of editorial copy they produce. A news story in a local paper will typically generate £4 (Van den Bergh, 1995: 18). There are other disadvantages. Job insecurity is rife, it is hard to establish copyright on filed stories, extracting payment from newspapers is typically a protracted business and the capital equipment and set-up costs which have to be borne by the journalists are considerable (Keeble, 1994: 315 and Piggott, 1997: 11). Job cuts and union derecognition have had predictable consequences for local journalists' salaries. One in ten journalists earns less than £10,000 a year and one-quarter earn below £15,000; salaries are lower for journalists on local papers than the nationals (NUJ, 1994: 6). Four out of five trainee journalists earn less than £10,000 per annum; little wonder one trainee described his newsroom as 'an understaffed sweatshop' (Guild of Editors, 1995: 5).

The profession of journalism has changed in other ways. It is increasingly a graduate profession in which 48 per cent of entrants have a degree (Delano and Henningham, 1995: 12). Two-thirds of new journalists, moreover, describe themselves as middle class (ibid.: 10). Women journalists now constitute 37 per cent of the profession and promise to outnumber their male colleagues within a decade (NUJ, 1994: 3). But while their numbers are expanding, women are excluded from senior editorial posts (Sebba, 1994: 237), are represented 'disproportionately in the lower earnings bands' (NUJ, 1994: 6) and tend to work in broadcasting, especially local radio and independent television, rather than print journalism (Delano and Henningham, 1995: 9). Regrettably some things never change. In 1994, only fifteen of the estimated 8,000 journalists working in the local press were black or Asian – a remarkable and shocking statistic (Ainley, 1995: 57; see chapter 18)!

The training of journalists has also changed. New technology has rendered many of the journalist's traditional skills obsolete, although debate still rages about whether micro recorders have made shorthand competencies redundant (Delano, 1997). But the expansion of journalism as an undergraduate degree in universities, combined with newspaper companies establishing their own in-house training, has done much to undermine the authority and financing of the NCTJ since the mid 1980s. Local newspapers, however, still offer most new entrants to journalism their first job and consequently still provide a good deal of journalistic training (see chapter 5). A major problem in identifying training needs is that the activity of journalism is constantly changing.

Journalists' specialist skills are increasingly being eroded as managements encourage them to become generalists. In the 'revolutionised' newsroom at the *Birmingham Evening Mail*, for example, subeditors have been replaced by page editors who are all-round multiskilled designers, subs and picture journalists. Their brief is comprehensive and they will 'switch between news, sports and features depending on the pressures of the day'. In the longer term journalists will be required to work on all Midland Independent Newspapers' media outlets; the *Mail's* editor argued that 'one journalist should be capable of covering a story for the company's newspaper, cable, TV and radio output and we will be moving down this route' (Morgan, 1997a: 2; see also chapter 14).

These changes of task are largely driven by the perennial search for cost cutting. The growing tendency to regionalise production – for example UPN's decision in 1996 to centralise the subbing of all their Yorkshire titles in two regional centres – inevitably leads to newspapers' loss of local identity and feel for local news. Some journalists and editors are unhappy about these changes. In August 1997, the editor of the *Pontypool Press* launched a rival paper after the owners centralised subbing at the Bailey Group headquarters fifty miles away; following the move the paper had become 'totally irrelevant to our readership'. The editor claimed the purpose of the new paper was to 'give the people a local newspaper back' (Morgan, 1997b: 5).

These changes in the profession of journalism, its training requirements and the tasks involved in being a journalist, have occurred alongside a re-definition of the very *nature* of local journalism. Local newspapers have become tabloid in both size and content; and at a remarkable rate! In part this was simply following the strategy of national papers, which were moving their emphasis away from hard news towards entertainment and using more of the stories from public relations sources and freelance news agencies, in order to try and stem the haemorrhage of readers and cut editorial costs. The 'tabloiding' of local newspapers has resulted in a 'dumbing down' of the local press. The publication of shorter, brighter, 'frothier' stories and the increasing reliance on stories about entertainment, consumer items and 'human interest' stories, are the infallible hallmarks of the tabloid genre. Typographically it has involved the use of bigger headlines, more pictures, bigger pictures and the use of colour. One journalist cited competition and changes in readers' interests as the cause for this shift to tabloid journalism:

We live in a competitive world, so in the last five years or so we have tweaked our content. We are competing for that 25p for the cover price and I think increasingly we are looking for the lighter story. Readers have become more interested in soundbites or wordbites . . . we are catering for a public which has a grasshopper mentality and therefore you shorten the news items, you go for a big read and keep the story count as high as possible in order to keep your audience's attention.

(Interview, April 1996)

The conversion from broadsheet to tabloid has certainly been rapid and comprehensive. Less than a dozen of the seventy-two local evening papers still publish the broadsheet format and almost half of these operate as a tabloid on Saturdays; only one of the Sunday regional and Scottish titles is broadsheet. The regional morning market is more traditional with nine of the seventeen papers remaining broadsheet (Griffiths, 1997: 12). The advantage claimed for the tabloid shape is that it is preferred both by readers and advertisers. It is easier to handle in a crowded bus, offers twice as many pages and, significantly, offers double the number of right-hand pages which are so beloved by advertisers. In truth, the push to tabloid seems to have been driven by the wholly untested belief, which seems prevalent in many parts of the newspaper industry, that the way to keep readers and even to enhance circulation is to 'go downmarket' editorially. The strategy offers obvious financial as well as these presumed marketing advantages; the provision of 'infotainment' is considerably less demanding on editorial resources than investigative journalism or hard political news.

The final trend apparent in the local press which reflects changes to the pattern of local newspaper ownership is no less significant for being left until last. The ownership of local newspapers has developed through two distinct phases (see chapter 6). First the gradual process of acquisition and growth in corporate size began to change as large combines diversified into related areas such as marketing, market research and the organisation of business systems. Using the sophisticated printing plant which they had acquired, companies expanded their activities into specialist consumer and trade magazine publishing. Newspaper groups restructured their assets through a succession of local deals in which titles and smaller newspaper groups were transferred between corporations such as Thomson and Reed in order to build local monopolies and provide the best opportunities to take full economic advantage of their substantial printing capacity. Groups also moved sideways and began to buy into regional television companies and independent local radio (Franklin and Murphy, 1997).

Thus from what might be called an 'organic' process of concentration there developed a pattern of increasingly monopolistic regional concentrations owned by large corporations and characterised by cross-media ownership and involvement in media-related activities. These groups invariably had some transnational element. EMAP, for example, began to acquire specialist magazines published and sold in France. International Thomson and Reed International were both multinational companies – Reed emerged with the Dutch publishing group Elsevier to become Reed Elsevier. The ownership of local and national titles became increasingly coterminous. Associated Newspapers, for example, own the Mail group but also control a large local and regional empire. United Newspapers owned the Daily and Sunday Express titles before they were taken over by Lord Hollick, the owner of the MAI group which owns Meridian, Anglia, a share in HTV and Channel 5 Broadcasting as well as a 20 per cent stake in ITN (Franklin, 1997: 207).

The second phase of change in the pattern of local newspaper ownership took place in the early 1990s and was the outcome of a process that was disjointed rather than continuous. A number of multinational companies suddenly abandoned their holdings, seduced by the higher profit margins available on scientific publishing titles, and were replaced by two quite distinctive types of new owners. Lonhro sold its British newspapers. The Reed and Thomson groups moved out of ownership of the British local press. There was a spate of selling of papers and groups which was preceded by severe cutbacks in personnel levels.

The first result was that Trinity International, which owns the *Liverpool Daily Post* and the *Liverpool Echo*, became the largest owner of local newspapers, while the Guardian Media Group, which now owns the *Guardian*, the *Observer* as well as shares in GMTV and Piccadilly Radio, became a major player. This reflected a trend towards firms like Johnston Press, with specialist interest in the local news media and a commitment to that business, replacing the multinational as the main owners (Bourne, 1996: 4). But at the same time the American holding company Kohlberg, Kravis and Roberts (KKR) financed the management buy-out of Reed Regional Newspapers. Newsquest was born; £205 million of KKR capital served as midwife. This represented a move in a quite different direction. KKR is a group of recent origin which has made money largely from the retailing area by taking over companies and then 're-engineering' them – i.e. trimming down the running costs in relation to income in order to increase the firm's capital value. This would suggest the opposite of a commitment to newspapers, or any form of media, as anything other than a financial investment and would ratchet up the level of commercialisation and marketing orientation already mentioned to a level previously unanticipated.

In sum, the changes in ownership of the local press have been dramatic. During 1996, ownership of one-third of all regional newspapers changed hands. A predictable outcome has been to intensify concentration of ownership with 89 per cent of the market by circulation now in the control of twenty publishers; the ten largest companies account for 71 per cent of circulation. (See table 1.3.) Thomson, EMAP, Reed and Pearson are no longer publishing regional newspapers; TRN, EMAP Newspapers, Reed Regional Newspapers and Westminster Press have each been sold. In July 1997, Mirror Group Newspapers (MGN) bought Midland Independent Newspapers (MIN) for £297 million (Sharpe, 1997: 13).

While this outline represents what we identify as the dominant trends in

Table 1.3 The market share of the ten largest local newspaper publishers (December 1996)

	Dailies		Weekly paid-for		Weekly free		Total	
	Circ. (000)	% total	Circ. (000)	% total	Circ. (000)	% total	Circ. (000)	% total
Trinity International	4,659	15	1,007	15	2,725	10	8,389	13
Northcliffe	5,885	19	334	5	1,673	6	7,892	12
Newsquest	2,872	9	615	9	4,211	15	7,698	12
United Provincial	2,242	7	250	4	2,296	8	4,788	7
Johnston Press	835	3	1,024	15	2,526	9	4,385	7
Midland Independent*	1,797	6	194	3	1,691	6	3,681	6
Guardian Media	1,167	4	281	4	1,335	5	2,783	4
Eastern Counties	959	4	199	2	1,192	4	2,350	4
Midland News	1,732	6	42	1	571	2	2,345	4
Southern	950	3	177	3	1,210	4	2,338	4
Others	7,385	24	2,487	38	9,291	32	19,166	29
Total	30,483	100	6,610	100	28,721	100	65,815	100

Source: Newspaper Society
* Approval for sale to Mirror Group expected by the end of 1997

the development of local newspapers across the past three decades, the process of change has not been simple or unidirectional. Two exceptions to this predominantly consumerist, depoliticised thrust can be identified. The first was the growth of the alternative press in the 1970s and 1980s (see chapter 8). The development of the new print technology allowed small undertakings to print their own newspapers at minimal running and capital costs. It was almost reminiscent of the radical press of the early nineteenth century. In big metropolitan centres such publications were established as co-operative ventures with a news agenda based on the notion of revelation and investigation of the political and business system, rather than the conservative celebration of the existing order so evident in the traditional press.

This was combined with listing pages and arts sections focused on rock, jazz and film. In London there was *Time Out*; in Leeds there was *Leeds Other Paper* latterly *The Northern Star*. They probed the land dealings of councillors, police violence and corruption and gave a voice to local groups who were engaged in social and political struggles for recognition: Asian workers, gay and lesbian rights groups, tenants of slum landlords.

They have all now succumbed to the market through one of two processes. Either as in the case of *City Life* (now owned by the Guardian Media Group) in Manchester or *City Limits* in London they have become listings magazines focused on entertainment and life-style journalism. Or, as in the case of *Leeds Other Paper* which outlasted all others as a radical paper, they have not been able to generate enough income from advertisements and sales in order to survive. Only in the unlikely and un-urban Highlands and Islands has the *West Highland Free Press*, run by English radicals, survived as a viable newspaper. Perhaps the difference is that it serves a series of communities where respectable people of all ages have a tradition of rebellion against landlordism and entertain the perfectly reasonable belief that everything emanating from south of Fort William and East of Fort Augustus is absolute rubbish!

Another non-market emanation from the possibilities generated by the new print technology in the 1970s was the local government newspaper. Many Labour authorities, witnessing themselves pilloried in the tabloid press as 'loony lefties', set up their own publications to provide news of their policies and to give people the information they needed to take advantage of the facilities that were being provided (Franklin, 1988). The magazines often resembled the alternative press in style but were essentially one strand within municipal public relations and lacked any critical or investigative dimension (see chapter 12). In the course of the 1980s the Thatcher government gradually applied more and more draconian financial controls over local government so that such ventures were squeezed out of existence. The Local Government Acts of 1986 and 1988, moreover, denounced their contents as propaganda and, via a number of clumsily worded paragraphs, declared their contents subject to central government regulation. In any case, the Labour Party realised that if it was to be elected it could not be both loony and left wing. It therefore followed the example of the Tories and ceased to be left wing while remaining as loony as ever.

Overall, the dominant tendency which has characterised the last three decades of change, not simply in the local press but in the local media (see chapters 2, 3 and 4), has been the constant, apparently remorseless advance of the market as the arbiter of the nature, the content, the form, the labour relations and mode of production and the ownership of the local media. Technological innovation has been both a product of this process and has helped this process to accelerate. At the same time national politics have been used to generate and sustain this while multinational business has been the corporate vehicle of much of the change. New technology such as cable television, combined with retailing and marketing transnational ownership, project a future which is increasingly unstable and in which the prospect for the local press as investigators and informers of the public in the process of local democracy looks even bleaker than that for the democratic process itself.

REFERENCES

The Advertising Association (1997) *Advertising Statistics Yearbook 1997*, London: Advertising Association.

Ainley, B. (1995) 'Blacks and Asians in the British Media: A Study in Discrimination', unpublished Ph.D. thesis, London: London School of Economics.

Bourne, C. (1996) 'Reshaping Regional Newspapers', *Free Press*, no. 94, Sept./Oct., p. 4.

Delano, A. (1997) 'The Power of Shorthand', *British Journalism Review*, vol. 8, no. 2, pp. 59–64.

Delano, A. and Henningham, J. (1995) *The News Breed: British Journalists in the 1990s*, London: The London Institute.

Franklin, B. (1988) 'Civic Free Newspapers: Propaganda on the Rates?', *Local Government Studies*, May/June, pp. 35–57.

—— (1997) *Newszak and News Media*, London: Arnold.

Franklin, B. and Murphy, D. (1991) *What News? The Market, Politics and the Local Press*, London: Routledge.

—— (1997) 'The Local Rag in Tatters: The Decline of the Local Press' in Bromley, M. and O'Malley, T. (eds) *The Journalism Reader*, London: Routledge, pp. 214–29.

Gall, G. (1996) 'New Technology, Industrial Relations and the Regional Press' unpublished Ph.D. thesis, Manchester: UMIST.

Goodhart, D. and Wintour, P. (1986) *Eddie Shah and the Newspaper Revolution*, London: Coronet Books.

Griffiths, D. (1997) 'The Irresistible Advance of the Tabloid', *Press Gazette*, 1 August, p. 12.

Guild of Editors (1995) *Survey of Editorial Training Needs*, London: Guild of Editors.

Hayes, A. (1996) *Family in Print: A History of the Bailey Newspaper Group*, Gloucester: Bailey Newspaper Group.

Keane, F. (1996) *Letter to Daniel: Despatches from the Heart*, London: BBC/Penguin.

Keeble, R. (1994) *The Newspapers Handbook*, London: Routledge.

Morgan, J. (1997a) 'Newsroom Revolution at Evening Mail', *Press Gazette*, 8 August, p. 2.

—— (1997b) 'Editor Sacked for Planning to Launch Rival', *Press Gazette*, 1 August, p. 5.

Murphy, D. (1976) *The Silent Watchdog: The Press in Local Politics*, London: Constable.

National Union of Journalists (1994) *NUJ Membership Survey*, conducted by the Trades Union Studies Unit, London: Ruskin College Oxford, available from NUJ.

Piggott, M. (1997) 'Don't Give Freelances the Brush-Off', *Press Gazette*, 15 August, p. 11.

Porter, J. (1986) 'Distribution of Frees in Europe' in *AFN News*, June/July.

The Press Council (1987) *The Press and the People*, 34th Annual Report, London: The Press Council.

Sebba, A. (1994) *Battling for the News: The Rise of the Woman Reporter*, London: Sceptre Books.

Sharpe, H. (1997) 'Monty's Regional Shopping Spree May Not Be Over', *Press Gazette*, 18 July, p. 13.

Smallman, A. (1996) 'Telling the Editorial from the Advertisements', *Press Gazette*, 10 May, p. 11.

Tunstall, J. (1995) 'From Gentlemen to Journos', *British Journalism Review*, vol. 6, no. 3, pp. 54–9.

Van den Bergh, P. (1995) 'What's My Lineage?' *Press Gazette*, 23 October, p. 18.

Chapter 2

Local radio: attuned to the times or filling time with tunes?

Andrew Crisell

In one sense, the launch of the present system of local radio in Britain, which occurred in 1967, could be seen as an instance of history repeating itself, for it marked the arrival of a technology for which there was no apparent demand. We commonly assume that most inventions and new technologies are developed in response to a felt need, or at least that their potential is fairly clear from the outset, but this was not altogether true of the birth of radio in the first years of the twentieth century.

As a means of *private* or point-to-point communication between individuals, wireless telephony, the atmospheric transmission of sounds over distances, had obvious enough uses: during a period which partly coincided with the Great War (1914–18) many of these were naval and military. But *broadcasting* was seen as a negative side-effect of wireless telephony. What was the value of exchanges between diplomats, military allies and business associates if they could be heard by anyone who possessed a wireless receiver? Even before the War problems were created in America and elsewhere by 'irrepressible [wireless] amateurs, already numbering thousands, who were anathema to the military; their chatter was said to interfere with military communication. They were even accused of sending fake orders to navy ships, purportedly from admirals' (Barnouw, 1977: 17).

There was no initial demand for wireless broadcasting because it was not perceived as a separate technology with distinct uses although these were fairly rapidly anticipated. In 1916 David Sarnoff, an employee of the American Marconi Company, announced:

> a plan of development which would make radio a 'household utility' in the same sense as the piano or the phonograph. The receiver can be designed in the form of a simple 'radio Music Box' and arranged for several different wavelengths, which would be changeable with the throwing of a single switch or pressing of a single button ... This proposition would be especially interesting to farmers and others living in outlying districts removed from cities. By the purchase of a 'radio Music Box' they could

enjoy concerts, lectures, music, recitals etc., which may be going on in the nearest city within their radius.

(Armes 1988: 107)

Once the uses of this form of wireless telephony were apparent – as a medium of entertainment, information and education – demand for it could be stimulated through those institutional models of broadcasting which are now familiar to us. In America it was established as a means of delivering audiences to advertisers, and in Britain as the embodiment of a public service philosophy largely conceived by John Reith, first the Managing Director of the British Broadcasting Company and later the Director General of the British Broadcasting Corporation.

LOCAL RADIO: A BRIEF HISTORY

In Britain wireless broadcasting began on a local scale, but as an infant technology which could span great distances, and moreover one which because of the scarcity of wavelengths was a fairly precious resource, it was soon developed as a national system under the centralising sway of John Reith, and local radio virtually disappeared (Gorham, 1952: 78; Harvey and Robins, 1994: 41). What persisted were regional variations within what was in essence a network service controlled, if not originated, from London (Scannell and Cardiff, 1991: 15).

It was with the arrival of VHF/FM technology in the 1950s and 1960s that the history of radio repeated itself, for though its uses were obvious enough there was again an absence of demand. The first test transmissions took place at Wrotham, Kent, in May 1950, and heralded the 'reintroduction of low power programming for very specific audiences, a return in an age of television to the first broadcasting patterns of 1922' (Briggs, 1979: 561–2). Henceforth scores of local stations would be able to find a place on the waveband; moreover during the 1960s, when the government was at last ready to authorise a spread of such stations, localism was very much the *zeitgeist*. Some of the offshore pirates appealed to local loyalties (albeit rather superficially) by giving themselves names like Radio Kent and Radio Essex and by publicising events and activities within the regions to which they broadcast, and there was much general political discussion about the need to stimulate local democracy and raise awareness of local issues. Unlike early broadcasting technology, then, the new technology of VHF/FM had a use which was obvious enough.

Nevertheless, what the pirates illustrated above all was that if local radio was to be a commercial activity, the content which would draw the biggest audiences and thus attract the most advertising revenue was pop music, a phenomenon whose origins and manifestations were hardly 'local'. In the public sector, the BBC's local radio operation certainly aimed to raise local political awareness, but the problem it encountered (and still does to a considerable extent) was a widespread conviction that this was already being accomplished quite satisfactorily by the local press and regional television. The consequent lack of demand for local radio was expressed in the fact that as late as 1972 only about 40 per cent of the radio audience had bothered to equip themselves for VHF/FM reception (Briggs, 1995: 842). To bolster interest, the government allowed the BBC and later the Independent Broadcasting Authority (IBA) to give many of their new stations a low-power AM frequency to support the 'prime system of transmission' on the FM waveband (Briggs, 1995: 647). It was only at the end of the 1980s, when the four national BBC networks switched to VHF/FM in the interests of better sound quality, that the bulk of the radio audience followed suit.

During its first six years local radio was a BBC monopoly. The Labour government under Harold Wilson was ideologically hostile to the pirates, forcing them off the air by the Marine Broadcasting (Offences) Act of 1967. It then gave the BBC the exclusive right to meet the huge demand for a service of continuous pop music which the pirates had identified, and the result was Radio 1, which went to air on 30 September 1967. At the same time it followed the recommendations of the Pilkington Report (1962) and entrusted the Corporation with the development of local radio. After an earlier experiment the service, which has always been based on speech, was launched with Radio Leicester in 1967.

For many years to follow, the administration of local radio in Britain reflected the innately conservative, Reithian view of sound broadcasting which was shared by the BBC and the government, whatever the political complexion of the latter. Neither fully appreciated the radical change in listening behaviour which television had prompted. Television was now the primary vehicle of entertainment and culture, and radio was a medium which was most commonly used to provide background for other activities. But the cheap and portable transistor sets which had become massively popular during the 1960s meant that radio could be used as a background medium in many more situations than ever before (Crisell, 1994: 28–30). The brief and relatively uncomplicated tunes of pop music were well suited to this secondary, intermittent mode of consumption, as also were segmented forms of news and current affairs which could bring the listener up to date much more quickly than the viewer or reader. The provision of separate, constructed and various programmes, which was the cornerstone of Reith's public service philosophy, was no longer sustainable beyond a single network for dedicated, attentive listeners: Radio 4. Yet in its infancy BBC local radio also made feeble, underfunded moves towards a mixture of programming: news, music, sport, religious, features and educational programmes, even dramatisations.

The early structural and financial problems of the service have been eloquently described elsewhere (Lewis and Booth, 1989: 95–6). We might summarise them here by saying that because the BBC is an essentially metropolitan organisation, its local operations have always seemed ancillary to the networks. They have been poorly financed and perceived both by the public and, apparently, within the Corporation, as existing primarily to feed the networks with locally originating news stories and with promising technical and creative staff.

The old Reithian attitude to sound broadcasting coloured even the birth of commercial or 'independent' local radio (ILR) in 1973. The Conservatives returned to power after the 1970 general election, and the Sound Broadcasting Act of 1972 expressed their determination to expose the BBC to competition in radio, just as its television service had been exposed to the competition of ITV. The service would be local because it was at the local level of VHF/FM transmission that competition could be maximised: a far greater number of commercial operators could gain access to the spectrum than at national and regional levels, thus affording unprecedented choice to the listeners and opportunities to advertisers.

It was evident at the outset that in order to attract a large audience the service, like that of the pirates in the previous decade, would have to be driven by pop music. Yet even here, the government, through its regulator the IBA, imposed residual Reithian obligations. With the exception of LBC in London, which offered an all-news format, the new stations were obliged to offer a 'balance of programming' for the communities they served, including full news provision (Barnard, 1989: 74–5). With the arguable exception of Radio 4, this was a level of service which the individual BBC networks were no longer offering even at national level – and such a service was not only costly in itself but too heterogeneous to enable prospective advertisers to identify the kind of audience that might be attracted to it.

It is possible to exaggerate the weight of these burdens. To meet their Reithian duty to provide range and variety, most of the ILR stations scattered a palatable miscellany of interviews, announcements, news summaries and short features within what was essentially a sequence of pop records: but during the 1970s and early 1980s some of the smaller stations went under or were forced to merge with others, and even the larger ones showed poor profits.

It was not until the mid 1980s, when ILR was hit by a new, land-based generation of pirates targeting ethnic groups as tightly as it could without any concern for 'balance', that the IBA at last began to loosen the fetters of its licensees. It eased restrictions on the cross-ownership of stations and on programme sponsorship, no longer insisted on a balance or range of output, and at a nod from the government allowed the stations to split their frequencies by offering Top 40 on FM and 'gold' music for older listeners on AM (Donovan, 1992: 135) – a measure which at last created well-defined audience segments for prospective advertisers.

The Broadcasting Acts of 1990 and 1996 further reduced the regulation of independent radio in order to allow as many stations as possible onto the spectrum, and so create competition and choice within the commercial sector as well as between the commercial sector and the BBC. The 1990 Act created two bodies from the old IBA: the Independent Television Commission and the Radio Authority. The latter was empowered to license stations at national and regional as well as at local level, and the 1996 Act then lumped newspapers, radio and television into a single 'media market', removing many restrictions on cross-media ownership and in-area radio holdings. Henceforth any merger or acquisition would have to satisfy a 'public interest' test according to three criteria. What economic benefits would it bring about? What effect would it have on competition and choice? And would the diversity of information sources be reduced? The third criterion clearly related to the provision of news, but at local level that horse had already bolted, for following the 1990 Act the Radio Authority was able to point out that 'there is no requirement for [independent] local radio to carry local news and insofar as it does so there is nothing to prevent that local news being bought in from the local newspaper' (1995: 13).

At the beginning of the 1990s, with ILR about to be set free to chase the market, the BBC saw its opportunity to capture a niche at local level: news programming. It is also interesting to see how, at both local and national level, the provision of news has increasingly claimed to be 'public service broadcasting' as the older meanings of that term have been made less and less tenable by technological and political developments. In its pristine, Reithian sense, public service consisted in offering not merely news but the fullest range and variety of material, partly to satisfy the greatest number of audience tastes but partly to introduce individual listeners to subjects and interests they had not previously cared for or known about. As Reith saw clearly, this kind of public service was justified by the shortage of frequencies and made possible only by a monopoly.

The argument was in essence this: frequencies were scarce enough to make broadcasting a precious national resource, and so precious a resource should be devoted to the most comprehensive service the BBC could provide. But there were just enough frequencies to allow a competitor or two, and Reith insisted on a monopoly because competition would force the BBC to abandon its range of programming, which included a service to minorities, and merely offer inferior, populist fare to the greatest number of people. The argument, however, came perilously close to self-contradiction, for it seemed a bit like saying: 'We insist on keeping broadcasting scarce in order to protect a service which is justified by broadcasting's scarcity.'

Competition with commercial broadcasting was blunted initially by imposing public service obligations on ITV, and also by the different sources from which the BBC and ITV derived their income. But from the 1960s the new technologies of VHF/FM, fibre optic cable and satellite transmission made room for many more stations and channels in both television and radio. The scarce, precious nature of broadcasting evaporated, and with it much of the justification for the kind of public service which aims to provide a whole range of programming on a single frequency. With the new channels came 'narrowcasting' and specialist formats.

Hence the BBC quietly sought a new definition of public service: the provision of programming for otherwise neglected minorities – programming which would not be commercially sustainable. But with the 1980s came Thatcherite proclamations about the sovereignty and disciplines of the market: how could the BBC command a universal licence fee for providing programmes that few people wished to watch or listen to? In 1985 the government even appointed the Peacock Committee to consider whether at least some of the BBC's operations might be paid for from advertising (Peacock, 1986: 1).

To be able to define public service almost exclusively in terms of the provision of news and information has therefore been a godsend to the BBC. Even if only a minority of people wish to avail themselves of it, financial considerations cannot be allowed to stem the flow of news and information in a democracy – and in any case the minority who seek it are likely to be sizable. In terms of local radio the BBC believes there is a significant demand for news and spoken word among older listeners, who are less keen on back-to-back music – a view which finds some support in academic research (Barnett and Morrison, 1989: 30).

It has also been pointed out that the provision of local news has a particular rationale, for the very ease with which national and global news can be delivered by satellite and other technologies means that the local is more likely to be overlooked. This has given BBC local radio its 'unique selling proposition' (McNair, 1994: 162–3).

From 1990 the focus on news at local level was masterminded by Ronald Neil, the Managing Director of BBC Regional Broadcasting. Henceforth BBC local radio would provide a genuine alternative to music-based ILR, which found news and speech too costly to deliver and insufficiently attractive to a large audience. The service would embrace sport, traffic and travel, and leisure interests as well as hard news, and an important part of it would be targeted at the various ethnic populations within the community (Neil, 1993: 4–5).

At first, the aim was that 80 per cent of BBC local radio output would consist of speech, much of it hard news and current affairs, but aside from the fact that the smaller stations were hard pressed to find sufficient news to broadcast, this proved too spartan a diet for many listeners, and from a typical market share of around 20 per cent the BBC stations' sank to about 13 per cent. It eased up again later, but was hit anew in 1995–6 by the re-launch of BBC Radio 5 as Five Live and by the debut of Talk Radio UK. There has been a further recovery to about 15 per cent of the market. In 1996 Neil was succeeded by Nigel Chapman, Controller of BBC Local Radio in England, who has been keen to broaden the service's speech repertoire into the arts, lifestyles and cultural history.

Notwithstanding these efforts, the general impression of local radio which has evolved over the years seems to be that it does not contribute significantly to the provision of local news and culture – that ILR is insufficiently local in content, and that although the BBC does offer local content, it is insufficiently funded. The rest of this chapter will consider the performance of local radio in the light of this impression and explore the extent to which its contribution to local news and culture is distinctive and valuable and likely to remain so. I shall draw my examples from stations in my home region, the north east of England, as being representative of local radio in general, but shall make it clear when I believe that they are not. However, I shall take no particular cognisance of the impending arrival of digitalisation, which could vastly increase the number of channels available to local radio – a third instance of broadcasting technology which is in advance of any perceived demand for it!

LOCAL RADIO: THE CONTRIBUTION TO LOCAL NEWS AND CULTURE

Since it is now free of any obligation to provide local news, does ILR seem destined to provide nothing but Top 40 music and occasional network news feeds – a service which is devoid of all local identity? Many of the portents are certainly dismaying. There are now about 180 ILR stations in Britain, virtually all of them under sustained financial and listener pressures to reduce the ratio of news and speech to music. Typically, they offer 'capsule' news about once an hour (an unhappily medicinal metaphor suggesting that news should be administered as a bitter pill only to those who are sick enough to need it). Each capsule might consist of a two-minute bulletin which combines local with network news and includes just one audio clip, though there is sometimes an extra minute for sport.

Speed and frequency are radio's special strengths and consequently it strives to be first with the big stories and to repeat and update them at short intervals – there are few, if any, exclusives at local level. Because everything is geared to the next bulletin, news staff have no time to take a longer view, for that independent investigation of facts and cultivation of informants from which most exclusives emerge. Hence ILR relies for its news on the same stock sources as the newspapers: the events diary, the police and courts, the press releases. This is why so many of its bulletins seem derivative and lacking in distinctiveness, and though sometimes more up to date than the newspapers they provide much less in the way of detail and backgrounding.

Two Newcastle stations provide sobering insights into the current state of ILR news. Metro FM, which serves the Tyneside conurbation, Sunderland and surrounding areas, presently has a staff of just four news journalists, three of whom are 'first jobbers'. Century Radio, a station wholly owned by Border Television, was awarded the north east regional franchise by the

Radio Authority in September 1994 for a service which would consist of 55 per cent speech and only 45 per cent pop music. The station would be heard as far as Teesside to the south and Berwick to the north, and the speech would include a two-hour daily news programme, half of national and half of local items, chat shows, phone-ins and 'tradio', on-air swop shops. In March 1996, however, the station successfully applied to the Radio Authority to scrap the news programme, a move which resulted in the departure of almost all its reporters.

There are also worrying trends in BBC local radio, despite its commitment to news, information and other forms of speech output. In the BBC's overall radio structure, network and national shade into regional and local. Below the five networks are the 'national regions': Radios Scotland, Northern Ireland and Wales, which have native language equivalents where appropriate (for example, Radio Cymru) and contain local opt-outs such as BBC Radio Orkney (BBC, 1996a: 36). Then in England there are thirty-nine local radio stations (BBC, 1997: 1).

In fact, the BBC's sub-network radio system is something of an unsung success story. Nearly 10 million people, over 20 per cent of the UK's adult population, listen in to its local and regional stations, making it the BBC's most popular service after Radio 1 (BBC, 1996b: inside front cover). But here as in ILR, where many of the stations have been absorbed by one of three big groups: East Midlands Allied Press, Great Western Radio and the Capital Group, economies of scale are developing, and these are potentially inimical to the very idea of localness. Programme content which once originated in the area that a station serves might now be either provided from elsewhere or replaced by networked material – still, perhaps, a service *to* the locality but not one which originates *from* it.

In such a metropolitan-centred organisation as the BBC, the very notion of a local service seems almost a contradiction in terms (see above), but while the system has always been underfunded it has fared worse since 1990. The licence fee has been pegged to the retail price index, but inflation has risen faster, and in recent years all the terrestrial networks and stations have been squeezed in order to pay for the new digital services. In July 1997, the BBC announced a cut of thirty-nine posts in regional journalism as part of a five-year scheme to save £4 million from its regional budget in order to capitalise the new digital services. Presently about 15 per cent of the BBC's total broadcasting budget is being set aside for this purpose.

So what of the future? Further cuts in staffing and in off-peak programming are almost inevitable, measures which the larger, urban stations will be able to withstand better than their country cousins. Savings will also be made through technology, notably the Electronic News Production System (ENPS), which enables news items, interviews and pieces of sound actuality to be centrally assembled within a region that might comprise three or four local stations. The items are packaged by a single presenter, known as 'the golden voice', and each station within the region can then select and priori-tise the stories in order to create a news bulletin of its own. The rather melancholy calculation is that ENPS could replace up to five news staff within a given region, a saving of over £100,000. The system is simply another form of networking, a phenomenon which is bound to increase. Those programme packages and documentary features which used to char-acterise individual stations will soon have to serve several stations, and there will be fewer of them. There is no doubt that BBC local radio will actually be less of a local service: what its managers are counting on is that the benefit in financial savings will outweigh the extent to which the loss of localness is perceived by the listeners.

This hope seems less unrealistic when we remember that networking can in some respects *enrich* the provision of local services: for instance, certain kinds of specialist music such as jazz or country-and-western are beyond the resources of individual stations but can be provided on a regional scale. Nor is it just networking, the regional collaboration of stations, which can enrich local provision but the institutional backing of the BBC as a whole – a backing which ILR lacks. The obvious example is ethnic programming. Syn-dications from the BBC World Service at Bush House mean that although the Tyne and Wear area, for instance, contains a relatively small population of ethnic minorities, Radio Newcastle can provide some three hours a week of programming for Chinese listeners and groups from the Indian sub-continent, an amount which will shortly be increased by 20 per cent.

But apart from these isolated compensations, are there any solid grounds for optimism about the future of local radio, whether public or commercial? Notwithstanding the relentless pressure of economics, local radio would appear to have certain invincible advantages which spring from the very nature of the medium. At this point it might be worth addressing the ques-tion of how far radio *complements* the other news media and how far it *competes* with them.

We saw earlier that the local media cover much the same stories, though since the press is a spatial rather than temporal medium it is able to cover many more than radio and even television. Nevertheless radio could not compete with the other media unless it could offer audiences something distinctive – something which could thus be seen as complementary – and we also saw that speed and frequency are its particular strengths. What newspapers can offer above all is *detail* – explanation, backgrounding, con-text – but radio, like TV, is faster than print. Despite the accelerating effects of new technology the papers must at some point treat their news as defini-tive and go to press, and by the time they are distributed it is dated. The concept of 'rolling news' could not have predated the arrival of broadcast-ing, and because of the speed of the latter it is not unknown for newspaper reporters, especially sports staff, to refuse to question their sources in the presence of broadcasting journalists.

Radio, however, lacks the moving pictures of television. Yet its blindness is by no means a straightforward disadvantage. On the terrestrial channels regional television gains limited amounts of airtime until the early evening – and even if digitisation leads to twenty-four-hour regional TV news, as seems quite likely, most people are not in a position to watch it at other times of the day. But because radio is secondary, listened to by many of us as an accompaniment to other activities, its news can reach us much more promptly. It can give instant and frequent, often even continuous, access to events, and is for this reason much more *pervasive* in its impact on the audience than are the primary media. I have discussed these characteristics of radio in much more detail elsewhere (Crisell, 1994: 3–15, 121–5, 221–4).

Even ILR, which for most of the time settles for music and disc jockey chat, has not totally lost sight of the special power of radio. Though by no means all the stations are as fortunately situated, Metro FM, serving an area with an acute sense of regional identity and a fundamentalist fervour for soccer, carries a three- to three-and-a-half hour sports programme on winter Saturdays which includes live commentary of local matches. Similarly, mid-week evenings are cleared for coverage of all key games involving Newcastle United and Sunderland, and it is interesting to note that Metro's sports staff are much more experienced than its news team and subject to a much slower turnover.

We might sum up by suggesting that thanks to its key qualities of 'instantaneity' and secondariness, the historic achievements of local radio have been twofold: it has uncovered a whole new *stratum* of news, and it has brought a new *perspective* to news. The new stratum is news which is too trivial for the national media; too trivial, too 'secondary' and often insufficiently visual for regional television; and too ephemeral for the local press. Yet what is interesting is that it often blends the reportage of events with practical information, something for certain groups of its listeners to *act upon*. Some obvious examples are traffic and travel reports, weather updates, agricultural and maritime information, local market prices, and local appeals which also have the status of news stories. The latter might include an account of how vandals have damaged a local theatre just before the opening night of a play – an account which is combined with a request for volunteers to help repair it or find another venue. As far as the local papers are concerned, many of these items would cease to be news in the time it takes them to go to press.

Yet perhaps even more important is the new *perspective* which radio has brought to news and current affairs – a perspective which though not peculiar to local services is of special importance in them. Despite the quantitative limitations of radio news, Tony Fish, the Manager of BBC Radio Newcastle, claims that BBC local stations 'do more issues-based stuff' than the papers, seeing this as part of the Corporation's public service duty to give its listeners an informed view of contemporary topics and events.

It is worth exploring the guises that issues-based radio assumes. One is the studio discussion or debate, and another is the phone-in, which may or may not be mediated by a studio 'expert' as well as a presenter. The phone-in made its debut in Britain at the end of the 1960s, at about the time the first local stations were being launched, and since it is a mainstay of local radio's speech content their histories are closely connected. The first regular phone-in programme seems to have been heard on BBC Radio Nottingham in 1968 (Donovan, 1992: 203).

There is no doubt that both discussions and phone-ins are a cheap and easy way of filling air time, but at their best their contribution to current affairs on the radio is valuable and original. Local papers and regional television report news stories and issues, but as well as needing explanation these things stimulate opinions and debate among the recipients. However, there is little sense of these recipients in the newspapers. Local radio also offers news stories and issues but can use the studio discussion and/or phone-in to locate reactions and responses to the news *within the same medium*. Its professional broadcasters act as brokers between the people in the news, or the experts on the news, and 'the public' in the form of the studio guests or phone callers: this is largely what is meant by radio fostering community debate. Moreover, the interaction between the news and the responses to it, the latter sometimes informed and sometimes emotive, can itself become newsworthy. The notion of 'the news' is bracingly extended from news as the mere relaying of information to news as a matter of dialogue or debate.

But the association between news, in its broad sense of contemporary issues as well as specific events, and 'views', need not be close or direct – nor is it wholly absent from modern ILR. Metro FM in Newcastle may be atypical in serving a locality with an extraordinary sense of its own identity, but for four hours a night, five days a week, Metro listeners can tune in to Alan Robson's *Night Owls*, predominantly a phone-in/talk show with a presenter whose Tyneside accent is astutely broad. Discussion embraces current social and moral debates as well as hard news, but the listener is left in no doubt of the impact of the contemporary world on 'ordinary people' and the passions it arouses.

The press manages this less well and television manages it less often. Newspapers always carry commentary, explanation and interpretation alongside the news itself, but as well as lacking the inflections of the human voice they can convey the community's responses only in the delayed, dead prose of readers' letters. Regional television does include local debate on public affairs, but as we noted earlier, air time is scarce, and even if it becomes more plentiful, viewers are for much of the day a less 'available' species than listeners.

Even though ILR has not entirely lost sight of the medium's ability to treat events and issues as a matter of audible opinion and debate as well as mere things to report, the BBC stations are continuing to exploit it vigorously. Studio discussions and phone-ins cost little to produce and perhaps achieve less than they might. But they help to ensure that radio's contribution to the local provision of news and current affairs is a unique as well as valuable one.

ACKNOWLEDGEMENTS

I am indebted to three people for some of the factual material in this chapter. Tony Fish, Manager of BBC Radio Newcastle, generously provided me with much information about the recent history, present position and future prospects of BBC local radio. Sharon Thomas, a former student of mine at the University of Sunderland and now a news reporter at BBC Radio Newcastle, was a ready and efficient provider of contacts and sources and gave me a vivid impression of what it is like to be a journalist in modern local radio. Jon Driscoll, sports reporter at Metro FM, gave me a patient and lucid account of news and sports reporting in both ILR and independent regional radio.

REFERENCES

Armes, R. (1988) *On Video*, London and New York: Routledge.
Barnard, S. (1989) *On the Radio*, Milton Keynes: Open University Press.
Barnett, S. and Morrison, D. (1989) *The Listener Speaks: The Radio Audience and the Future of Radio*, London: HMSO Books.
Barnouw, E. (1977) *Tube of Plenty: The Evolution of American Television*, New York: Oxford University Press.
BBC (1996a) *Annual Report and Accounts 95/6*, London: British Broadcasting Corporation.
—— (1996b) *Going Digital: The Challenge for BBC Regional Journalism*, London: BBC Regional Broadcasting.
—— (1997) *Local Radio Factsheet*, London: BBC Regional Broadcasting.
Briggs, A. (1979) *History of Broadcasting in the United Kingdom,* vol. IV: *Sound and Vision*, Oxford: Oxford University Press.
—— (1995) *History of Broadcasting in the United Kingdom,* vol. V: *Competition*, Oxford: Oxford University Press.
Crisell, A. (1994) *Understanding Radio*, London and New York: Routledge, second edn.
Donovan, P. (1992) *The Radio Companion*, London: Grafton Books.
Gorham, M. (1952) *Broadcasting and Television since 1900*, London: Andrew Dakers.
Harvey, S. and Robins, K. (1994) 'Voices and places: the BBC and regional policy', *Political Quarterly*, vol. 65.
Lewis, P. and Booth, J. (1989) *The Invisible Medium: Public, Commercial and Community Radio*, London: Macmillan.
McNair, B. (1994) *News and Journalism in the UK*, London and New York: Routledge.
Neil, R. (1993) *Extending Choice: The Role of BBC Journalism in the Regions*, internal briefing paper issued by BBC Regional Broadcasting.
Peacock Committee (1986) *Report of the Committee on Financing the BBC, 1986*, Cmnd 9824.
Radio Authority (1995) *Media Ownership: The Government's Proposals (CM 2072) – A Response by the Radio Authority*, London: Radio Authority.
Scannell, P. and Cardiff, D. (1991) *A Social History of Broadcasting,* vol. I: *1922–1939: Serving the Nation*, Oxford: Basil Blackwell.

Chapter 3

News and current affairs in regional television broadcasting

Ralph Negrine and Rachel Eyre

Regional television services are changing; and rapidly. Occasionally the pace of change has prompted paradoxes. Takeovers and buyouts, in the wake of government policy, have resulted in the ownership of Channel 3 companies being increasingly concentrated in the hands of a few cross-media conglomerates. At the same time, concern to target local audiences more closely has led some companies to subdivide their regions to offer a more 'local' news service to their viewers. In the public sector, BBC services have been plagued by cuts in regional broadcasting with a further £1 million cut announced in July 1997 to prepare for digitalisation of services. This chapter reviews recent developments in regional television news services and explores their changing nature through a comparison of output drawn from 1986 and 1996. The first section looks principally at the changes in the commercial television sector over the last decade and raises some key questions about the performance of regional television. Section two considers the distinctions which can be drawn between regional, local and community provision and draws on a series of interviews conducted with media practitioners working in regional and local media. Section three offers a brief overview of regional television news by comparing news output from two weeks in 1986 and 1996 on both public and private sector television services. The chapter concludes with a broader examination of contemporary and possible future regional and local news services.

CHANGES IN REGIONAL TELEVISION BROADCASTING

The regional map of commercial television was initially drawn with financial and technical considerations in mind with the large population centres being covered first so as to allow the new industry to become established and provide funds for other areas. Over the years, changes have often been made to the original franchise areas. For example, in 1980 the Midlands and Southern England were subdivided by the Independent Broadcasting Authority (IBA) into dual regions (Johnson, 1989: 13). Such changes had not, however, significantly affected the federal structure of commercial television and each franchise remained relatively independent in terms of ownership even though increasingly more attention was being paid to the centralisation of scheduling and production facilities. But by the 1990s, the commercial television map had gone through radical changes.

Within two years of the 1990 Broadcasting Act and the franchise awarding round of 1991, the Conservative government liberalised the rules governing the ownership of commercial television franchises and made it easier for companies to 'change hands'. A number of mergers took place very soon after this change in the rules: Carlton and Central merged, as did MAI (controllers of Meridian) and Anglia, and Granada and LWT. Proposals for a further relaxation of the ownership rules were announced in May 1995 which 'maintained the ... two-licence limit on regional Channel 3 licences', but enabled 'broadcasters to expand to up to 15 per cent of total television audience share thereafter' (Department of National Heritage, 1995: 27).

The significance of the 15 per cent audience share figure is easily appreciated when one looks at the Carlton–Central group. According to the Department of National Heritage, the audience share of this group is 9.4 per cent (3.4 per cent and 6 per cent or 1.8 million and 3.6 million households respectively) thus leaving some opportunity for further mergers with, or takeovers of, other regional television companies. Many of the smaller companies have a relatively small audience share: HTV with a share of 2.8 per cent (Department of National Heritage, 1995: 34), for example, was bought by MAI in July 1997.

The prospect of a small number of companies controlling a large number of different regional television licences is therefore not too far-fetched. Granada Television's takeover of Yorkshire–Tyne Tees Television in the summer of 1997 has concentrated ownership of a large part of the ITV franchise map into three large groups: Granada, Carlton and United News. The chairman of Granada even went as far as to suggest that the ITV ownership rules be abandoned and that there should only be one single ITV operator (King, 1997: 22).

The implications of this for regional and local identities – often constructed by the regional and local media themselves – and for the larger question of diversity of content across the commercial sector cannot be underestimated. What, for example, would happen if the Central company logo and its other regional specific elements were to be replaced by the Carlton imprint? Or Anglia's by Meridian's? Who would object and what would be lost in the regions and by the regions? The Acting Editor of *Central News East*, for example, acknowledged the importance of the Central logo. For her, the logo was a familiar symbol with which audiences identified and she believed that this identification created a feeling of comfort and security and came to stand for quality programming. Without it, would regional television vanish altogether in the pursuit of a national commercial television structure?

It could be argued that part of the answer to these questions lies in one other change which took place in the 1990s which also needs to be documented. Changes made subsequent to the 1990 Broadcasting Act affected the role of the ITC *vis-à-vis* the individual regional television companies. Under the old regulatory system, the Independent Broadcasting Authority (IBA) was 'the legally-accountable broadcaster. The new (post-1993) system . . . delegates broadcasting responsibility to the licensees.' The ITC, therefore, now has a monitoring role in the sense that it reviews on an annual basis the performance of each regional television company which 'have separate regional programming obligations. Each licence specifies minimum amount of regional programming, expressed in weekly average, which each licensee is required to broadcast' (ITC, 1994: 1).

These obligations are important in maintaining the distinctiveness of each regional company and in ensuring that the regional dimension of a company's work is not subsumed within a larger conglomerate and a non-regionally based entity. Inevitably, though, a 'lighter regulatory touch' and concentrated ownership of regional television pose dangers to diversity of content amongst different franchisees.

How does the system work? Performance and results for local and regional output

The IBA's annual report for 1989–90 sets out the requirements for each specific regional television company. The weekly requirement for Central Television, the licensee for the Midlands region, was 14 hours per week of new productions of local interest. This requirement included a minimum of 4 hours per week for each of Central's three sub-regions. Central exceeded this minimum by 2 hours and 7 minutes, and it exceeded the weekly requirement for each of its broadcasting sub-regions by between 9 and 37 minutes. The weekly minimum requirement for Central Television increased to 16 hours and 25 minutes by 1991 (ITC, 1991: 30) but dropped to 15 hours and 21 minutes by the time of the 1996 Performance Review of commercial television companies (ITC, 1997: 32). Central Television has always met these requirements and usually by a good margin: for example, by 3 hours and 49 minutes in 1996. But what does this output consist of?

The Performance Review is necessarily sketchy and it does not offer a very detailed breakdown of these figures. News and sport contribute much to this weekly requirement. The 1997 Review verdict on Central is mixed: the '30 minutes per week of regional drama dealing with ethnic issues' requirement of the licence was not met directly though 'a new music, events and entertainment programme' did redress the balance somewhat; 'there was also a shortfall of 7 minutes per week against the current affairs requirement but this was compensated for by other factual material'. However, *Central News* exceeded 'the licence requirement of 4 hours per week in each sub-region, and equally significant, more than 95 per cent of regional programmes are produced in the region' (ITC, 1997: 34).

These figures illustrate both the nature of the monitoring exercise and the diversity of requirements regional licence holders have to meet. Without doubt, the competitive and constantly changing nature of the industry requires some flexibility in the monitoring process but at the same time it does need some detailed supervision to ensure that requirements to meet the diversity of regions and sub-regions are not forgotten. Nevertheless, and as the Review highlights, the range of formats used to celebrate the region is not large and franchisees carefully balance the need to meet the requirements of the licence with the need to appeal to an audience bombarded by other media: so news and some current affairs, discussion programmes, and a range of arts and entertainment programmes dominate.

The comments made by the ITC in its reviews imply a degree of flexibility within the requirements but, at the same time, a degree of monitoring and supervision which can extend to severe warnings for recalcitrant operators. Whether such warnings lead to more serious actions of a kind which endanger the positions of the licensees is another question altogether. In a sense, the flexibility which is apparent is a consequence of the newer and more competitive broadcasting environment in which commercial television now operates: the licensees need to meet their obligations but they also compete for viewers in an increasingly crowded media world. When the ITV companies were first established, they simply competed with the BBC. Now, they compete with the BBC for a share of the audience and Channels Four and Five, and cable and satellite services for both a share of the audience and a share of the advertising revenue available. In such circumstances, obligations are to be met but the environment may be less conducive for more adventurous or demanding material.

REGIONAL AND LOCAL NEWS IN THE REGIONS: A LOOK AT THE MIDLANDS

The centrality of local news provision in the licence requirements has not usually translated into academic interest. As Cottle rightly pointed out, 'charged with a statutory responsibility to provide news and other forms of programming produced in, for and about the region, regional television is an area of broadcasting deserving of serious attention' (1993: 37). He goes on to point out that the value of regional news programmes should not be underestimated; they attract and engage audiences because of their particular form, with the emphasis being placed on human interest stories, conveyed through the 'familiar friend' image of the studio presenters, and the familiar, comfortable visual scenes from the audience's region. They also play a significant role in attracting and keeping an audience loyal to a channel for the whole evening's viewing.

Much of this emerges in a review of Central Television, the Midlands contractor since 1982 and the contractor with the largest audience share of ITV licensees (at 6 per cent of the total audience). The franchise area was split into three sub-regions, East (Nottingham), West (Birmingham) and South Midlands (Abingdon) in the mid-1980s on the grounds that the region as a whole was not only too large to broadcast local news to but that it also lacked any sort of regional cohesion. One can translate this move into more specific, and perhaps parochial, terms: the Nottingham centre covers such cities and towns as Leicester, Derby, Melton Mowbray and Market Harborough, even though these areas do not, in themselves, have much in common. In this respect, the East Midlands may be more of a construct than a real and unified regional entity. To viewers in Leicester, events in Nottingham some thirty miles away are events at a distance, they lack a point of resonance and contact.

But this is not a problem that is unique to Central Television. The BBC Pebble Mill studios which broadcast *Midlands Today* to the West region are also based in Birmingham (serving a 'region' that includes Shropshire, Gloucestershire, and Hereford and Worcester), whereas the East region (which covers Nottinghamshire, Leicestershire and more) is served via the Nottingham studios. These divisions which still leave large areas to be covered by one studio have none the less grown out of the realisation that the original areas were too large and too indistinct to allow for viewers to relate to them easily. As one of our respondents, a BBC regional television producer, explained:

> In the 1950s, there was a concept of the Midlands as being a separate part of the country. It seems now to have become more locally broken down. Nottingham people don't associate with Derby people. . . . There is no common ground. The idea of the region is very odd. There were sometimes strange groupings of areas for administrative purposes.
>
> (Interview, 1997)

And, as with Central Television, if the choice of items in the regional news broadcasts emanate from within a small radius of the studios, those viewers who live in towns and cities outside these radii may feel somewhat aggrieved to the extent of questioning the regionalism of the service. So, for broadcasters working in a region, what makes a region is not an idle question: does a regional identity of some sort have to exist before regional media can succeed or can regional media succeed in creating a regional identity?

Such problems do not arise in the context of local – as opposed to regionally based – media such as local newspapers or local radio services. Within the cities and towns covered by regional television, there are thriving local newspapers (e.g. in Leicester, Nottingham) and local radio stations, including ethnic ones (BBC Radio Leicester, Leicester Sound, Sunrise Radio, etc.). Each of these media perform different roles within their respective communities and each provide their readers and listeners with different things. For the citizen in any one of the Midlands towns and cities, it is that interplay of media which is a significant factor in assessing their access to local and regional news. As these proliferate, the question of their construction of regional, local and even ethnic identities increases in importance.

David Morrison's analysis of regionality supports the concept of the regional and the local as being defined by cultural rather than simply by spatial/geographical distinctions. He defines regionality as an awareness of belonging to an area which has characteristics distinct from those of other areas. He further suggests that some people have a strong affinity with an area, and the region then becomes a focal point for self identity. However, he maintains that for a majority of individuals the concept of a region, or of 'our region', provides a person with no more than an increased interest in a particular area. Morrison further argues that any television company wishing to create a 'region' can be tested if their broadcasting definition does not correspond with the cultural definition held by the audience in that area (1989: 15).

Johnson has also argued that regional commercial (and non-commercial) broadcasting 'highlights' and 'reinforces' those aspects of a region that make it different and reflect this to other parts of the country. Regional provision, he continues, also encourages the viewers' involvement so offering the opportunity of creating a regional identity (1989: 13). For media practitioners this may mean bringing to their viewing publics the news from the local/regional area, raising issues that are important to those publics regionally and locally and reflecting their particular region, at work and at play. Such a service could never be provided by the national media since it is too distant both physically and culturally from the locality of the local and regional media audience.

According to the Acting Editor of *Central News*, before Central created the East sub-region, it was never seen as the 'East' Midlands region:

> the East is a region now. . . . The key is to appear local to the audience and identify with them. This needs to be in the context of a region rather than a particular town. Central have built this region called the East Midlands and people relate to Central and see themselves as an entity. Granada did this well because they created something called 'Granada land', with a kind of wall dividing this from other regions.

One could, nevertheless, query the nature and depth of the regional identity/identities created by a service that covers Lincolnshire, Leicestershire, Nottinghamshire, Derbyshire and parts of Cambridgeshire. As previous research has suggested, unless news is local and therefore in an audience's immediate area, it finds very little with which to identify. So however well intentioned, the editor's conviction that Central have created a region is a problematic statement, because it relies on the audience identifying with the region thus defined. Many factors can influence a person's sense of regional identity (if indeed such a thing exists). These can include the place that they live, work and were born. Contemporary societies are so cosmopolitan that it may be more useful to think of individuals having not one but several identities constructed around such factors as ethnicity, localities, work, leisure, communities of interest and the like.

Local city-wide newspapers may be able to develop stronger links with their readers because of their fairly limited geographical areas and their abilities to engender attachments within that limited cultural and geographical space. The *Leicester Mercury* (circulation just over 100,000) – which exists very healthily within the Midlands television region alongside other similar media – is able to flourish because it understands what readers want and mean by local news. According to its editor, its own audience research suggests that the readers (viewers) believe that what is happening in local communities is important: 'Community is the key to a newspaper being involved and doing things . . . it is part of our role . . . we have to help and be seen to be helping.'

One attempt to move academic research towards a more detailed consideration of such questions as the audiences' (viewers') identification, affinity and orientation towards regional television services was Halloran's exploratory work for Central Television (1989). One measure employed by researchers was to evaluate the extent to which members of the audience cared for, or were interested in, Central Television or other regional channels. Other measures included relating viewing patterns to patterns of leisure, work and travel, friendship networks, and the like. In this way, some attempt was made to find out how members of the audience/public oriented themselves towards the various regional television services provided.

Perhaps not surprisingly, a common criticism voiced by interviewees living in the fringes of the regional broadcasting areas was that the news focused disproportionately on the large cities, usually those near the main studios, at the expense of smaller towns and outlying districts. Two recommendations made in the study addressed such criticisms head-on and suggested that the coverage of fringe areas of television broadcast news needed to be improved and, following from this, that ways should be found to allow viewers to identify with the regional news programmes more easily. In these ways, regional broadcasting must not only take into account spatial considerations, e.g. the size of the area covered, where the main studios are located, etc., but also cultural and political ones, e.g. football clubs, in order to begin to create a sense of regionalism.

But these sorts of issues transcend the specific locale of the Midlands; regional broadcasters overseas have also thought long and hard about the question of regionalism and localism and the place of 'the media in the regions' and particularly about the puzzle of whether 'regions create the media, or the media create the regions' (Musso, 1991).

Such questions apart, there is much evidence to show that regional media do have significant numbers of readers and viewers. Whether the act of viewing a regional news programme or reading a regional/local newspaper is an indication of an affinity to a region or locality is another, albeit related, matter, but it does lend support to the view that such media play an important part in the lives of individuals. According to our respondent at Central, *Central News East* has the highest audience rating over all other regional companies in England and its audience is larger than that of the BBC. Such statements are partial: a report in the BBC's *Ariel* magazine trumpeted that in the first two months of 1997 combined audiences for BBC regional news across the UK hit their highest level for five years and pulled ahead of ITV for the first time in two years. The same piece put the audience for *Midlands Today* at an average of over 1 million, though it omitted to mention the figures for Central.

If we treat the global figures as broadly correct, they suggest that in any one month some 15 million viewers tune in to regional news broadcasts, a considerable figure. How that audience is shared between the services, however, is in dispute. The above figures suggest a BBC lead, albeit in a short time span, while a recent survey for the ITV companies suggested that the Channel 3 regional news service is preferred by 58 per cent of viewers, the remaining 36 per cent choosing the BBC news service as alternative (*Financial Times*, 13 May 1997).

These figures form part of the continuing struggle between the major broadcasters in Britain to attract audiences and also reflect the different strategies used by the services in the pursuit of this task. The Acting Editor at Central suggested a range of factors which could be used to attract viewers: contemporary popular music and more 'viewer friendly' presenters being two factors identified. In many ways then, presenters come to represent a type of regional programme, and a type of approach to regional programming, which can lead to allegiances amongst the viewing population. Overall though, a programme such as *Central News East* is carefully crafted to appeal to a wide audience. As she expressed it:

> The trick is that you like the people you are broadcasting to and so you try to entertain them. We cover the hard stories better . . . more seriously (than other channels), the viewers feel safe to come to us to get the information that they want.
>
> (Interview, 1997)

The self image of *Central News East* is one of straight, 'report it as it is' hard news, human interest stories, mixed with approachable, safe, friendly, 'sexy' presenters; all of this within an entertaining package. And this is often contrasted with the more educational and informational approach used by the BBC (whether intentionally or not). Such interpretations of the programme vehicle inevitably spill over into decisions about content.

NEWS OUTPUT

If the main national broadcast news services provide the hard news on national and world events, and on local events if they are catapulted into the national forum, the regional and local services remain very firmly tied to their area. Their aim is to focus on what happens within the region with a strong emphasis on news and events but given a strong human interest (and entertaining) treatment without succumbing to dullness. Subjects that do not meet such criteria for good regional television are unlikely to be aired. Over the 1997 election period, the Acting Editor of *Central News East* described the programme's role as a 'politics exclusion zone'. She explained that 'in the six weeks Central will talk to the three main political leaders and every Friday night the political editor will do a "piece to camera" that is amusing'. (This included a montage sequence of visual images of the week's political events, filmed to a background of music.) More detailed coverage would have been seen as boring because of the amount of political coverage in other media. The day the 1997 general election was announced, *Central East News* did not run the story in the opening headlines but relegated it to the middle of the news programme. By contrast, on the same evening the BBC *Midlands East Today* news programme dealt with the election in the opening headlines and gave it prominence by using the item as the lead story. Subsequent coverage confirmed this pattern. The BBC's coverage was more intense with many of the weekly items focusing on regional issues and regional contestants as well as the political leaders visiting the region. *Central News* was, on the other hand, giving comparatively little coverage in the run-up to the election and happy to run items on 'how to shred election literature', 'how to get away from the election' and similar 'fun' items. Clearly, the contrast here was between an attempt to inform and an attempt to entertain first with little information provided and then only as the election loomed large. These different approaches not only reflect the way the services view their different roles but also the ways in which nationally significant events are always refracted through local concerns (Sreberny-Mohammadi, forthcoming).

The analysis of two weeks of regional news programmes in 1986 and 1996 is given in tables 3.1 and 3.2.[1] Both tables provide a breakdown of the major categories of items; the tables exclude all links, introductions and summaries to each individual programme and usually treat sports information and news as one single item to reflect the point that sport is concentrated into the latter part of the programme. Although the data are, on the whole, unproblematic it is important to appreciate that the nature of regional news coverage is less formal than that of national news coverage and, crucially, more personalised. Even items on health and medicine, for example

Table 3.1 Items (%) and length of items as percentages of total time (excluding links, summaries, weather news) on *Central News*

	1986 (n = 104) 8 days	1986 (13,037 secs)	1996 (n = 90) 8 days	1996 (11,038 secs)
Health	5	2	8	6
Sport	9	18	9	22
Exhibits etc.	16	26	11	13
Accidents	10	4	8	5
Human interest	6	5	9	13
Crime	22	8	23	15
Industry/employment*	6	8	4	2
Royalty	3	2	—	—
Features	—	—	6	5
Council/local politics	5	4	5	4
Others**	19	23	17	15

* Includes 4 items on the launch of the Rover 800.
** In 1986 includes items on education (3), transport (1), policing (2), Northern Ireland (2), Olympic bid (4). In 1996, on BSE (2), sex discrimination (2), policing (1).

on autism or on medication for children, are constructed around the personal experiences of individuals, whether mothers, fathers or children, so blurring the distinction between, say, a 'medical' story and a 'human interest' one. While the programme makers may perceive that they each have different styles and approaches, significant differences may be more difficult to discern either across the whole programme or within the approaches to each individual item. Furthermore, they are not immediately obvious from the empirical data (see tables 3.1 and 3.2).

The programmes analysed differ in length: BBC *Midlands Today* ran for about 24 minutes in 1986, and about 27 minutes in 1996. *Central News*, on the other hand, varied more widely in 1986 often reaching 29 minutes though sometimes it was extended to include features on country life and leisure in the region (these are not included in the content analysis). In 1996, *Central News* was between 27 and 29 minutes in length.

Such variations – minutes here and there – complicate the comparison between the services, as does the difference in the number of days for which we have data. Nevertheless, certain patterns emerge:

- For *Central News*, 'sport' is a consistently important category taking up about one-fifth of all programme time. By 1996, this is also true of BBC *Midlands Today*, though it was less true of the same programme in 1986.
- 'Crime' is another important category. For *Central News* in 1986, 22 per cent of items were about crime and 23 per cent in 1996. For BBC *Midlands Today*, the 1986 figure is 29 per cent but only 11 per cent in 1996. This

Table 3.2 Items (%) and length of items as percentages of total time (excluding
links, summaries, weather news) on *Midlands Today*

	1986 (n = 134) 9 days	1986 (9,976 secs)	1996 (n = 97) 10 days	1996 (12,848 secs)
Health	6	7	3	3
Sport	7	11	11	22
Exhibits etc.	7	14	1	1
Accidents	9	3	7	2
Human interest	4	5	3	3
Crime	29	19	11	13
Industry/employment	11	8	11	7
Royalty	2	5	1	1
Features	—	—	12	13
Council/local politics	4	4	4	3
Education	2	3	10	12
Other*	18	21	25	20

* For 1986, includes 3 items on transport, 3 on policing, 1 on Northern Ireland, 2 on Birmingham's Olympic bid, 2 on agriculture, 2 on the environment, and assorted others. For 1996, includes 4 items on medical matters, 2 on medical/health matters, 3 on BSE, 3 on water charges and related issues, 2 on transport, 2 on policing, and assorted others.

category took up 19 per cent of time in 1986 but only 13 per cent in 1996 suggesting a change in that programme's agenda. The large number of items and comparatively lower amount of time they take up is due to the practice, at least in 1986, of having many short items about crime. Overall, it is an important category as Cottle also found in his research. According to his detailed and extensive analysis of 288 programmes, crime news 'comprise[d] a quarter of all regional news items' (1993: 128).

• Two other categories are worthy of comment. In both years, there were many items about 'exhibitions, festivals, etc.'. Such items are a mixture of publicity, information, reviews and forthcoming events. They took up considerable time in 1986 for both programmes (26 per cent for *Central News*, 14 per cent for BBC *Midlands Today*) but less in 1996 (13 per cent and 1 per cent respectively). On the other hand, 'features' were more important for the BBC in 1996. One week's worth of programmes contained a daily item about people with unusual occupations, for instance.

• National political actors play a minor part in regional news. They rarely feature and then mainly as secondary actors: if a display requires their presence, a statement from an MP wraps up the item, or a bye-election is taking place and their presence is called for.

What is apparent from this data is not only what does get covered in regional news but, perhaps more significantly, what does not. In Simon Cottle's case, the 'wider public understandings of the inner city problem ... find uneven representation within the routine contours of regional inner city news' (1993: 128). As did politics during the 1997 election on *Central News*, and as does national and local politics generally since it is defined as 'boring on television' (Interview, 1997), the allocation of power and resources within a locality or localities remains largely unexplored.

There is one final point about these data which needs to be mentioned: there are fewer individual items broadcast in 1996 than in 1986 although the consequences of that vary from one programme to another. For *Central News*, the average length of an item is 125 seconds in 1986 and 123 seconds in 1996; for BBC *Midlands Today*, the figures are very different: 75 seconds in 1986 but 132 seconds in 1996. This can be explained by the practice in 1986 of broadcasting a large number of items of a very short (20 seconds or so) duration in the middle section of the programme. Such findings contradict the view of our BBC respondent who felt that in the mid-1980s items would often run to two-and-a-half to three minutes, whereas today the average is well below that. However, it is more in line with the view at Central that a typical story runs to 'about one minute and thirty seconds' again, and possibly shorter than in the past. The real difficulty here is determining what a typical item is: some were (and continue to be) of a very short duration, others last much longer. It is that mix of pace, subject matter, and running order that is distinctive of the news magazine programmes that make up regional television news.

REGIONAL NEWS PROVISION BEYOND THE MILLENNIUM

Regional news programmes have developed and adapted to meet the needs and wants of their various, and overlapping, audiences. And this is broadly true for other media working in the area. Local newspapers exploit their ability to cover local events in great detail and to provide a range of news material and *advertising material* to help the local reader/citizen make sense of his or her local environment. Local radio works in the same way (see chapter 2). The BBC Radio Acting Managing Editor commented that:

> News on the radio is very important to the public. People will tune in just to hear the news itself. With hourly bulletins if something happens we will bring it out just about quicker than anyone else.
>
> (Interview, 1997)

Cable television, on the other hand, works in a different way as it seeks to involve local people in the programme making process (see chapter 4). Unlike the other media, it does not necessarily seek to develop its own news agenda, or something which is recognisable as such to other media practitioners. Its intention is to 'look at local people and events' rather than simply mentioning the city. More than this, it is 'community access television . . . local people are not just watching but making the programme' (Interview, J. Ludlum, Channel Manager, Cable 7, Leicester, 1997).

At one level, each of these media reinforce and lend support to each other: by emphasising local news in a geographical and spatial sense, they all help to construct a locality, however extensively defined. From the community level of cable to the local level of local radio and newspapers to the more regional level of television news broadcasting, it is the identification with a core and anchoring location that is important. But beyond this, these media can also be in a competitive position against each other: the BBC versus ITV, as we have seen; newspapers against television, local BBC radio against local commercial radio, local BBC Asian services against other commercial Asian services, and so on. Consequently, the interplay of forces looks different when viewed from the 'top-down' media perspective rather than the 'bottom-up' perspective of the more active 'audience'.

Among the main services, then, there is a certain similarity of content as each develops its own way of appealing to the viewer/reader/listener. Part of the reason for this is undoubtedly the links built up between journalists working in different media but within the same regional space, for example local radio reporters would contact local television regarding a story item. Such simple connections are perhaps inevitable but they can often lead to similarity rather than a diversity of output, something that is also common across national and international media.

But how will regional television news provision fare in the next century? As we have seen, the regional television structure has changed with respect to organisation and ownership but the fundamental idea of providing something for the regions has remained unchanged. In the foreseeable future, and in spite of possible changes in the rules of ownership with regards to commercial television, it is difficult to see the regional requirements being abandoned. This does not mean, however, that the content of those vehicles which satisfy the requirements will remain unchanged: cuts in expenditure and in resources, greater collaboration between regional centres, a more populist approach to attract larger audiences – all these things can impact on the range and diversity of what is on offer.

Certain changes within regional television are likely. Both our respondents from the main services felt that multi-tasking, multi-skilling, bi-media working would become much more the norm in the future. The crew or team would disappear and be replaced by a single journalist–cameraman – the video journalist – who could single-handedly produce individual items ready for transmission. But the presence of journalism of a kind in the regions was not likely to disappear, if anything the regional presence would be supplemented and/or complemented by the presence of other media, cable television being an important one.

Although still largely undeveloped, cable could offer the most local of services and so, in theory, threaten the regional providers. But cable penetration is still low and few operators have seen the need to invest vast resources into building up a local community presence as a news and information provider (see chapter 4). Compared with the regional companies, local cable community services are in a different league. Whether this will change in the future is difficult to tell: experience elsewhere suggests that local cable community providers benefit by building up working relationships or alliances with other news providers such as local newspapers or local radio, rather than creating their own news provision facilities. At present, they remain largely separate from the other media in their regions though co-operation clearly does take place. The editor of the local newspaper acknowledges that his paper is not in direct competition with the local cable company, however he clearly recognises the potential of the new media and the possibility for changing demand. The editor commented:

> Whether ... via local radio or cable television or internet, the *Mercury* needs to be aware that if any one of these becomes more popular than a newspaper then they (the newspaper) need to be there offering that service.

So the mix of media will persist. The local press, itself undergoing change and retrenchment as it has since the last century, will survive if it provides the combination of national and local news, leisure and feature content and local advertisements which make it such a valuable local resource. Somewhere in between, local radio will find a niche. A situation clearly articulated by the Acting Managing Editor of BBC Radio Leicester:

> The BBC have realised that the 40 BBC local radio stations combined add up to listening figures of ten million ... twice Radio 4 and at a tenth of the cost. They (the BBC) realise that there is a value for money aspect to local radio ... it is a BBC presence in the locality, people know of local BBC radio.

This need to signify a strong local presence was supported by the concluding comments made by the Acting Editor at *Central News East*:

> Central need to be a 'pivotal point' for viewers to keep off competition. At twenty past six at night they need to be sure of what they are getting – this familiarity and identity with Central will keep the viewers.

Finally, it was suggested by media practitioners that survival of local media forms part of a broader economic issue which to some extent transcends questions of regional or local identity and the need to appeal to audiences. The future depends on the economic priorities of large media companies and so for some media practitioners the battle will be for resources and the need to encourage financial backers to develop and expand existing services.

NOTES

1 Samples taken from two weeks in May and July 1986 and two weeks in February and March 1996. Which service is accessed depends on the direction one's TV aerial is facing: East (BBC) and West (Central) can be accessed within a mile of each other in the centre of the Leicester area.

REFERENCES

Collins, R. (1990) *Television: Policy and Culture*, London: Unwin Hyman.

Cottle, S. (1993) *TV News, Urban Conflict and the Inner City*, Leicester: Leicester University Press.

Department of National Heritage (1995) *Media Ownership: The Government's Proposals* London: HMSO.

Halloran, J. (1989) 'A Qualitative Exploratory Study for Central News', unpublished, Leicester: Centre for Mass Communication Research.

ITC (1991) *ITC Annual Reports and Accounts*, London: ITC.

—— (1994) *ITC Performance Review 1993*, London: ITC.

—— (1997) *ITC Performance Review 1996*, London: ITC.

Johnson, M. (1989) 'The Regional View' in *Airwaves*, London: Independent Broadcasting Association.

King, I. (1997) 'Call for a Single TV Operator', *Guardian*, 12 June, p. 22.

Lewis, P. (1978) *Community Television and Cable in Britain*, London: British Film Institute.

Morrison, D. (1989) 'A Question of Identity' in *Airwaves*, London: Independent Broadcasting Association.

Musso, P. (ed.) (1991) *Regions d'Europe et Télévision*, Paris: Miroirs.

Sreberny-Mohammadi, A. (forthcoming) *A Study of Regional Coverage of Women Candidates*, Leicester: Centre for Mass Communication Research.

Wilson, J. (1993) 'Rooting for the Regions', *Spectrum*, London: Independent Television Commission.

Wilson, R. (1994) *Local Television: Finding a Voice*, Shropshire: Dragonflair Publishing.

Chapter 4

Local visions
Cable television: the new local medium?

Granville Williams

The relationship between local and regional newspapers and the developing cable industry, which is also keen to identify local markets for news and other entertainment and information services, promises to be at best uncertain and, at worst, problematic; and for all parties! The character of the eventual relationship will be influenced by factors such as the nature of the company which holds the local cable franchise, the attitude other local media groups adopt to the new technology, or the strategy which some of the bigger national media groups take to issues of cross-media ownership. Another vital dimension will be the extent to which cable companies are successful in persuading potential customers to become subscribers to their television and telephony services. It is against the backcloth of the cable industry's future prospects that assessments of the likely relations between cable and other local media must be made. It is not the intention here to re-rehearse the early debates and false starts within the cable industry so typical of the 1980s, but to look at the key contemporary features of the industry and the factors likely to influence future development.[1]

THE DEVELOPING CABLE INDUSTRY

Cable, along with satellite, were the media technologies which were heavily promoted by visionaries of the new media age. The much vaunted claim was that these 'new' technologies would break the old barrier of spectrum scarcity which so severely limited terrestrial television. Cable would enable audiences to enjoy a wide range of programmes based on a multiplicity of channels to which individuals would choose to subscribe or 'pay to view'. In the United Kingdom, in marked contrast to the United States, it was the financial muscle behind British Satellite Broadcasting (BSB) and Sky Television which guaranteed the development of satellite television ahead of cable. Substantial sums of money were invested in both satellite services, but losses were heavy, resulting in the merger of the two services to create BSkyB in 1990. Rupert Murdoch's News International, which effectively controlled BSkyB, continued to invest heavily in the promotion of its satellite channels, and the purchase of broadcast rights to key cricket, boxing and football fixtures, in order to persuade people to buy satellite equipment and win audiences for satellite television. The vital factor in the success of BSkyB from a marketing point of view was the heavy emphasis on advertising and the promotion of televised sporting events in News International's own UK newspapers. Rupert Murdoch described his control of the rights to transmit key sporting events as the 'battering ram' which drove forward the increase in subscriptions to BSkyB, but this increase was also linked to a powerful and unified promotion of the brand image of BSkyB (Chippindale and Franks, 1991).

During the 1980s, cable development stalled because there was neither the financial power nor a favourable regulatory regime to provide a sufficiently fertile terrain on which it might be nurtured. The Cable and Broadcasting Act 1984, moreover, excluded non-European companies from ownership of UK cable companies. This changed with the 1990 Broadcasting Act and American corporations began to acquire substantial interests in UK cable franchises. The new, more favourable regulatory regime created the possibility for cable companies to provide both telephony and television services, while British Telecom was excluded from providing this full range of services because of its dominant market position. Across the same period, there was a remarkable growth in the number of cable franchise licences awarded, so that 80 per cent of homes in the UK fell within a franchise area, compared with only 20 per cent in 1988.

The cable industry took a serious step forward with heavy investment in building the network infrastructure necessary to carry the cable signal. By 1997 around £7.5 billion had been invested, with the industry forecasting a final spend of £12 billion by the year 2000. The technology associated with this investment is mainly broadband, constructed with fibre-optic cable, which is able to carry a much higher capacity of data and television services. The old narrowband technology now represents only 6 per cent of connections.

The prospects for the cable industry, however, are not very positive, in spite of the considerable investment monies which are literally being buried below the ground. Because it has created a patchwork of franchises, cable has not matched the dynamism, marketing flair and insistent promotional campaigns of BT or BSkyB which might have placed cable services firmly in the public eye. It was as late as 1996 that the cable operators began collectively to address this brand image problem; they ran a £12 million advertising campaign, co-ordinated by the Cable Communications Association. The other major problem hindering the expansion of the industry has been 'consumer resistance'. Estimates for cabled households have constantly been revised downwards. Predictions that the penetration of cable would rise from 20 per cent to 46.6 per cent between 1994 and 2000 are being revised, with cable companies becalmed at around 22 per cent.

But despite a sluggish start, it seems inevitable that concentration and consolidation in the cable industry will continue for a number of reasons. First, it will require a much more powerful grouping to break BSkyB's dominance of subscription television channels. Cable companies have complained to the Office of Fair Trading (OFT) about being forced to pay very high prices to carry channels such as Sky Movies and Sky Sports which makes effective competition with BSkyB impossible. But the regulators are also looking at the concept of compulsory 'bundling' of pay channels which requires cable subscribers to pay for channels they do not want in order to access those which they do. This has some implications for the fate of local news channels which will be considered later.

The second important factor favouring concentration is the emerging competition promised by the imminent launch of Rupert Murdoch's digital satellite television. The award of the digital terrestrial franchise to British Digital Broadcasting (BDB) (main stakeholders Carlton and Granada, but with BSkyB providing programming) and the roll-out of Internet modems (for example, BT and News International's Line One) will all intensify the competition for audiences and advertisers and test cable's ability to hold on to its subscribers.

Table 4.1 reveals that the major UK cable operators have consolidated in recent years, with the most dramatic merger being between Mercury Communications, the telephone business, and the cable operators Videotron, NYNEX CableComms and Bell Cablemedia taking place in October 1996. This gave the new company 525,026 cable connections, and 32 per cent of the share of the total number of UK connections to cable. This merger, which created the company Cable and Wireless Communications (C&WC), was given a mixed reception by the business press. *The Times* headlined it as the creation of a 'cable colossus' but the city columnist, Tempus, described the merger as 'long on hype and short on substance . . . the real challenge is

Table 4.1 Main UK cable operators (October 1996)

	Connections	% share of total connections
TeleWest	457,560	28
NYNEX Cablecomms	242,800	15
Comcast	229,495	14
Bell Cablemedia	145,967	9
Videotron	136,259	8
CableTel (UK)	120,139	7
General Cable	96,092	6
Telecential Communications	97,261	6
Diamond Cable	50,109	3

Source: Cable Communications Association

to turn their franchises into customers' (23 October 1996). A *Guardian* leader described it as the 'marriage of two failed cultures' with Mercury Communications 'supposed to provide an effective alternative in the domestic market for BT' and the cable companies 'set up to provide alternative television services without so far making much impact'. It concluded that there was no longer any justification for the government's ban on British Telecom entering the market for providing television services: 'If Britain is to maximise the gains of the information revolution, access must be both affordable and nationwide [it] . . . will be more likely to happen if BT doesn't have its hands tied behind its back' (*Guardian*, 23 October 1996). Not much comfort in comments like these for the future prospects of Cable and Wireless.

In the summer of 1997 two other large UK cable companies, TeleWest and NTL (formerly known as International CableTel), were in preliminary talks about a merger. The cable map will probably end up with two or three companies dominating the UK cable industry, but the jury is still out on whether the early prediction, that cable would be the delivery system of the future, can be realised. Indeed a recent forecast suggests that the cable industry will have difficulty in competing against satellite where price and ease of access are preferred by consumers to promises of unlimited bandwidth through fibre-optic cable and full interactivity. The report's author, Michael Katz, asserts: 'the truth is still that however many channels you deliver into the home, customers will watch only six or seven. There is also some doubt over whether interactive services over the television will find a market.' Superior technology doesn't necessarily impress consumers who are largely untroubled by dish versus cable arguments and operate with the 'dustbin lid' theory of distribution – it doesn't matter how it gets there so long as it gets there. In July 1997 ITC figures revealed more than 2 million people viewing television via broadband cable (ITC, 1997) but 3.3 million households enjoying satellite television (Bell, 1997).

If this assessment of cable's potential is relatively cautious, compared with the success of direct-to-home satellite television, it is still the case that cable, unlike satellite, can provide through the 'return path' two-way communication and with it a range of services, including Internet access, video-on-demand, home shopping and all the other conveniences associated with interactivity on the 'information superhighway'. These aspects of cable led the Newspaper Society, which is the body representing Britain's regional and local press, to identify cable television as 'perhaps the most attractive alternative to local newspapers in the future'; the Society added 'this potential threat is also a glaring opportunity' (Newspaper Society, 1997; see also chapter 11).

Clearly, local and regional newspapers seek to provide a range of news and entertainment, and attract advertising which has a direct appeal to readers in its circulation area. Could this also be the same for local television in the UK? One modest experiment in the Lancashire village of Waddington in the spring of 1989 suggested it could be, when Granada Television wired up households to see how viewers would respond to the multi-channel television world then emerging. Ten per cent of the village households – a cross-section of the demographic make-up of the village population – received the satellite services, but the regulatory body, the Independent Broadcasting Authority (IBA), gave a special dispensation for a low-powered local UHF transmitter to be set up which enabled all villagers to receive the 'village channel' – Waddington Village TV (WVTV). It was a hit. While it was a modest and unrepresentative experiment which lasted only a month, WVTV demonstrated vividly the appeal of local television – in this case local people, without any experience, making programmes which local people wanted to watch (Wilson, 1994: 32–4).

Another factor which some newspaper groups might also have considered is the impact on circulation from the entry of a new competitor into their territory, especially when sales of local and regional newspapers have been steadily slipping (see chapter 1). So what has been the response of newspaper groups to the development of cable television?

CABLE TV, LOCAL NEWSPAPERS AND MEDIA SYNERGY

One of the clearest views of the commercial opportunities which could flow from an integrated approach to the local media of cable, radio and newspapers was given by Sir David English, Chairman of Associated Newspapers and Channel One, the cable news channel. The group's ownership of Northcliffe Newspapers also makes it a dominant player in local and regional newspapers. From 1993, through an umbrella organisation with other newspaper owners, the British Media Industry Group (BMIG), English was active in lobbying for changes in media ownership legislation. The 1996 Broadcasting Act was the successful outcome for these efforts, and when in July 1996 he gave a key speech at the Radio Festival, he was enthusiastic about the commercial opportunities for cross-media ownership which liberalisation of media ownership in the Act (then awaiting Royal assent) heralded.

Setting the scene, he argued for the inevitability of convergence and pointed out that regional newspapers were a 'mature' industry with declining sales and cost-cutting affecting the quality of the journalism:

Newspapers are the core foundation of local and regional communications. They must be free to build on these foundations by extending into every branch of the media ... TV, electronic and radio. I'm convinced that by becoming multi-media publishers, newspapers have a lot to give to future partners.

(English, July 1996)

In his analysis, Sir David English pointed out the economies possible through exploiting cross-media commercial opportunities:

A local radio station owned by and working in conjunction with a regional evening newspaper can cut costs and improve content. Clearly the news content can be lifted immediately. Local radio stations often only have three or four journalists working for them, usually less than the BBC competition. Regional newspapers have an average of about 80. The combination of those forces would be formidable for the radio station . . . and I might add the newspaper. A joint sales force will make the cost of selling air time cheaper, overheads can be shared and it will produce a higher yield through packages and cross-media deals. And then there is whole-hearted cross promotion.

(Ibid.)

This is a familiar argument in one respect – it was at the heart of the case for relaxing limits on cross-media ownership rules put forward by the BMIG. The consequent synergies, combined efforts on advertising and promotion, and (although it didn't feature in the BMIG case for cross-media ownership liberalisation) economies through staff cuts, were the key issues which made this business strategy attractive. And Sir David added another ingredient to the approach towards local media: local cable TV.

Associated Newspapers launched Channel One in London in November 1994. It was seen as an obvious extension to their dominant position in London news reporting through their ownership of the London *Evening Standard*. In a deal announced in November 1993 Associated Newspapers was awarded a ten-year contract by a consortium of six cable companies, the London Interconnect Group, to supply twelve hours of television programming daily. Channel One subsequently developed operations in Bristol and Liverpool. In his Radio Festival speech Sir David English acknowledged that the group's cable TV plans were 'not going as quickly as we hoped but that is only because the cable TV companies are not connecting up homes at the speed which they promised'. None the less he highlighted the 'fascinating' cross-media opportunities:

The advertising packages will become textual, audio and visual. Management costs can be cut again, with central services providing all three media outlets. And, once again the editorial becomes enhanced. Video journalists can handle radio stories in almost the same breath as they cover Channel One stories. Radio journalists can become VJs; both can provide information to the newspaper, though they will not have the time to actually write stories. Newspaper reporters though will have the time to make radio broadcasts.

(Ibid.)

This approach of integrating local media into a unified media group raises a number of issues about the resultant range, quality and diversity of the product carried by the different media, with homogeneous viewpoints

almost certain to replace the distinctive perspectives of the previously different news organisations. When Channel One was launched there was a great
deal of publicity about the type of journalist that the channel wished to
recruit. Thirty young journalists were given a month-long training course in
low-cost television journalism, using lightweight Sony cameras to both prepare the story, interview, film and edit on return to the office (Brown, 1994).

Sir David English alluded to this approach in his Radio Festival presentation, but broadened it to suggest it was applicable across different media:
'Multi-skilling is the future in electronic journalism and the colleges are
turning out young journalists who will, after sufficient training, be able to
turn their reportorial skills to all outlets.' But what might be logical from a
commercial perspective is in danger of ignoring the fact that people use the
media in different ways depending on a number of factors. To the extent that
we begin to receive the same news via different media because it has been
covered and reported by the same news organisation's reporter could eliminate the particular appeal which motivates groups to watch or read particular
media.

One survey, for example, identified television as the main source of world
news (68 per cent), followed by newspapers (19 per cent) and radio (8 per
cent); whereas for local news, newspapers were named by 41 per cent of
households as their main source, followed by television (32 per cent) and
radio (13 per cent). Also newspapers have a greater appeal as a source for
local news for older people in A and B social groups, whereas television has a
larger appeal to those in D and E groups and in the age range 25 to 34
(Slattery, 1997: 11).

The consequence of the approach outlined by Sir David English, where
one news organisation supplies the different media of radio, cable and newspapers, could be a diminution of choice and diversity for the consumers;
local and regional media might become a one-note chorus with stories
repeated, without including alternative perspectives, across the different outlets. People might question why they should buy a paper, listen to local radio,
or subscribe to a local cable news channel if they are not sufficiently distinctive. In this respect the development of an integrated cross-media news
channel also supplying general entertainment and other features in different
formats, might be self-defeating (Greenslade, 1997).

The principle of diversity, however, which requires the Radio Authority
under the 1996 Broadcasting Act to assess the public interest when radio
stations are taken over, can sometimes block this commercial strategy. When
the Northcliffe group, which owns the *Leicester Mercury*, sought to take over
the local radio station, Leicester Sound, the Radio Authority ruled against it.
Cable however is much more lightly regulated, and a simple licence is all that
is required, which places few demands on the cable operator, above basic
requirements under the Broadcasting Act, of taste and decency.

The other interesting aspect of the strategy outlined by Sir David English involves the notion of synergy. Northcliffe Newspapers have powerful regional monopolies of newspapers in the East Midlands and South West regions, but Channel One haven't featured in any development plans with papers they own in these regions, with the exception of Bristol where they have a minority stake in the *Bristol Evening Post*. Channel One Liverpool is jointly owned by the *Liverpool Daily Post* and *Liverpool Echo*, part of another large regional newspaper group, Trinity International. Keith Ely, formerly Editor of the *Liverpool Daily Post*, runs the Liverpool Channel One operation, and has indicated some of the factors which influenced the joint venture. In contrast to Channel One London, where journalists from the *Evening Standard* rarely work with the cable programme, in Liverpool the journalists on the *Post* and *Echo* are integral to the operation. The Channel One Liverpool studio adjoins the paper's newsroom and a dividing window overlooking the print reporters is the backdrop for the presenters. There are twenty-four staff working on the venture, and it transmits thirteen hours' daily programming which comprises news and sport for the first half-hour of every hour, except between 7am and 9am when there is continuous broadcasting. The back half-hour comprises lifestyle broadcasting supplied from Channel One London. A senior producer sits in on the *Liverpool Echo*'s morning news conference, the paper's sports reporters carry camcorders on certain stories to feed the channel, and experts from the paper are used to comment on stories. The output of Channel One Liverpool also includes local programming such as the arts and entertainment show *Scene on One* and *Sports Page*. However, the use of material made by Channel One London can jar with Liverpool subscribers who do not relate to material which has a London emphasis and content on their local channel. For example, a thirty-minute programme *The River* deals with events and issues centred on the River Thames, but for Liverpool viewers this is hardly local programming, especially when for them it would be the River Mersey which looms large in their consciousness. Research on local audience responses to Channel One Liverpool highlighted this uncomfortable duality between home-grown programmes and news, and the imported London originated programmes.[2]

By mid August 1997, Channel One was still a loss-making venture. The Daily Mail and General Trust drastically reduced its spending budget from around £10 million to £4 million a year. Its London workforce was cut by a half with seventy jobs going, including video journalists, news editors and presenters. Announcing the cuts, Managing Director Julian Aston blamed the channel's failure to generate profit on a lack of subscribers, with the target of around 1 million actually nearer 500,000. The new plans to run the service 'more cost effectively' and reduce losses from £8 million to £1 million a year include selling the satellite link truck (which will make it difficult to cover live, breaking news) and dropping feature-led programmes to concentrate on covering local human interest news stories similar to those found on the inside news pages of the *Daily Mail* and *Evening Standard*. In addition a local news text-only service from the Press Association would be used as well as video material. Editor Martin Dunn denies that these major editorial changes will lead to a 'dumbing down' (Kelly, 1997: 4).

TALKING TO YOURSELF? L!VE TV

L!VE TV espouses a different set of values compared to Channel One in the way it promotes local cable news and entertainment. After the ousting of Janet Street Porter, former *Sun* editor Kelvin MacKenzie created publicity for the city television channel with the News Bunny, topless darts, weather forecasts in Norwegian, and a product described as 'tabloid television'. When the channel was launched in June 1995 from the Canary Wharf studios, purpose-built and costing £5 million, the claims were grandiose. Mirror Group Newspapers (MGN) would invest £30 million with break-even established three years later; the group's newspapers would launch and sustain L!VE TV with the same kind of promotion that Rupert Murdoch's titles offered Sky Television when it was established.

MGN, with 24 per cent of the national newspaper market, is excluded under the media ownership rules in the 1996 Broadcasting Act from owning television and radio franchises. In July 1997 the £297 million purchase of Midland Independent Newspapers (MIN), which publishes the *Post* and *Mail* in Birmingham, where there is also a L!VE TV station, seemed to indicate a move into the regional newspaper business, as well as an attempt to repeat Sir David English's strategy of regional cross-media groups with a mix of newspapers, exhibitions, magazines and local television programming.

Two years after its launch, L!VE TV's revenue was around £5 million and its costs £12 million, with programming costs at around £2,000 an hour. BARB, the Broadcasters' Audience Research Board, lists audience figures for thirty-four satellite and cable channels, but L!VE TV doesn't figure because its audience is neither national nor large enough to be measurable. In a cutting verdict, William Phillips, *Broadcast* magazine's rating expert, said, 'I really would have thought you were talking to yourself most of the time if you're working for L!VE TV. These cable channels have been rubbished so much I can't see what possible use it is for the cable companies to keep subsidising them' (quoted in Nevin, 1997).

But L!VE TV continues to expand its city stations. It has opened local services in Liverpool, Birmingham, Manchester, Edinburgh, Westminster and Newcastle with plans to operate in twelve cities. Kelvin MacKenzie is relentlessly optimistic about the prospects for city television, seeing cable as a challenge to what he considers the inferior product of local newspapers. The mix of L!VE TV is half local, with vox pops and fairly straightforward information, interspersed with the wackier programming which has allowed MacKenzie to publicise his cable channel.

Two issues are crucial to the success of L!VE TV. The first is subscribers, and the second is persuading local advertisers to use the medium. Before L!VE TV launched it had contracts with two-thirds of the cable industry, which will run for nine years with no-break clauses, but which are based on subscribers rather than actual viewers. It may have seemed a good idea at the time for the cable companies, but experience has revealed a number of problems with what subscribers perceive to be the quality and value of the various channels on offer to them.

The result has been *churn*. While the take-up of subscriptions to cable has been disappointingly low, the more worrying problem has been those who fail to renew. It's at the top of the telecommunication industry's concerns, and one conference, entitled *Building Loyalty and Reducing Churn*, addressed issues like 'save and winback strategies', 'building lasting relationships with high value customers' and 'programmes to secure customer loyalty'. It's a very serious business, and the publicity leaflet for the conference highlighted the strategies to tempt back 'defectors', 'create innovative lifestyle packages', and so on. The problem is that for some cable channels L!VE TV doesn't quite fit the bill when they do research on what subscribers think about their channel. Joyce Taylor, Managing Director of Discovery Communications Europe, has pointed out that research revealed subscribers assign a high value to the *Discovery Channel*, but because of the problem of 'bundling' channels they are also receiving L!VE TV in the same package, and it doesn't carry the same level of approval, to put it mildly. In other words any strategy to boost cable television penetration rates has to appeal to particular niche interests, and whilst the *Discovery Channel* has identified and won an audience, the wacky, low-cost output of L!VE TV may get publicity but not audiences. Consumer resistance is connected to their perception of value for money and the move is towards dismantling a big basic subscription with a range of channels towards creating smaller packages offering better value to sub-scribers, and hopefully driving up subscriptions to the 30 per cent level and above. The key question will be where L!VE TV features in these better value packages, if at all.[3]

On the other issue of winning local advertisers to use L!VE TV, even Kelvin MacKenzie is uncertain about a time-scale, suggesting at least two or three years before they will use the medium in the same way they currently use local newspapers. With local newspapers there are of course certified figures for circulation of both paid-for and free papers, but potential advert-isers will be very wary of using a local cable channel with a low level of subscribers and uncertain viewing figures. We should be cautious about the prospects for survival of L!VE TV. Like Channel One and the Daily Mail Group, maybe MGN will have to learn the painful lesson that L!VE TV will never match costs with revenue and have to cut back.

LOCAL CABLE FUTURES

In 1997 regional newspaper managers were invited by accountants Coopers and Lybrand to assess the greatest long-term threat to the regional publishing industry; their response was that the Internet and on-line services, much more than cable television, posed the biggest threat. At the same time, these newspapers, with over 80 per cent of local advertising, were clear that cable companies were not going to erode that share without hard battles. Cable companies attempting to set up, commission and package deals in their franchise areas have been rebuffed. In addition, the majority of managers thought regional press journalists did not have the skills to present television or radio news. So it seems clear that many of the predictions made by Sir David English in his Radio Academy speech are unlikely to be realised (Sharpe, 1997).

That does not mean however that cable companies are going to leave the local programming area unchallenged. The UK cable industry has correctly identified local television as one area where viewers can be attracted to the right kind of programming. As the cable programme build is slowly completed and subscribers are won, so too will local television programming develop, but in most cases it will be developed in-house by the cable companies. It's clear also that the economies of scale in creating large cable groups covering several franchise areas mean that local television services won't be provided by staff working from studios in all the franchise areas, or even co-ordinated at a local level either. CableTel, for example, has a person appointed to develop local programming but she works from the head office in Farnborough, with little in the way of resources at the local level in a franchise area such as Huddersfield.

From a positive point of view, cable television could provide a valuable training ground for people who have come through the diverse range of film and video production courses now provided in the universities and colleges, but it will never provide lucrative salaries for journalists. Programming budgets for local cable franchises are in most cases tiny or non-existent. In many areas cable television will be reliant on volunteers and students from local colleges and universities to make programmes almost as showcases for local talent. Wilson devotes a chapter in his book to 'Volunteers in Local Programming' and argues: 'Staffing costs are the biggest single cost in a TV channel operation and a significant volume output is only possible if the main output of local programmes is made or provided on a nil or extremely low-cost basis' (Wilson, 1994: 114).

Finally, there is a general trend across all media to cut costs, on staffing and programming. As more and more channels come on stream, and audiences are increasingly fragmented, pressures to drive costs down further will be enhanced. In the ten years from 1986 to 1996 the UK has moved from four to seventy-six channels. In terms of hours of television, this means a move from 25,000 to 350,000 television hours per year; the introduction of digital will multiply this by a factor of ten (ITV Association, 1996). Amid this welter of television, cable is going to have to fight very hard for its share of viewers, as well as to retain a share of the telephony services which are the key to profitability. If this is a pessimistic assessment for the future of cable television, and the role for local programming within it, there is a comforting implication for that old, traditional piece of communication, the local newspapers. Maybe the local rag shouldn't be written off too soon.

NOTES

1 Two publications survey some of this ground. The initial interest in cable was stimulated through the publication by the Cabinet Office in March 1982 of the *Report on Cable Systems* by the Cabinet's Information Technology Advisory Panel. This led to the establishment of the Hunt Inquiry and the subsequent report on Cable TV published in October 1982. A booklet dealing with this stage in policy formation is *Hunt on Cable TV: Chaos or Coherence?* by P. Hughes, G. Wensky, N. McCartney and J. Ainsley, (CPBF, 1982). *Local Television: Finding a Voice* by Roger Wilson (Dragonflair Publishing, 1994) has a clear account of the developments in the cable industry up to the 1990s.
2 Information on Channel One based on discussions with Keith Ely, General Manager of Channel One, at the 1996 Manchester Symposium.
3 The two-day conference, *Building Loyalty and Reducing Churn*, was organised by the Institute for International Research, and held in London, 30 September /1 October 1997. Joyce Taylor's comments were made at an Institute for Public Policy Research seminar, 'Quality in Broadcasting', 15 July 1997, in a session, 'Competing concepts of quality'.

REFERENCES

Bell, E. (1997) 'Rising Satellite Leaves Future of Cable in the Air', *Observer*, 15 June.
Brown, M. (1994) 'Switched on to Cheap TV', *Independent*, 8 March.
Chippindale, P. and Franks, S. (1991) *Dished! The Rise and Fall of British Satellite Broadcasting*, London: Simon and Schuster.
English, Sir David (1996) 'Cross-Media Ownership: How Can Radio Develop?', speech to the Radio Academy Festival, Birmingham, 17 July.
Greenslade, R. (1997) 'Hack of All Trades, *Guardian*, 23 June.
ITC (1997) 'Over Two Million Homes Tune in to Cable TV', press release, ITC, 4 September.
ITV Association (1996) *Leading Britain in Regional Television*, London: ITVA.
Kelly, T. (1997) 'Channel One Rejigs Output after Job Cuts', *Press Gazette*, 8 August, p. 4.
Marks, N. (1996) 'Entering a Cable Relationship', *Press Gazette*, 22 November, p. 15.
—— (1997) 'Inside Channel One Liverpool', *Press Gazette*, 28 March.
Nevin, C. (1997) 'L!VE: But for How Much Longer?', *Guardian*, 24 February, pp. 2–3.
The Newspaper Society (1997) *The UK Cable Industry*, Market Factsheet Number 7, 17 February.
Sharpe, H. (1997) 'On-line Services Main Threat to Regionals', *Press Gazette*, 21 February.
Slattery, J. (1997) 'Television Tops for World News but Trailing Locally', *Press Gazette*, 25 April 1997, p. 11.
Wilson, R. (1994) *Local Television: Finding a Voice*, Shropshire: Dragonflair Publishing.

Part II

The economics of the local press

Chapter 5

Instinct, savvy and ratlike cunning: training local journalists

Peter Cole

Journalism training is for some, particularly older, male journalists on national newspapers, an oxymoron. The ability to be a journalist is seen as God-given, though why, if it was let to Him, He bothered to provide the gift at all is unclear. The school of journalist that takes this rather gung-ho approach to the need for training tends to be the old-fashioned sort (younger journalists are no longer great drinkers) that after the eighth gin and tonic reminisces about old so-and-so who was such a 'complete professional' that in a state of considerable inebriation he managed to file on some notorious international story, still beating the competition, and earning a herogram from his editor.

The story gets better as the gin and tonics are reordered. It is a peculiar aspect of the hack's character that he (it almost always is 'he') feels the need to reduce an activity requiring very great skill to accomplish well to something so easy it can be achieved to maximum effect when roaring drunk.

Other professions take a diametrically opposite view: that they require not only peculiar and specific skills, whose acquisition demands great ability, time and effort, but also the occupation must protect itself and its standards by limiting the right to practise it to those who have the necessary qualifications. This is often reinforced by membership of a professional body.

IS TRAINING NECESSARY?

This sterile argument about journalism as a profession or craft or trade has occupied much debate. Why does the journalist flee from the acceptance of his or her own abilities, flee from the possibility of acquiring, passing on, developing or refining those skills, while at the same time using the word 'professional' as the ultimate compliment? It is of course tied in with self-image. The journalist likes to see him or herself as the outsider, the rebel, and a profession is inclusive as well as exclusive. The journalist's romantic image of him or herself is of performing against the odds in difficult conditions and bringing the story home.

The journalist fortunate enough to have crossed that so resolutely undefined line and become a journalist, especially a national newspaper journalist, or even a foreign correspondent on a national newspaper, has perhaps a subconscious desire to exclude others by refusing to define the criteria for inclusion. 'You can't put your finger on it, old boy, you've either got it or you haven't. You can't teach a person how to write, any more than you can teach them how to find the crucial contact in the middle of Beirut. It's instinct; it's savvy; it's ratlike cunning.'

It always comes back to ratlike cunning. Nick Tomalin, a *Sunday Times* journalist of some distinction who was killed in his prime, wrote a famous essay in 1969 called 'Stop the press, I want to get on'. It was published in the *Sunday Times Magazine* in October 1969, and because it was engagingly written, full of genuine insight and understanding of the journalistic process and journalists, and above all funny, it has been taken ever since as the last word on journalism training, particularly by those already on the inside who undertook no training themselves.

> The only qualities essential for real success in journalism are ratlike cunning, a plausible manner, and a little literary ability. If you look at the jewels of the profession you will see that this must be so. . . . The ratlike cunning is needed to ferret out and publish things that people don't want to be known (which is – and always will be – the best definition of News). The plausible manner is useful for surviving while this is going on, helpful with the entertaining presentation of it, and even more useful in later life when the successful journalist may have to become a successful executive on his newspaper. The literary ability is of obvious use.
>
> (Tomalin, 1969)

Tomalin goes on to describe the difficulties of getting a job on a national newspaper, the usefulness of having a famous mother or father, and provides a brilliant description of the composite national journalist. His main point, however, is to decry training for those who will become the best and the most famous and the most influential and the richest national journalists.

> We are obsessed with professionalism, and convinced there is not only a mystery to our craft, but a whole spectrum of laboriously learned techniques. We demand an apprenticeship, examination results, and years of drudgery before we allow entrants a proper chance to show their talents, and yet virtually all the really successful (and really good) journalists have somehow or other managed to escape such a cumbrous ordeal.
>
> (Ibid.)

In one sentence Tomalin dismisses schools of journalism and academic courses as worse than useless. But this was 1969! However, and the reason I quote Tomalin at some length, many of the attitudes he exhibits are current today, and equally many of the views he expresses remain true. There was the National Council for the Training of Journalists then; the NCTJ is with us today. Local newspapers had apprentices then, and trained them; local news-papers have trainees today – we will examine how much they train them. The point Tomalin is making is that this training is of no usefulness or relevance for national newspaper journalism, and that the best national journalists will come, untrained, from other sources than the local press. He is saying that national and local journalism are so different they are separate activities requiring different skills and different people. In effect he is saying that the locals require trained journalists whereas the nationals require their journal-ists to be untrained. Surely a preposterous notion. Except that it is still held – if not articulated in precisely this way – by many national journalists. And many senior national journalists have undergone no formal journalism train-ing whatever, although that becomes less and less the case.

I should declare an interest. I am one of the great untrained. I entered journalism from university on to a London evening newspaper, had no apprenticeship, took no exams, acquired no certificate of competence. And I practised as a national newspaper journalist, as reporter and editor, for many years. Did I suffer from the training deficit? Well, yes and no. I was fortunate initially to have as my immediate boss a man who shared wisdom, inspired and encouraged. By example and helpful reference to my own writing and reporting mistakes he developed my journalism. Of course there were many occasions, particularly in court and the Commons, when I wished I had shorthand. The knowledge of the workings of government, to the extent that it is taught to journalism trainees, I brought with me from university. Newspaper law, avoiding the traps of contempt and defamation, I had to acquire for myself, often through embarrassing encounters with the duty lawyer pointing out that something I had innocently reported would prob-ably be in contempt of court. And I had to learn a lot more when later as a newspaper executive I was handling the legal cases.

Perhaps because journalism is full of non-experts and dilettantes – the good journalist mostly knows a little about a great deal, rather than having deep knowledge of one subject – there is a reluctance to acquire expertise. There is a perverse belief in some quarters that training in some ways dimin-ishes journalism, removes its flair and creativity. It is a peculiarly British attitude, and peculiarly foolish.

Perhaps, too, it is changing, and has changed a great deal already. No longer can journalists disregard the acquisition of skills; the technology has seen to that. Journalists require computer skills, electronic communication skills, electronic research skills. The page-planner and modern equivalent of the subeditor require more advanced computer skills. None of these are hard to acquire, but they must be learned. The stubborn resistance to new tech-nologies is no more than a self-indulgence for those at the end of their careers, or seeking a premature end.

So the technology itself – essentially the replacement of hot-metal type by direct computer input by journalists – has contributed to the culture where training of journalists is essential. But these computer skills are not central; necessary but little to do with journalism itself. For all the technological changes, for all the changing attitudes towards content, journalism remains the identifying, collecting, selecting, ordering, and presentation of information. Much of this can be taught, and is taught. Interviewing skills, research skills, writing skills can be taught, and are taught. The idea that journalism is instinctive, based on innate ability and flair which cannot be improved upon by training is manifestly as absurd as suggesting that world-class athletes simply compete and have no need for the training which fills 99 per cent of their lives.

For all that Nick Tomalin is right about the differences between national and local journalism, and there are still entrants to journalism who find their way directly on to national papers through nepotism, luck or ratlike cunning, most newspaper journalists begin their careers on local newspapers. This, then, is where we should look to see training provided.

This has traditionally been the case. Today, while there have been considerable changes in the organisation of training, the educational background of those entering journalism, and the qualifications to which journalism training leads, most journalists begin their careers on local papers, either weeklies or evenings. Trainee journalists used to sign 'indentures' with their employers, in effect an apprenticeship contract where the newspaper would support the training of the recruit, putting him or her through the various block- or day-release courses and then the requisite examinations, until the trainee became qualified and moved from the status of junior to senior, with a consequent adjustment of pay.

A high proportion of these trainees were teenagers who had grown up in the catchment area of the newspaper in question. Far fewer young people went to university, and not many graduates were to be found in the regional press, or indeed the national press away from the upmarket broadsheets. It is very different today.

JOURNALISM TRAINING AND THE NCTJ

Journalism training was supervised by the National Council for the Training of Journalists (NCTJ), which was born in 1952 following recommendations on the need for co-ordinated training from the 1949 Royal Commission on the Press. The National Council was intended to represent all interested bodies: the proprietors, the editors, the unions. To this day the board of the NCTJ is made up of representatives of, respectively, the Newspaper Society, the Guild of Editors, the National Union of Journalists and the Institute of Journalists. It was to be funded by the industry, essentially the regional press who paid a per capita levy on their editorial staffs. The Printing and Publishing Industry Training Board organised the funding and acted as the supervisory body for the NCTJ.

The NCTJ was responsible for setting and marking examinations in newspaper journalism, law, public administration and shorthand, at a preliminary level and at a final, National Certificate (formerly Proficiency) level. It acted as a clearing house for entrants into journalism, approving day- and block-release courses. It also approved lecturers, who were always ex-journalists. The NCTJ would seek to control some near match between vacancies on local papers and numbers entering journalism training. Its control of journalism training remained unchallenged from the 1950s to the mid-1980s. It gave the NUJ an influential role in journalism training, and indeed in access to journalism. For example, in the late 1960s the NUJ successfully persuaded national newspapers that they could not hire any journalist who had not worked for three years (two in the case of graduates) in the regional press. It is hard to imagine today the NUJ wielding such power, and it going almost unchallenged by editors or proprietors (only the editors of the *Financial Times* and *Observer* refused to accept the ruling and continued to recruit new graduates directly). Editors, particularly of the text broadsheets, would complain that they were not allowed to hire the bright recruits they wanted straight from the universities, and said that many of these young people would not work in the provinces for two years while waiting to enter national journalism.

Meanwhile the BBC and independent television companies were recruiting just such people through their own training schemes. Some national newspaper groups, notably the IPC Mirror, ran training schemes geared towards feeding their national titles on local papers they had purchased. The Mirror owned a series of local papers in Devon, where it trained mainly graduates specifically for their nationals. It was very successful, and a number of later well-known reporters passed through the scheme. It represented in some ways the shape of things to come. The present Chief Executive of Mirror Group Newspapers, David Montgomery, has recently decided that training of national journalists on his own papers is again required, and has set up an 'academy' to provide such in-service professional development. The Mirror training scheme is running again, and trainees are taken off university journalism courses or straight after a first degree to be trained for MGN newspapers (Morgan, 1997: 1).

Journalism training, and more importantly the dominance of the NCTJ, began to fragment in the mid-1980s, at the time when so much that was traditional in the newspaper industry began to unravel. It was the time of the breaking of the stranglehold of the print unions, the introduction of the new technologies, of Eddie Shah and Wapping. While the change in the balance of newspaper power was then portrayed as increasing the power of the NUJ, passing responsibility for inputting copy from print workers to journalists, that was not to last. Other, more general, Thatcherite influences were in play, and these had the effect of limiting all union power. (See chapter 7.)

All this had a bearing on journalism training. The previously mentioned Industry Training Board was abolished in the mid-1980s, breaking the hegemony of the NCTJ. And the changing trade union environment brought to an end the National Agreement between the employers, the Newspaper Society and the NUJ in 1986 (the agreement with the IoJ ended in 1991), although they continue to this day to sit together on the NCTJ board. No longer were newspaper publishers obliged to fund the NCTJ, and many began to take a fresh look at training and its funding.

It remained the case that only the NCTJ offered a nationally recognised qualification, and many local newspaper editors, themselves trained through the NCTJ system, still saw NCTJ measures of ability as the only ones they could accept. That remains true for some local editors. But with the NUJ losing its clout, no longer being able to insist on NCTJ training for recruits, newspaper managements entering a new era of cost-cutting to maximise the benefits, to the bottom line, of new technology, and higher education institutions moving into journalism training, the whole area became a melting pot. Only now are serious efforts being made to construct some sort of order out of the training chaos.

The NCTJ had enjoyed the universal support of the regional and local press. It had been supported by the per capita levy on newspaper editorial staffs. By and large editors, and to a certain extent publishers, were happy to take advantage of, and pay for, training arrangements which were externally provided. The change in attitude came in the late 1980s and early 1990s. Various factors came into play.

The dominant two were potential for cost-cutting and concern about the content and relevance of NCTJ training. The bigger publishers, making the biggest contribution to the NCTJ because they had the biggest editorial staffs, began to wonder whether they could not provide their own training more cheaply than paying the NCTJ annual levy. They wondered, too, whether they might not be able to provide training more relevant to their own group needs.

Thomson Regional Newspapers was a good example of this approach. They started their own training centre, based around their daily and evening titles in Newcastle. The group withdrew from the NCTJ, ceasing to pay the levy or put its trainees through NCTJ examinations. Instead trainees joining TRN would be put on the in-house sixteen-week course, covering the same sort of syllabus as the NCTJ – writing, law, public administration, shorthand – but expanded to deal more with audience awareness and to be more focused on the specific editorial requirements of TRN. The scheme took particular advantage of the TRN Newcastle titles, housed in the same building as the training centre.

The courses achieved a good reputation, and TRN demonstrated its commitment to training by giving the centre a high profile and its head significant group status. When Trinity took over TRN, and became the biggest regional newspaper group in the UK, it decided to continue running the Newcastle training centre, not only for its own trainees, but for others sent by different employers or paying their own way. The Mirror Group trainees are sent on the Trinity sixteen-week course.

Other big groups, like Westminster Press, now taken over by Newsquest, and United Provincial Newspapers, also developed their own in-house training schemes, usually giving their own qualification. The NCTJ found its sphere of influence greatly reduced. Most of the big groups were no longer entering their trainees for NCTJ examinations, and there was a massive reduction in NCTJ funding as a result of the removal of income from the big publishers. Smaller groups and independents continued to support the NCTJ, but it went through a crisis in the mid-1990s, before a new business plan was produced by a new chief executive and some stability was restored. By now, however, journalism training had moved up many agendas and was the subject of intense debate in many corners of the industry. Life for the NCTJ would not remain the same. Other factors were in play. Most important of these were the development of the National Vocational Qualification (NVQ) and the growing influence of the higher education providers of journalism training.

NVQs AND MODERN APPRENTICESHIPS

NVQs began to be discussed at the start of the 1990s. The government, aware that the number of people going to university had increased vastly and the need for a skilled (trained) workforce was increasing all the time as only the high-tech industries had a future, sought to develop formal vocational qualifications. The NVQ was to be a measure of competence, acquired and initially assessed in the workplace but independently verified. The employer would provide, or arrange to have provided, the underpinning training. Trainees would build evidence of achieved competence, through such means as portfolios, and these would be progressively 'signed off' so that eventually the trainee had his or her NVQs.

Were these relevant to journalism? The Newspaper Society, the regional press employers' body, certainly thought so. They took a central role in the development of level four (supposed to be the vocational equivalent of a degree) NVQs in newspaper journalism, covering writing/reporting, production and photography. The Royal Society of Arts would be the awarding body. The NCTJ was very cool about this development. So were many editors and proprietors. Better the devil they knew, the NCTJ's National Certificate, or the devil they had recently invented, the company diplomas earned through the in-house training scheme.

The main objections to NVQs for journalism were the complexity of the administration, the form-filling and verification needed to legitimise the continuous assessment of a trainee's work, and the absence of a one-session examination to prove that the trainee understood, for example, the nature of contempt of court. How much easier for the trainee to disappear from the office for a day to take his or her National Certificate Examination (NCE), organised, set and marked by the NCTJ, or to take the tests involved in the in-house company diploma. So take-up was slow, with initially just a few believers speaking up enthusiastically for the new qualification.

But then money began to talk, as it will. The government, anxious to get a better take-up of NVQs and to demonstrate a commitment to training (the more cynical talked of massaging the unemployment figures), supported the development of Modern Apprenticeships. These would provide money for employers who took on young people and trained them, provided that the training culminated in the acquisition of NVQs. The government would contribute funds, through local Training and Enterprise Councils (TECs), towards the training for a period of up to three years of recruits under the age of 25.

Again the Newspaper Society played a key role in developing Modern Apprenticeships in journalism, and pilot schemes were running by 1995. Word got round that there was government money available for training. The regional press was in some turmoil, with ownership changing hands throughout the industry, restructuring, merging of operations, essentially massive cost-cutting, going on. Training is seen by the less enlightened in the industry as an area where money goes out and cost-cutting can easily be achieved. The prospect of actually getting some external income into the training budget was an attractive prospect. Training managers started mugging up on NVQs and Modern Apprenticeships.

It quickly became clear that TEC funding could be acquired for graduate entrants as well as school-leavers, for those who had done pre-entry courses, for those on company training schemes. As long as the trainee was put through the NVQ programme, then some state funding would be provided. The big groups, who had regarded the qualifications they provided themselves as not only adequate but preferable to alternatives, began to seek TEC funding for their trainees. This could amount to as much as £7,000 for a trainee, a direct tax-payer subsidy for big and profitable publishers to do what they had previously been doing, training recruits. Some publishers took the view that they had to make little financial provision themselves for training; the money would come from the TECs.

Modern Apprenticeships were piloted in 1995. By 1997 take-up took off. By April of that year there were about a hundred Modern Apprentices on newspapers, 80 per cent of them over 20 years old, suggesting they were graduates. The breakdown of sexes was 55/45 per cent female/male.

It was not therefore surprising that NVQ registrations were also rising, since they were a prerequisite of Modern Apprenticeship funding. In 1992/3 just over 200 registered for NVQs. By 1995/6 the figure was more than 350, and in 1996/7 it was over 220 for the first half year. Criticism of NVQs still came through loudly from editors, but the financial inducements were working.

There were consequences for the NCTJ. Having taken an antagonistic view towards NVQs, it subsequently realised the way the wind was blowing, and began to doubt whether its own National Certificate had a future. A working group was set up to examine the prospects for the NCE, and at the time of writing it seemed very likely that the NCTJ would drop its own post-entry qualification. It intends to provide verification and training support for NVQs.

THE GUILD OF EDITORS AND TOMORROW'S JOURNALIST

But much more is going on in the training area. After decades of very little changing, the years 1996/7 saw a vigorous debate taking place on what form journalism training should take. The Guild of Editors, itself having been through something of an internal revolution aimed at making itself more relevant to the industry it served, decided to take a detailed look at training. The Guild, formerly the Guild of British Newspaper Editors, is made up of editors and deputy editors from all over the country, mainly regional editors but with some national involvement. It is also broadening to include representatives of the broadcast media. It has long had a training committee, but this had been somewhat quiescent, and it was decided that the 'new' Guild would make training one of its major areas of activity. This has had a catalytic effect on the training debate.

The Guild first carried out a survey of its membership to discover attitudes to training among editors and those responsible for training. About 420 editors and 600 trainees responded to the survey. The results were published in 1995, presented to the Guild's annual conference, and discussed at a series of conferences around the country. The survey found that the typical modern entrant into newspaper journalism was a middle-class graduate. It identified the main concerns of editors and trainees:

Editors: the standard of basic English demonstrated by trainees; their lack of curiosity; too few working-class recruits with local knowledge; the wrong people being recruited to college journalism courses.

Trainees: pay – four out of five trainees starting on less than £10,000 a year; inadequate on-the-job assessment; inadequate pre-entry training in several basic areas; disparity between in-paper training policies.

(Guild of Editors, 1995: 3–8)

Editors told the Guild that their favourite recruits were those with pre-entry qualifications tested by work experience. The most important skills they sought were basic English and recognition of news values. In terms of what they wanted out of training in the future there were again separate lists for editors and trainees:

Editors: a common standard of assessment; broader training covering newspaper finances, circulation and advertising; more emphasis on ethics and the Press Complaints Commission (PCC) code of practice; accepted minimum standards for the whole industry; and recruitment from a wider social background.

Trainees: greater value to be placed on in-house training; a change in the 'sweatshop' culture of some newsrooms; minimum standards of training across the industry.

(Guild of Editors, 1995: 1)

The survey was widely read and similarly discussed. When one looked at the detailed responses from editors it was clear that there were different factions. There remained the old-fashioned editors, who had little taste for graduates and wished they could hire 'boys on bikes from local estates'. There were those who stood by the NCTJ, and many who thought its syllabus too limited and old-fashioned for the present industry. There was a strong 'back-to-basics' tendency, a bemoaning of the present standards of literacy, punctuation and general knowledge. There was a significant desire, particularly from the bigger groups, for more awareness among trainees of the 'business' side of the operation, the marketing and circulation. Trainees, thought these editors, needed to know about targeting readers, understanding the market place.

Shortly after this training survey, the findings of another piece of research emerged. This was *The News Breed*, a study of British journalists in the 1990s carried out by Anthony Delano and John Henningham for the London Institute. Training and the background of trainees were but a small part of this research, but there were some relevant findings. For example, many more journalists are graduates. Six times as many as forty years ago. About 70 per cent of all journalists went to university or college. Journalism degrees and postgraduate diplomas are held by around 10 per cent of those working in journalism, a figure that is growing rapidly. Such qualifications have been around a relatively short time.

The News Breed states:

Despite there being no formal barriers to entry into journalism or career progress, the near preponderance of graduates suggests that a higher education qualification has become a de facto prerequisite. Present-day journalists (and employers) may say that they do not regard any educational or vocational credentials as essential but the evidence suggests that within the span of a single working generation journalism has come to offer fewer opportunities to anyone with a limited or unconventional education. Its practitioners seem to be drawn from narrowing socio-economic strata and, notwithstanding the increasing enrolment of women, to be predominantly white, male, and, although largely non-practising – Christian.

(Delano and Henningham, 1995: 20)

Those conclusions apply to all those working in journalism at present, not to recent recruits. The balance between the sexes is no longer predominantly male; recruitment figures, on to courses and on to newspapers, now show a balance, even a majority of women. The socioeconomic point, however, is undoubtedly born out, and is likely to become more so as we shall see when we look more closely at university and college courses.

The Guild of Editors' training survey led to the setting up of a working party to examine training in detail and make proposals for the future. The working party was made up of working editors plus one higher education representative, this writer. It set out to examine in detail the present fragmented nature of training, to see if agreement could be reached on a new national curriculum for journalism training. Inevitably that begged questions about the NCTJ, about whether there would be a new national qualification, and who would administer it. There were further questions about who would provide pre-entry training, what that would comprise, and who would accredit training institutions.

It was a huge task, and it was to take place against the background of an industry in some turmoil. Regional newspaper ownership was changing by the week, with familiar players moving out and new ones coming in. Modern Apprenticeships were gaining importance, and with them the NVQs. The working party has not completed its work, but a description of the present state of play can be given.

At the end of 1996 the Guild published a 'green paper' entitled *Tomorrow's Journalist*, which was circulated all over the industry and was the subject of much debate. It looked at the current fragmented state of journalism training, the role of the NCTJ, NVQs and company training schemes at the post-entry level, and the role of the NCTJ, college and university courses at the pre-entry level (Guild of Editors, 1996).

It put forward a three-tier curriculum for a new National Diploma in Journalism. Stage one, for raw recruits with no pre-entry training, would take place either on newspapers or on pre-entry college or university courses. It would cover the traditional basics of news writing and research, interviewing, shorthand, law and public administration. It would add ethics, basic subbing and design, an understanding of how a newspaper works, and a look at the electronic media.

Stage two would take place post-entry, on the newspaper, and provide a qualification analogous to but amplifying that provided by the NCTJ's NCE. It would develop the core journalism skills, the law and the public administration, add financial journalism, sport, page design, basic graphics and photography, features, and understanding the audience.

Stage three, which it was assumed would be embarked upon by only a small number of trainees, or indeed more senior journalists, would include editorial management, marketing and the use of databases, and a thesis or project.

Reactions were invited, and poured in, indicating a widespread interest in and concern about training. There were, as intended, all manner of detailed observations, some critical, but overwhelmingly there was enthusiasm for unifying and modernising journalism training and bringing to an end the fragmentation which had developed.

That work goes on, but there have been other developments. The growth of NVQs through the financial support of the Modern Apprenticeships led to their adoption by big groups such as Trinity and United. The NCTJ too seemed to be accepting that they were here to stay. It also seemed that criticisms of the complexity of administration surrounding them might be overcome. The NVQs were up for revision, a process now under way. The Newspaper Society is playing a central role in this.

The government support for NVQs has not diminished, and the responsible department has now indicated that it would like to see core NVQs embracing periodical and broadcast journalism as well as newspaper journalism. Although initially resistant, the representative training bodies for broadcast and periodicals now seem supportive of the 'common core', and development work is under way. A new 'industry training body' is being set up at the time of writing, likely to embrace newspapers, through the Newspaper Society, periodicals, through the Periodicals Training Council, and Broadcast, through Skillset. The revision of the NVQs, probably with the 'common core', is likely to deal with one of the big objections from the industries, the lack of any formal examinations to back up the continuous assessment and development of portfolios. Known as 'standard external testing', it seems likely that in the future trainees could be given, for example, law exams as part of their acquisition of NVQs. The new training body would be the link with government, and would be the link with the industries over funding.

JOURNALISM AND THE ACADEMY

There is one other, and vital, component to this training melting pot, and that is higher education. Media courses have proliferated in Britain, and are tremendously popular with students. It is not uncommon for an undergraduate journalism course to be oversubscribed by a factor of thirty to one.

But here too there are problems. Media and communication represents a large and diffuse area of study, usually broken down into the vocational area and the media studies area. There are one-year courses, usually postgraduate, which all fall into the vocational category. The best of these are seen as the sure way into journalism. Newspaper editors like them and like their products, and anybody who is successful in getting a place on one of the top courses will undoubtedly get a job a year later. Initially there was suspicion on the part of editors – these pre-entry trainees were, after all, graduates – but that has passed. One-third of all young people now go to university. A fourth year learning journalism skills, undertaking work experience on a paper, in some cases taking NCTJ preliminary exams, represents excellent and relevant pre-entry training. It has the added advantage of costing the newspaper which then hires the trainee nothing. They can then be signed on as Modern Apprentices to bring in more financial support for the publisher.

These postgraduate courses were established in the 1980s. The 1990s brought the undergraduate courses, and more suspicion from the industry. Most editors use the expression media studies as an expletive. The present problem is that these undergraduate courses vary enormously – from cultural studies to practical reporting – and are often confusingly badged. Some are branches of linguistics or sociology and involve no practical journalism, no writing, reporting, interviewing or work experience. They can be taught by lecturers who have never seen the inside of a newspaper office. Some editors describe some curious job interviews with media studies graduates who know very little about journalism.

Other courses are light on media theory and put their emphasis on teaching people to become journalists, rather than to study the products of journalism. These are courses concerned with 'doing', and will involve work experience, journalistic products, and relevant knowledge like law and ethics. Editors have been slow to come round to the undergraduate experience as a suitable preparation for employment as a journalist, but that is changing.

Then there are any number of hybrid courses, with both practical and more academic content. Pity the poor school-leaver lacking good information about the industry and its requirements and trying to decide on the right course. There is prejudice in the industry, and prejudice in academe. There is not enough contact between the industry and academe, which is absurd when academe is providing so much of journalism's pre-entry training at no cost to the industry. But then there is too little contact between the NCTJ and academe. Although the NCTJ accredits some college courses, which meet their criteria, they tend not to engage in dialogue with the main providers. There is no higher education representation on the NCTJ board, despite the fact that most pre-entry training is now done by higher education colleges and universities. And those who do the accrediting, the teams the NCTJ sends to institutions to determine whether they are fit to teach journalism, tend to be made up of long-retired journalists or on occasion people who have hardly been journalists at all.

The victims of all this confusion are the aspiring journalists themselves. They build up debt through their university undergraduate days (much more from 1998); they pay substantial fees for a postgraduate course, adding to their burden of debt; and if they are lucky enough to secure employment at the end of all this education they will be doing very well if they are paid more than £10,000 a year. And they will need a car. And the bank manager would like to see a start on paying off the debt.

Yet they queue up for courses and they queue up for jobs. Why? Because they believe, rightly, that journalism can be a wonderful and rewarding and exciting career. But should they be so severely fined for taking that view? Only a small proportion of them will make it on to national papers and the better money they pay.

Editors complain about the calibre of entrants, and pay them next to nothing. Editors complain about the middle-class bias of those recruited on to courses and then applying for newspaper jobs. Is that surprising when the pre-entry training insisted upon by most publishers is so costly? Wealthy parents will pay; students from less affluent backgrounds will build up debt. Editors hark back to the days when the local school-leaver joined the local paper and didn't bother with university. Do they really want to exclude the one-third of school-leavers who now go to university? Of course not. They hire graduates. And are aspiring journalists leaving school wanting to go on short courses and get straight into newspapers? By and large no; they want to go to university first.

Many of these problems do not exist abroad, where it is taken for granted that journalism is highly demanding and, increasingly so, requiring entrants who are both educated and trained. If the regional and local press is to recruit the talent it needs to make better newspapers and their new digital offspring, it has to become more sophisticated about training. Journalism may not be a profession, although it so often thus describes itself; but it needs to professionalise. You can't get good journalism on the cheap, or by taking a philistine attitude to teaching aspiring journalists to think. The better publishers know that. But there are too many of the others.

CONCLUSIONS AND POLICY QUERIES

We are now at a stage where the nature, content and fragmentation of training are being addressed by a number of bodies, from government to editors and publishers. The very examination of the problems is underlining how complicated a subject it is, and how difficult it is to end the fragmentation, if indeed there is a universal desire to do so.

The questions are more simply put:

- What should the trainee journalist be taught? Can there be agreement on a national syllabus?
- Who should provide that training, both pre-entry and after joining the newspaper?
- Should there be a universally recognised portable national qualification,

sought by all entrants into journalism and demanded by all employers? Is that inevitably NVQs, necessarily revised?
- Will there still be a need for, and/or an insistence on providing, a further in-house qualification such as several of the big publishers are now providing?
- Will there remain a need for a pre-entry qualification such as the present NCTJ Pre-Entry Certificate, an external examination taken by students at colleges and universities in addition to their own examinations and qualifications they are bound to provide? If so, who should administer that external qualification? Or should it be accepted that universities and colleges are in the business of assessment and should be left to do their own? An accrediting body could moderate or check on the institution's assessment to ensure it met desired industry standards.
- Does there need to be accreditation of higher education institutions providing pre-entry journalism training, as is currently provided by the NCTJ? If so, who decides the criteria and who grants accreditation?
- In an age when higher education students are increasingly having to pay their own way, does the newspaper industry feel any obligation to provide any funding for the pre-entry training of which it takes great advantage?

Local and regional newspapers are now recruiting better-educated young people, most of whom have been to university. The way they are trained and developed in the workplace is very variable. National news organisations, like Mirror Group and the Press Association, are now making their own significant contributions to training, and are seeing the importance of links with the higher education providers of pre-entry training. So are some of the regional and local publishers. NVQs look as though they are here to stay, and if that is to be the modern post-entry qualification, then it is important that editors, publishers and the providers of pre-entry training talk and work together, in the interests of providing better journalists and better journalism.

REFERENCES

Boyd-Barrett, O. (1980) 'The Politics of Socialization: Recruitment and Training for Journalism', *The Sociological Review*, Monograph no. 29, University of Keele, pp. 181–202.

Delano, A. and Henningham, J. (1995) *The News Breed. British Journalists in the 1990s*, London: London Institute.

Guild of Editors (1995) *Survey of Editorial Training Needs*, London: Guild of Editors.

—— (1996) *Tomorrow's Journalist: A Green Paper on Editorial Training*, London: Guild of Editors.

Morgan, J. (1997) 'Monty Plans Journalistic Elite', *Press Gazette*, 6 June, p. 1.

Tomalin, N. (1969) 'Stop the Press, I Want to Get On', *Sunday Times Magazine*, 26 October.

Tunstall, J. (1996) *Newspaper Power*, Oxford: Oxford University Press.

—— (ed.) (1970) *Media Sociology*, London: Constable.

Chapter 6

Earthquake undermines structure of local press ownership: many hurt

David Murphy

The local and regional press, partly because of its long history, is seen as an institution bedded in the locality, and ownership has been traditionally conceptualised in terms of its political–institutional significance. The local press is seen as a set of organisations participating in a social and political process which is owned either by local business or by chains which may or may not influence the content of the press and therefore its institutional efficacy. The existence of local monopolies and the growing domination of national and multinational chains may have been seen as a central issue to do with understanding ownership. When ownership patterns were static or moving in a predictable direction such an institutional view may have been useful as a means of understanding the data. This chapter argues that recent changes in ownership patterns, which have involved the abandonment of their local and regional newspaper holdings by four of the ten biggest chains, including the two largest, reflect a new and sudden increase in the rate of change. This means that we need to focus on the processes of ownership and on the nature of these changes in order to understand it as a phenomenon in its own right.

THEORISING LOCAL PRESS OWNERSHIP

Discourses among academics about the ownership of the media in general and the local and regional press in particular have focused on the demonstration or refutation of the proposition that the supply side of the market is dominated by a small number of national or multinational companies and that this has significance for the health of civic society. This is because the existence of a free mass media is central to the operation of a liberal democracy in providing citizens as voters with a plurality of views and accurate news. Concentration of ownership is seen as a means to control the consciousness of the population.

The way in which ownership is presented in such analysis is an empirical state of affairs – monopoly or oligopoly – which either exists or towards which developments are moving. And as a result one of two possible outcomes will follow: either, in the simplistic version, owners will be in a position to use their own corporate control to expand their political influence, or, in the more sophisticated Marxist analysis, the resultant newspaper chains will form the corporate structure which generates and reinforces a hegemonic ideology.

James Curran's view of ownership and concentration in reference to recent history of press ownership (including the local press) argues 'commercial newspapers became increasingly the instruments of large business conglomerates with political interests' (Curran and Seaton, 1993: 102). The implications of this view of the legitimacy and function of proprietorship are explicated in Peter Golding's and Graham Murdock's analysis of the nature and effects of ownership and ideological control. They argue that control over the production of ideas is concentrated in the hands of capitalist owners of the means of production which results in their views being promulgated to other subordinate social groups and this generates an ideological domination which helps to maintain class domination (Golding and Murdock, 1978).

Nicholas Garnham's view of ownership and concentration does not assume that concentration necessarily leads to unbridled control either of the public agenda or of the audience's consciousness (for reasons that are beyond the scope of this argument) but his analysis of the 'cultural industries' is concerned with the strategies of firms to obtain audience maximisation which in turn generates high levels of concentration, internationalisation and cross-media ownership 'which lead to a number of strategies including monopoly or oligopolistic controls over distribution channels' (Garnham, 1990).

In the context of an argument whose purpose is to explain the limiting effect of capitalism on ideological pluralism, Brian Whitaker's book *News Limited* combines the control by newspaper moguls with the need for any newspaper in a capitalist system to make a profit as the basis for ideological control over what appears in the press. He writes: 'And ultimately everyone knows where the wages come from. Even if newspapers no longer further the political ambitions of their owners in print, they are still ready to be used to safeguard company profits' (Whitaker, 1981).

Writers who challenge part or all of such propositions remain wedded to the idea of ownership as a phenomenon which forms the framework or structure within which things happen. For instance, Jeremy Tunstall has cast doubt on the argument that choice is as limited as is suggested by the concentration/hegemony argument (Tunstall, 1983: 173) and Ralph Negrine has critically examined the implications of Marxist-oriented ideological hegemony arguments (Negrine, 1989). But they still examine what happens in terms of reader/viewer choice or the power of workers within the cultural industries to resist the powers of owners, on the basis of an assumed rather than examined meaning of the concept of ownership itself.

Two characteristics of the ownership of the local press in particular have traditionally been the focus of critical attention. The first is the dominance of newspaper chains owned by single companies, often the fiefdom of a particularly repulsive or mad nabob. The classic formulation of the supporting data for such an argument is that some percentage of the total circulation of the local press was or is in the hands of some given limited number of companies (Curran and Seaton, 1993: 92). The implication of this state of affairs is that ideological power is concentrated in the hands of a relatively small number of companies owned and controlled by a small number of men from the same economic and social class backgrounds: the further implication being that they will therefore promulgate a narrow range of political views or a specific slant on the news either frankly identified as Conservative or in most cases masquerading as 'Independent' but in fact profoundly wedded to the status quo, conservative with a small 'c' and manifesting a difference from formal Conservatism invisible to the naked eye. Such corporations – EMAP, Reed Elsevier's Reed Regional Newspapers – have been typically cross-media combines and to a greater or less extent conglomerates.

The second characteristic defect of the sector is the separate issue of local monopoly. First the big regional evening and morning newspapers all enjoy a more or less total local monopoly in their local newspaper market and second there is a growing monopoly in the ownership of weekly chains. Often it can be demonstrated that where there is apparent competition between different chains of weekly paper, both are owned by the same big corporation. Indeed, I and others have tried to show that these corporations have done deals with one another to exchange titles and production facilities in order to regularise agreed arrangements for local control. And such details have been underpinned by agreements to refrain from competition within agreed circulation boundaries. And, what is more, where such cases have been scrutinised by the Monopolies and Mergers Commission they have not been challenged (Franklin and Murphy, 1991).

Such an argument implies that this build-up of monopoly and corporate control by cross-media conglomerates is a gradual process tending towards a limit which will be an ecology of local monopolies with no local pluralism and no effective competition. The number of large companies involved on a national scale, unlike the case with national newspapers, will not matter, since they will have entered into non-aggression pacts with one another and at local level competition and therefore plurality will not exist.

CHANGES IN LOCAL PRESS OWNERSHIP

But evidence of the past two years suggests that this is not an adequate analysis of the way in which the ownership of the local media has developed, and that the framework of the liberal democratic polity in tension with the 'free market', tending towards monopoly and the elimination of pluralism, is becoming less appropriate as a model for understanding the nature of media ownership at any level. A sudden fluidity seems to be characterising the proprietorship of local newspaper chains which at their core have been stable for decades and which had apparently been slowly tightening their grip on the industry. This fluidity seems to mark a move away from capitalists as owners of media enterprises, or any other sort of enterprise, as the primary focus of activity towards capitalists as controllers and raisers of funds by which ownership of enterprise itself merely becomes a commodity which is bought and sold on the market.

In order to understand this process and then to examine some of its implications it is first necessary briefly to reprise the situation in the fairly stable pattern of ownership of the local press which applied until the mid 1990s. The trend of ownership from the war until this point has been one of concentration into local monopolies controlled by large combines. By the early 1990s over 60 per cent of the British local press was owned by the largest ten companies (MMC, 1991: 11; MMC, 1992: 16) and over 80 per cent was in the hands of the top fifteen companies (MMC, 1991: 11). This concentration was not substantially brought about by big combines launching new publications, but by taking over existing titles. For instance, the 1992 Annual Report for the tenth largest combine, EMAP revealed that while £17 million was spent in three years on launches, £65 million was spent in one year on acquisitions. This was in the context of a total annual turnover of £269.4 million and an operating profit of £33.9 million. Such a high level of activity in takeovers was typical of all the combines.

A number of these acquisitions were brought about by the exchange of titles between conglomerates in order to establish local monopolies, a process which the Monopolies and Mergers Commission examined on a number of occasions but never impeded. This inter-conglomerate exchange of titles became a characteristic form of geographic reorganisation in the industry. In 1991–92 Reed Regional Newspapers, the second largest publisher of local newspapers in the country, exchanged with Thomson Regional Newspapers, the largest, a series of weekly titles in Tyneside for the *Blackburn Telegraph* and associated weeklies in Lancashire. This helped to consolidate Reed's strength in the north west while Thomson achieved the same consolidation in the north east (Reed Annual Report, 1992).

Similarly, the fourth ranked, United Newspapers, and EMAP sold each other outliers from their empires and consolidated in their own areas of strength. EMAP bought the *Northampton Chronicle and Echo* and *Cambridge Town Crier* from United and in turn sold them the *Western Telegraph*, the *South Wales Guardian*, and the *Cardigan and Tivy-Side Advertiser*. There was a net inflow into United of £5.5 million as a result of the deal (EMAP Annual Report, 1992; United Newspapers Annual Report, 1992; MMC, 1992). Such deals also involved agreements not to encroach on one another's circulation areas.

But at the same time as these acquisitions by the market leaders through such exchanges were taking place, the gradual process of consolidation by such leviathans devouring small fry was also continuing a trend which dated back to the nineteenth century. Well-established, independent local newspapers fell prey to the logic of the market and offered themselves for sale to firms with the financial reserves and the economies of scale to cope with the new market conditions and to weather the recession. For instance, Southern Newspapers Plc, whose origins dated back to 1823 and who published among other titles the *Bournemouth Echo*, was sold in 1991 after an auction involving five of the 'big fifteen' (MMC, 1991).

This process, however, has been subject to a sudden change in its substance since the mid 1990s as a result of the differing business politics of the companies involved, as well as by the external market conditions under which they operate. Some of the major players who have figured prominently in the 'top ten' have left the field and been replaced either by the new entrants or by the expansion of companies which already figured largely in the industry. Thomson Regional Newspapers and Reed Regional Newspapers, the two biggest groups, both local newspaper companies of long standing, were sold off by their parent companies. Pearson Plc disposed of the fifth biggest group, Westminster Press Ltd, in 1996 and in August of the same year, EMAP, the tenth biggest group, sold its regional and local press holdings.

The Thomson empire has been broken up and sold in three large helpings. The Barclay brothers, owners of *The European*, have paid £90 million and Northcliffe's Associated Newspapers £82 million for their respective parts of the TRN Scottish titles, while Trinity Holdings has acquired the TRN local titles for a further £24.5 million. This represents both a reassertion of the market position of Associated Newspapers and a continuation of the metamorphosis of Trinity from a medium-sized company based on the ownership of the *Liverpool Echo* and *Liverpool Daily Post* to one of the biggest regional newspaper combines in the country, with an increasingly multinational character. During the period from 1992 until the end of 1995 the company spent £63 million on acquisitions of titles in England and Scotland. It now controls about 13 per cent of the circulation of the UK regional and local press.

EMAP's sale of its newspapers to Johnston Press, the Scottish newspaper and book publisher, for £211 million means that Johnston has moved from being the UK's eleventh to the fifth largest regional newspaper owner. In the previous twelve months it had sold the *Bury Times* to Newsquest and had bought North Notts Newspapers from W. and J. Linney.

The Barclay twins' acquisitions in Scotland represents a move towards the acquisition of newspapers of conglomerate holding companies in order to compile a portfolio of assets. The twins' other holdings are based on their original property empire and include hotels, shipping, casinos and car dealing. They also own the *European* which they bought from Robert Maxwell. The participation of conglomerates in the ownership of the local press is not new. The multi-industry conglomerate, Lonhro, owned the *Herald* and other Scottish newspapers, before selling them to Trinity in 1992. It continues a tradition of companies and entrepreneurs with a taste for speculation for profit buying into the media as a means of making money and perhaps as a means for carrying out information wars on their rivals.

NEW DIRECTIONS IN PRESS OWNERSHIP

But the winter of 1995–6 was witness to a radically new departure from the familiar pattern of acquisitions in the British local and regional press. The first was the sale of Reed Regional Newspapers by Reed Elsevier to a management buy-out by Newsquest, financed by the American leverage takeover specialists, Kohlberg Kravis Roberts. This represents the first foray by the American venture capitalists into British media ownership. Its business is based on operations in retailing enterprises in the USA, and its media arm is K-111 Communications whose chief executive is a former Macmillan president, William Reilly. K-111 owns a television news-for-schools channel as well as numerous educational and other specialist magazines. It was founded as an 'investment vehicle for KKR' (Tomkins, 1995). The consequence of this is the subsumption of the local and regional press into companies where they are part of a range of media enterprises all seen as 'investment vehicles', and therefore likely to be disposed of when the returns are seen as less profitable than those which might be achieved from other investments.

KKR in its native America has been the subject of some criticism among the wild-eyed Marxists of the Wall Street stock exchange for the way in which it has conducted some of its leveraged buy-outs. Its mode of operation is to raise multi-billion-dollar funds from investors prior to launching takeover expeditions. In November 1996, Cinven, another 'venture capital group' and a new player in the regional newspaper takeover field, appeared with the aim of investing £48 million in the £305 million purchase of Westminster Press from Pearson. Cinven was itself formed by a management buy-out and plans to specialise in financing management buy-outs. It had raised £300 million from twenty clients in the UK, continental Europe, North America and the Middle East in months and had another £700 million available from other clients.

At the beginning of February 1996, MAI, the company owned by the Labour Lord Hollick which controls the ITV franchisers Meridian and Anglia, took over United Newspapers which owns Express Newspapers and was the owner of the third largest regional newspaper empire in the country. This was the first merger of a major newspaper combine with a terrestrial commercial TV company since the relaxation of the ownership rules for broadcasters in the autumn of 1995. The new firm metamorphosed into United News and Media and quickly began to divest itself in regional lots of its local press interests.

Some of this momentum comes from the established mode of acquisitions, but some from newspapers having to deal with competition from new technology and to consider new and alternative product markets. The *Yorkshire Post*, for example, is facing competition from the cable TV company Bell Cablemedia in Leeds, York and Harrogate. It seems probable that it will attempt to broaden the basis on which it competes in such areas. Local newspapers are already involved in local broadcasting. Prior to its abandonment of newspapers, EMAP, for instance, moved into local broadcasting (Snoddy, 1995).

Newspapers are also moving into the use of the Internet as a supplement or alternative to newsprint (see chapter 11). Evening newspapers are already providing online business information and advertisements and EMAP and Associated Newspapers are using the Internet to distribute information in parts of their operations outside the local and regional press. But if this proves commercially successful it is inconceivable that they will not extend their use of this technology into all their outlets (Waldman, 1995).

This concentration of ownership and technology change has taken place in the context of a general contraction in the industry, partly as a result of a long-term secular global trend towards lower rates of newspaper reading and in part due to the relentless tightening of labour marketing conditions which is a feature of modern capitalism. In a time of falling revenues Reed, for instance, maintained profits by 'cost savings' through shortening 'reporting lines' (which means sacking managers) and new technology. Overall it achieved staff reductions of 9 per cent in the year 1991–92. It lowered newsprint costs and closed eleven loss-making titles including the Birmingham *Daily News* (Reed Annual Report, 1992). This constant driving down of costs of course also improves such undertakings' takeover eligibility and price.

The case of EMAP is instructive. It was formed in 1947 as a local newspaper enterprise and its activities for its first forty-five years were securely based in the traditional notion of the local newspaper. It expanded by the normal method in the press, by the acquisition first of competitors and then by moving into new territories (Franklin and Murphy, 1991) and buying up existing chains. These acquisitions were predominantly local newspapers and their associated printing enterprises.

In the early 1990s EMAP boasted of 'cost reductions' in all divisions which showed through 'into a 22 per cent increase in the second half year profits'. It had its own native Midlands euphemism for the process of letting workers go: 'Along the way, sadly, there had to be some goodbyes.' The *Luton Citizen* was closed. The *Nuneaton Tribune* was metamorphosed into a weekly free sheet and sold to Coventry Newspapers Ltd (EMAP Annual Report, 1992).

But the pattern of takeovers during the 1990s shifted. During the first five years of the decade the firm spent £246 million on acquisitions of magazine enterprises, most of this in France. This compared with an outlay of £14 million on local newspapers – and even here the purchase of the *Northants Advertiser* and *Milton Keynes Gazette* brought with them the rivetingly interesting *Containerisation International*. Just under £14 million was spent on local radio acquisitions.

This shift in logic of the company's activities towards lifestyle and business magazines and away from traditional newspapers reached it apotheosis in August 1996 when the local press part of its activities was sold for £211 million to Johnston Press of Edinburgh, which doubled the size of Johnston and made it the fifth biggest owner of regional press in Britain.

Similarly United Provincial Newspapers faced a 2 per cent reduction in classified advertising volumes and 'most paid-for titles showed declines in circulation. The closure of eight loss making free titles enabled the free newspaper sector to increase profits substantially' (United Newspaper Annual Report, 1992: 12). Such a policy of ruthless cost reduction could be seen as a means of surviving in the newspaper market or as a means of making the group attractive for sale to a new owner. In a sense the specific reason is irrelevant: the outcome is directed by the logic of the market and reflects an universal move to cost reductions through shedding labour. This means that profits can still be increased, even in the context of a general recession and the firm always remains attractive in the takeover market.

Pearson decided to abandon its interest in the local press in the context of what its Managing Director Frank Barlow described as a 'global strategy for information'. This meant that

> in publishing, whether in newspapers or in professional areas, there had to be a potential for international growth. In electronic information, key opportunities lie in supplying the expanding demand for high-quality financial and business information. The information portfolio will therefore be focused on markets where the division (publishing) can build a significant international position. Consequently, Westminster Press no longer fitted this strategy.
>
> (Pearson Annual Report, 1996)

In short, for firms such as Reed, Thomson, Pearson and EMAP, all with an international focus, the returns from local newspapers do not pose an attractive future return compared with the alternatives. The reason is not hard to see. Magazines devoted to types of consumption and leisure, specialist business publications, online information services and broadcasting are expanding markets. They are also focused on groups united by a common interest in particular forms of consumption and advertising. Local newspapers are only focused on locality and are in decline.

CONSEQUENCES AND CONCLUSIONS

The implication of this is that the focus of competition is changing. Garnham, in summing up the nature of the cultural industries, identifies one of their characteristics as the drive to create bigger audiences for advertisers – with various consequences that flow from this (1990: 160). But the buying and selling of enterprises through the operations of venture capitalists mean that a new form of competition is taking place among firms which are driven to slim down their operations in order to make them saleable in the global market for shares. There is also competition among the buyers of enterprises, as in the case of the takeover of Westminster Press for instance where Newsquest as well as the Irish Independent group were among the bidders.

While not all the participants making up the market are venture capitalists, if their bids are helping to set the price and their strategies are successful, then they are generating a market logic which all the participating firms are subject to.

In the past it was a sensible interpretation of events to argue that acquisitions among local and regional newspapers owners could be explained by a general move towards *local* market control or dominance. But the existence of aggressive buy-out undertakings is part of the change in the nature of firms in that managements are influenced both as sellers to make their undertakings as attractive as possible for buy-outs and to consider setting themselves up as bidders using the management buy-out funds made available by groups such as KKR and Cinven.

The effect of such a state of affairs is that all the companies in the market for companies have to behave as if they were venture capital groups or as if they were multinationals such as Pearson with alternative sources of investment available to them – because this clarifies the nature of capitalism which is driven by the need to maximise returns on capital. Firms such as Johnston, the Independent Group, and Trinity or the Guardian Media Group although they remain regional and local newspaper producers whose operations still rely on being a local monopoly supplier of newspapers, none the less compete with groups such as Newsquest in the competition for possession. (They have all become successful by making acquisitions among the local press and broadcasting and by cutting production costs in their own enterprises.) This requires them to maximise the capital they have available which means that they must have either accumulated profits or loans available to do business. This involves in turn that they must either have maximised past profits or have available to banks or investors strategies for future profit maximisation.

Evidence to support this interpretation of events was provided in

September 1997 when Newsquest sold the first of its Westminster acquisitions. It was negotiating the sale of its Wessex Newspaper Division for £35 million to Bristol United Press. The main paper in the group, the *Bath Chronicle*, was losing around 5 per cent per year and BUP will need to look carefully at the fifty-two journalists and 150 other workers as sources of savings for the return on its pay-out for the group (which would realise about £2 million a year in a building society account at the most favourable rates currently available). The most revealing aspect of this proposed deal was Newsquest's identification of market forces as the reason behind the sale. Chief Executive Jim Brown claimed 'our ambitions are still to buy newspapers rather than sell but we appreciated that in this particular market place BUP was in a strong position to develop the Wessex business' (Morgan, 1997). In other words, only a large monopoly supplier in the region would obtain the returns necessary on the capital tied up in the venture. And there are only two ways in which such an analysis could make sense. Either BUP will be able to obtain economies of scale, by cutting back on staff and other variable costs and maximising the use of fixed capital such as printing plant, or it needs to be able to increase its readership and advertising income.

As others have demonstrated, however, in the press generally and in the local and regional press even more precisely, audience maximisation is not a route that has been available as a means of increasing advertising or sales revenue since the only accurately measurable sales – those for paid-for titles – have been in steep decline for the past decade and prior to that they were in gradual decline. This undermines the traditionally axiomatic syllogism that supplier monopoly implies control over the market which in turn implies some degree of determination of audience consciousness. The fact that the Guardian Media Group has a total monopoly of evening newspaper sales in Manchester, for instance, does not compensate for the fact that the sales of the *Manchester Evening News* at 130,000 are now only one-third of what they were in the early 1960s when the paper was in competition with a second evening paper the *Manchester Chronicle* which collapsed because it 'only' had sales of 240,000.

In this context there are two strategies available for survival in the market: the first is reduction in the costs of production achieved by the optimal use of new print technology and by laying off staff, and the second is to seek out audiences by moving into other areas of mass communication through investment in broadcasting, magazines or Internet services.

To understand this we need to look at ownership not as a static empirical state of affairs which involves the interaction of variables in the market in which managers and owners try to gain control over a fluid situation by the relentless pursuit of the maximum return on capital by cost reductions and by seeking the most effective product market for their enterprise to survive in.

This then focuses the analysis of newspaper ownership onto explaining it in terms of its own logic and data rather than being concerned a priori either with its relationship to questions about ideological hegemony or other Marxist superstructural issues or with the legitimacy of proprietorship in terms of pluralist liberal democracy. Such issues in themselves are worth considering but they do not explain or even illuminate the patterns of ownership in the regional and local press, much less why and how they change.

In fact the increasingly naked determination of the local and regional press by the forces of the market has a very direct effect on the content of the press and on its ideology. The cutting of production costs has resulted in drastic reductions in the number of journalists employed per newsroom and the consequence of this has been an increasing reliance on public relations handouts. The biggest suppliers of these are businesses who increasingly present them in ways which make them more or less ready for publication unaltered. At the same time the search for advertising involves the increasing use of business-friendly matter in terms of items about consumption and shopping and of advertorial to back up advertising features. In this sense it is possible to argue that the market both in ownership of the press and in its products is by-passing any supposed need to justify the power relations of capitalism which have now become a taken-for-granted assumption, and that news is increasingly addressing people as consumers of goods and services rather than voters and citizens.

REFERENCES

Curran, J. and Seaton, J. (1993) *Power Without Responsibility*, London: Routledge.
EMAP (1992) *Annual Report*.
Franklin, B. and Murphy, D. (1991) *What News? The Market, Politics and the Local Press*, London: Routledge.
Garnham, N. (1990) 'Public Policy and the Cultural Industries' in *Capitalism and Communication and the Economies of Information*, London: Sage.
Golding, P. and Murdock, G. (1978) 'Capitalism, Communication and Class Relations' in Curran, J., Gurevitch, M. and Woollacott, J., *Mass Communication and Society*, London: Edward Arnold.
Monopolies and Mergers Commission (1991) *Annual Report*, November, cm 1772.
—— (1992) *Annual Report*, October, cm 2057.
Morgan, J. (1997) 'Newsquest Sells Westminster Papers to BUP', *Press Gazette*, 12 September, p. 1.
Negrine, R. (1989) *Politics and the Mass Media in Britain*, London: Routledge.
Pearson Ltd (1996) *Pearson Newspapers Annual Report*.
Reed Regional Newspapers (1992) *Reed Annual Report*, London.
Snoddy, R. (1995) 'Survey of Leeds and the North: Microcosm of Media Change – Yorkshire Press, TV and Radio', *Financial Times*, 20 June.
Tomkins, R. (1995) 'International Company News: KKR-owned Media Company Plans IPO', *Financial Times*, 6 June.
Tunstall, J. (1983) *The Media in Britain*, London: Constable.
United Newspapers (1992) *Annual Report*.
Waldman, S. (1995) 'A Year on the Net', *Guardian*, 17 November.
Whitaker, B. (1981) *News Ltd: Why You Can't Read All About It*, London: Minority Press Group.

Chapter 7

Industrial relations and the local press: the continuing employers' offensive

Gregor Gall

INTRODUCTION

The provincial newspaper industry has experienced another decade of continual change, if not upheaval: the introduction of direct input technology in the mid-1980s; the removal of the well-organised compositors; the challenge of free newspapers; declining circulation of paid-for titles; and the widespread derecognition of the National Union of Journalists (NUJ). The industry is now undergoing a further bout of reorganisation and restructuring. After many years of attempting to offset declining circulations and recession-linked advertising revenue through an array of strategies such as switching to tabloid format, centralising production facilities and cutting the number of journalists, four of the six major multimedia groups have sold their entire portfolios of provincial newspapers to concentrate on other areas of media and publishing which produce higher returns such as magazine, scientific, technical, legal and electronic publishing. Table 7.1 outlines these changes.

This chapter uses these major changes in ownership as a prism to examine industrial relations in the local press. In doing so the focus will be on the editorial area rather than advertising, printing and distribution since the options for possible savings in labour and production costs in these other areas have already been exhausted. A brief outline of developments in industrial relations prior to the beginning of a sustained employers' offensive against journalists and the NUJ provides the context for examining the intensification and extensification of the editorial labour process under the new pattern of ownership. The chapter then assesses the implications of the drive to accumulate in the sphere of industrial relations in the new millennium.

THE CONTEMPORARY BACK-DROP OF EDITORIAL INDUSTRIAL RELATIONS

It is generally agreed that the collective organisation of journalists lacked cohesion and strength compared to that of the printers (compositors and

Table 7.1 Major ownership changes in provincial newspapers

Date of acquisition/ Acquisition	Vendors	Acquisitor	Price £m	Circulation ranking of acquisition	New circ. ranking of acquisitor	Total no. of journalists after acquisition
Nov. 1995 Thomson Regional Newspapers	International Thomson	Trinity International	327	1st	2nd	1,800
Nov. 1995 Reed Regional Newspapers	Reed-Elsevier	Newsquest	205	4th	(see below)	(see below)
July 1996 EMAP Regional Newspapers	East Midlands Allied Press	Johnston Press	211	10th	5th	1,600
Dec. 1996 Westminster Press	Pearson	Newsquest	305	5th	1st	2,100

press workers). None the less this should not preclude a recognition that journalists' collective organisation, embodied in the NUJ (rather than the ineffectual Institute of Journalists), developed into a much more combative and independent form of trade unionism from previously having been an ambiguous mix of trade unionism and professionalism (Gall and Murphy, 1996). In essence the NUJ developed a more collective trade union class consciousness with an accompanying development in organisational cohesiveness, albeit within a context of retrenchment for organised labour in the newspaper industry and elsewhere. Several key events and developments shaped this process: the journalists' wage strike of 1978–9 in England and Wales, a number of prolonged strikes at, for example, the *Nottingham Evening Post* and Dimbleby Newspapers and an increasingly assertive style of management. This followed earlier NUJ involvement in the struggles of the 1980s between the newspaper employers and the print unions (the National Graphical Association [NGA] and the Society of Graphical and Allied Trades [SOGAT]) over the conditions for introducing new technologies at Wapping (News International), Warrington (Eddie Shah), the Wolverhampton *Express and Star* and the *Kent Messenger*.

Despite the NUJ's part in inter-union disputes, sectionalism and rivalries, which ultimately only benefited the employers, large sections of NUJ members did increasingly come to see themselves as (labour) commodities and industrial workers. Consequently, the NUJ faced the employers as a more credible opponent than previously, but its continued weaknesses would come to be exposed far more so as the editorial area and the NUJ now became the focus of sustained managerial attention. Of course this process was neither linear nor without contradictions. The development of a greater trade union consciousness and cohesiveness of organisation was influenced by three inter-linked processes of the mid to late 1980s: the decentralisation of collective bargaining, the introduction of new technology called direct input and the growth of union derecognition.

In 1985, following their 'victory' at Wolverhampton, the employers through their federation, the Newspaper Society, imposed their terms and conditions for a new national agreement on the print unions. These terms then set the tone for the 1986 agreement offered to the NUJ: essentially they ended the substance of a national agreement while keeping its form so that companies would be able to pay journalists' wage rises as they saw fit according to their own specific conditions. The NUJ rejected these terms and, influenced by the experience of its Scottish membership, sought company-wide bargaining. The employers resisted this, establishing instead local bargaining, whereby each company e.g. Sheffield Newspapers, producers of the daily *Sheffield Star* and owned by United Provincial Newspapers (UPN), would negotiate with the NUJ on pay and conditions without reference to and separately from its sister daily newspapers in Leeds, Blackpool, Northampton, Newport, Preston and Wigan. Of course while UPN negotiated separately, it acted as a single entity while the NUJ became organisationally fragmented and undermined by localised bargaining. The result was that, in the prevailing conditions for organised labour in the 1980s (unlike the 1960s) of high unemployment, union defeats and a restrictive legal environment, the NUJ could not establish pay leapfrogging. In fact the reverse happened; employers were able to push wages and conditions down, for the NUJ could not use strong chapels (workplace union branches) to protect the weaker. Now the weaker were pulled down, with the stronger following in their wake.

Given this environment, it appears somewhat strange that the NUJ unlike any other union in Britain in the 1980s was able to establish new technology agreements (NTAs) which increased wages and conditions and provided for an element of control over the direct input (Noon, 1991). Direct input allowed the journalists to type and set their own text, whereas previously the setting of text was carried out by the compositors. The reason for this seeming contradiction was that, although the employers had already begun to shift the 'frontier of control' away from the journalists and towards themselves, at this particular juncture they were heavily dependent on co-operation from journalists and the NUJ to introduce this technology. Once introduced, the deepening of NUJ influence would require much more assertive behaviour.

This set the climate for the widespread derecognition of the NUJ. Under decentralised bargaining less than half of NUJ chapels failed to secure such local 'house agreements', these being mainly the smaller, weaker and non-daily newspaper chapels (Smith and Morton, 1990: 107). By 1994 the overwhelming majority of chapels were derecognised despite some concerted, local strike action. Little will be said of the specific reasons for derecognition, as this has been dealt with in detail in a debate elsewhere (Gall, 1993; Noon, 1991, 1992; Smith and Morton, 1990, 1992). Suffice it to say that the employers were intent upon removing any potential opposition to the exercise of their managerial prerogative in their pursuit of higher profits. In particular, the strategic position of the journalists in the production process as a result of the introduction of direct input meant that the employers sought to demobilise the NUJ so that their chapels would be unlikely to exercise this power to advance and protect their wages and conditions.

INDUSTRIAL RELATIONS IN THE PROVINCIAL NEWSPAPER INDUSTRY IN THE 1990s

Against this background, the chapter now examines the traditions of industrial relations in the Trinity and Johnston groups – in their existing portfolios as well as their recent acquisitions – to explain the considerable industrial relations changes implemented by both groups in their new acquisitions. Although Newsquest is a new player, its senior managers were formerly six of the senior managers in Reed Regional Newspapers. These managers created Newsquest as a management buy-out of the Reed titles. As such Reed stands as the precursor to Newsquest.

Trinity has in the majority of its existing centres recognised and bargained with the NUJ, not as the result of strong union organisation but a conscious management policy where the union is tolerated but only so far as this is deemed to assist the company in managing its journalists. Thus at Liverpool the NUJ makes and accepts moderate wage rises because they fear that to make greater demands would lead to derecognition. The chapel believed that accepting smaller than desired pay awards was the price of maintaining recognition and bargaining on other issues. Moreover the company has taken senior journalists out of the 'house agreement' by putting them on 'executive contracts' to let the chapel know that it could not take effective industrial action because of this ready-made team of strike-breakers. Trinity's pragmatic attitude to journalists and the NUJ can be seen by its actions in a number of earlier acquisitions.

Shortly after acquiring Scottish and Universal Newspapers in 1992 Trinity sought to reduce the starting rate for journalists by £3,000 p.a. because it regarded the rate as too high. This was made under the threat of 'accept or be derecognised', but the NUJ resisted and forced a compromise. Subsequently Trinity reverted to the old rates because of a tight labour market but was able to counterbalance this by the recruitment of new, younger and cheaper journalists as many journalists had left because of their dislike of the 'new regime': cuts in freelance pay and expenses, the ending of open competition for jobs and a policy of non-replacement of vacancies.

Trinity also introduced 'executive contracts' for senior journalists. At the

South London Press the vendors derecognised the NUJ shortly before the sale. Opposition from the chapel lengthened the time taken to implement this plan and this resulted in Trinity having to deal with this unfinished business after the takeover. It is clear from the resolution of the dispute that Trinity instructed the existing local management to reach a compromise to settle as soon as possible: an agreement on NUJ negotiated minimum rates and yearly across-the-board rises. But the editor has discretion to use merit pay to reward 'high fliers' while union recognition and collective bargaining remain on other terms and conditions of employment.

The NUJ's Provincial Organiser, Colin Bourne, commented in an interview that, like Trinity, Johnston Press 'had neither been hostile to the NUJ nor encouraged it' but had engaged in a 'constructive dialogue' in terms of industrial relations and furthermore was renowned throughout the industry for its policy of no editorial redundancies. While the NUJ chapels continue to be recognised, since the late 1980s wage increases have consistently been below inflation and expenses have not been increased in line with inflation. By contrast the Provincial Organiser characterised Reed Regional Newspapers' style of management as 'rapacious and bullying' while the chair of the House of Commons Employment Select Committee described the parent company, Reed Elsevier, as 'a very efficient dictatorship'. Prior to the spread of derecognition, allowances and bonuses were withdrawn and below inflation pay rises imposed. Merit pay and 'executive contracts' also began to be introduced. Between 1991 and 1992 Reed derecognised its daily newspaper chapels and then its weekly newspaper chapels first by terminating their 'house agreements' and second by requiring journalists to sign personal contracts through inducements and threats. Pay freezes were subsequently imposed for two years and staffing levels reduced despite protests from the chapels.

Like Reed, Thomson Regional Newspapers, EMAP and Westminster Press have derecognised the NUJ throughout their operations; only in a few exceptions did a couple of chapels maintain some kind of recognition and bargaining (Gall, 1993). At TRN despite, or indeed probably because of derecognition, union densities had remained quite high but union organisation has been severely affected where many chapels are only periodically active or are moribund. This remains true for the NUJ in EMAP and Westminster Press.

At EMAP executive contracts were introduced and followed by derecognition. Despite the EMAP *Northamptonshire Evening Telegraph* chapel having 70 per cent membership, it was informed by the editor there was no need for recognition because the company already operated 'an open-stance management . . . which allows all employees to discuss matters with their team leaders at all times' (*Press Gazette*, 3 October 1994). At Westminster Press the vast majority of the NUJ's chapels had been fully derecognised. At the four remaining chapels with some kind of truncated 'house agreements' (Bath,

Oxford, Bradford and Darlington) chapels were recognised not primarily as a result of their strength but their moderation and realism. While bargaining over pay formally existed, it had been de facto superseded by unilaterally determined performance related pay. Elsewhere, the value of journalists' pay and conditions worsened after derecognition in other groups but Westminster Press became known throughout the industry for its continual high level of redundancies among journalists, which it is believed was carried out to elicit a quick sale. Trinity, Johnston and Newsquest thus acquired newspaper centres where the NUJ had been overwhelmingly derecognised and had suffered a considerable setback. While membership levels remained high, this primarily existed on an individual rather than collective basis and chapel organisation was generally weak.

THE NUJ RESPONSE TO THE ACQUISITIONS

The NUJ's response was one of cautious optimism. Their Provincial Newspaper Organiser argued:

> There are two kinds of newspaper companies: those who are mainly interested in newspapers and those who are mainly interested in profit. The first aim to profit through the publication of good newspapers. The second see the papers as a means to ever-increasing profits for the benefit of big media groups. The difference between the two, for working journalists, is enormous.
>
> ... United, Northcliffe, Thomson, Reed and Westminster Press are in the second category. Some of the fast-expanding newer groups – notably Trinity and Johnston – are in the first, at least for the time being. That is why we should all cheer the decisions of Reed, United and Thomson to sell up. ... Their drive to increase profits at the expense of editorial quality has been relentless. They have cut all they can and it has not been enough. There are grounds for hope ... because Trinity is a Category One employer, and it cannot be a coincidence that its industrial relations [like Johnston's have] been much better.

(Bourne, 1995: p. 18)

The Provincial Organiser developed this line of argument further by arguing that the 'profits-through-papers' companies, because they intend to stay in newspapers and regard this as their sole or core area of activity, have accepted the levels of profitability that can be gained from newspapers (as opposed to electronic publishing) and recognise that editorial content and quality cannot be pushed down too far (or indeed must be supported) in order to prevent circulation falling. By contrast the 'profits-before-papers' companies have 'slashed and burned' their editorial resources and staff because they have sought to raise profits to levels comparable to other forms of publishing or to prepare their businesses for sale. Having failed to increase profitability to required levels despite many such initiatives, the majority of the large players have decided to quit the industry.

The profits-through-papers companies' strategy has implications for the editorial area, journalists and the NUJ, Bourne argued, in that staff levels are likely to be higher, staff receive better remuneration and the NUJ is held in higher regard in order to achieve industrial relations which are conducive to encourage and promote commitment and goodwill from the journalists towards the paper and company. Some support for this argument can be derived from the Newspaper Society (*Press Gazette*, 16 August 1996).

THE IMPACT OF ACQUISITION

Having laid out the previous management practices of the buyers and vendors and the response of the NUJ, we are now able to look at what we can call 'the impact of acquisition' on industrial relations. The task is trying to identify the essence of the likely impact in the period immediately subsequent to acquisition. Of course all subsequent changes and responses (for many years) may be in some way related to acquisitions but to extend the period of impact too far may make it harder to identify such a link as we may then be considering how a company, much as any other company, may react to prevailing market conditions. It should be noted that the Transfer of Undertakings (Protection of Employment) Regulations 1981 does limit the extent to which workers' terms and conditions of employment can be changed. It will be argued that while there are some differences between Newsquest on the one hand and Johnston and Trinity on the other, these are very slim and of little real benefit to journalists and the NUJ. What seems to make more of a difference is the activity of the NUJ.

Newsquest

Having refused requests from the NUJ nationally to meet to discuss its acquisitions, Newsquest stated:

> It's been a tough time for all the staff during [the] negotiations. I'm grateful to the staff particularly the journalists who have been hugely supportive of us, ensuring that they got out the very best papers during a time when all their futures were in doubt. It is our intention to substantially grow the company and keep on building and creating extra value. That has to be good news for our staff.
>
> (*Press Gazette*, 27 November 1995)

The NUJ responded by saying:

> We are hopeful this will mark a change in industrial relations between the workforce and the management because it's been clear that the policy of

derecognition [of the NUJ] has been a group-wide policy of Reed Else-vier. We would hope that the new management would take a more enlightened view.

(*Press Gazette*, 27 November 1995)

In an attempt to force the company to state its policy towards the work-force's trade unions, the father of the chapel of the *Bolton Evening News* at a staff consultative meeting asked the chief executive whether the new com-pany would recognise the NUJ given that it represents the majority of the journalists. He was told: 'No. We're not going back to those days.' Despite this attitude the chapel at Bolton succeeded in stopping the company intro-ducing Sunday working.

In April 1997 Newsquest served notice to the *Bradford Telegraph and Argus*, Darlington *Northern Echo* and *Oxford Mail* chapels that it was terminating their 'house agreements'. These were the only ex-Westminster Press centres which had retained union recognition. Newsquest stated that this was part of the process of integrating these business into its operations, that is derecog-nising all NUJ chapels: 'We don't recognise any trade unions and that is Newsquest policy as a whole' (*Press Gazette*, 18 April 1997). The precise timing of the derecognition was commented on by the NUJ (Ecclestone, 1997; *The Journalist*, May/June 1997) and *Press Gazette* (11 April 1997) to be connected to a move to prevent the chapels benefiting from imminent legislation on union recognition (see later). Such a move sparked a revival of union activity. The Oxford chapel, with 70 per cent membership, held an indicative ballot among all journalistic staff showing overwhelming sup-port for union recognition and representation. The Bradford (60 per cent membership) and Darlington (90 per cent membership) chapels held mandatory non-disruptive meetings and elected full complements of chapel officers.

Newsquest, largely as a result of the continuing NUJ agitation, has set up staff consultative councils after derecognition: its preference would seem to have been for no institutionalised forms of representation, however weak. But also to try to rectify the NUJ's marginalisation they have established these councils where employees are elected to represent their departments (not their union). Although these bodies are ineligible to discuss matters of pay and conditions, the NUJ chapels have used them as a point to organise around by successfully contesting the elections to the staff councils and to pressurise management on various issues within this forum.

Johnston Press

Johnston has not re-recognised any derecognised chapels, even where derecognition shortly preceded acquisition, despite requests to do so from the NUJ. Prior to the completion of the EMAP acquisition, Johnston instructed EMAP to consult with staff over the takeover as legally required. This was done with worker representatives rather than the NUJ. However, following completion the former EMAP editors told chapel officials that they were prepared to talk and discuss with them through an 'informal dialogue' issues of concern to the journalists such as work loads, staffing levels, training and the future of papers. This, given the previous EMAP policy, is likely to have been an initiative from Johnston, and represents an indication of a softening of attitude towards the NUJ because of Johnston's takeover. None the less this has not extended to positive encouragement of union membership or re-recognition, i.e. new 'house agreements'.

These developments could be said to either contrast or complement with another in an existing Johnston title. Johnston moved the *South Yorkshire Times* title into its newly created Doncaster division which comprises titles acquired from Newsquest. Upon the NUJ inquiring whether this had any implications for recognition, it was informed that within the new group, based on Reed's former titles where the NUJ had been derecognised, there is no recognition of the NUJ; the chapel was promptly informed it was derecognised. While in its acquisitions Johnston promised no redundancies, whether voluntary or compulsory, it has not ruled out a policy of non-replacement of vacancies. This policy would see the level of work for the remaining journalists rise. However, this 'no redundancy' policy did not last very long; eighty redundancies in former EMAP titles were made in 1997, of which nine were journalists.

Trinity

Trinity refused to meet NUJ to discuss implications of its takeover but has pledged no job losses. Where Trinity finds derecognition it has maintained this in the former TRN centres. The only exception, as a result of pressure from a strong chapel, is Newcastle. Shortly before takeover, the existing management derecognised the NUJ. This decision was not reversed by Trinity but, after a chapel campaign and under instructions from senior Trinity management, the scale of derecognition was reduced. While there will be no collective bargaining on pay matters, the local management signed a 'memorandum of understanding' over issues on which the NUJ will be consulted and have rights of representation.

PRESSURES AND RESPONSES: EXPLAINING EMPLOYER STRATEGY

The coercive nature of the capitalist marketplace places exigencies on each unit of capital to accumulate, be taken over or go bankrupt. Clearly, there is massive pressure on Newsquest, Johnston and Trinity to vindicate, and make reward from, these acquisitions to their shareholders and financial backers.

Newsquest's clear policy of anti-unionism stems from its belief that 'unions are bad for business' under the guise of the 'supremacy of the individualism' and direct communication with no third-party involvement in order to ratchet up the level of profitability (for example, see *Oxford Mail* editor's letter in *Press Gazette*, 2 May 1997). However, the specificity of Newsquest's takeover of Westminster Press titles means that additional pressure is placed on making savings through labour cost reductions because the geographical location of the new centres does not allow for rationalisation of printing facilities or regionalisation of subbing. In addition Newsquest has two sets of major loans to make returns on, whereas Johnston and Trinity have just one. However, that Westminster Press engaged in widespread redundancies prior to sale leaves little room for further redundancies as an obvious route. Johnston's aim of raising the profit margins of its EMAP titles (10 per cent) to those of its own (25 per cent) (*Press Gazette*, 11 April 1997) may be equally problematic for it has pledged no widespread redundancies; there is again no obvious room for redundancies given EMAP's 'slash to sell' policy but there is some scope for the rationalisation of production facilities in Yorkshire. As for Trinity, it has pledged no large-scale redundancies while it has little room for making rationalisations as a result of a lack of geographical match.

Putting these considerations together with their actions so far would suggest two strategies, albeit not entirely separate, being deployed. Newsquest sees union derecognition as key to controlling labour costs and enforcing managerial control. To date there has been no outright attack on the wages and conditions of journalists (for example by instituting various cuts) but rather by imposing poor wage increases and freezing the value of other elements of remuneration. Derecognition helps to demobilise chapels so that they are less able to reverse these actions. Trinity and Johnston are pursuing a path of not attempting to eradicate unionism but seeking to keep labour costs low, so by keeping derecognition where they inherit it as 'negotiating them costs time and money'[1] and having a constructive partnership-type relationship with the NUJ where, in the context of marginalisation, the union either agrees with their plans or where it does not, it reluctantly accepts them. Where this is not the case they are prepared to threaten derecognition. What the NUJ is experiencing therefore are not strategies of a different nature but a different tactic which seeks to emasculate the NUJ and increase profitability. Other than further reductions in labour costs, the groups may have to start exploring the possibility of disposing of or swapping titles/centres to create geographical proximity to allow scope for rationalisations of production. Already Newsquest has 'done' a deal with the *Manchester Evening News* (*MEN*) where the latter withdrew from the former's Bolton area in return for Newsquest withdrawing from *MEN*'s south Manchester stronghold. Now both have cut their costs and increased revenue. Of course journalists still suffered job losses.

INDUSTRIAL RELATIONS IN OTHER NEWSPAPER GROUPS

The picture painted of management attitudes towards labour costs, the journalist and the NUJ in the Johnston, Newsquest and Trinity groups is replicated elsewhere in the other major newspaper groups: United Provincial Newspapers (UPN), Northcliffe Newspapers, Southern Newspapers and Portsmouth and Sunderland Newspapers. Northcliffe, like Newsquest, is anti-union, while UPN, having derecognised all NUJ chapels, may be moving away slightly from this type of position as it is now prepared to acknowledge the union informally. Despite such variations of derecognition and/or union marginalisation, the general diminution of journalists' terms and conditions of employment is universally apparent. In these other groups, the NUJ response has similarly varied; it has been stronger in some groups than others and in some chapels than others for the same reasons.

THE POSSIBILITIES OF UNION RESURGENCE?

What of the prospects for the NUJ to regain lost ground in its ability to advance and protect the interests of its members? Despite a sustained employers' offensive, the NUJ is 'down but not out'; derecognition has not led to de-unionisation and the triumph of managerialism. After engaging in an internecine internal dispute over the direction of the union and the position of the general secretary in the face of widespread derecognition (see Gall, 1992), membership has stabilised and then grown while the union's finances are back in surplus. This in itself, however, is not evidence of a union 'fightback' but it does mean that the ground exists on which a 'fightback' could be organised.

To date there are a number of examples of chapels which have been able to mount rearguard actions (Gall, 1995) but so far no chapels have been able to regain recognition or win substantial improvements in wages etc. None the less, the election of the Labour Party to government has given a fillip to union activists, not necessarily as a result of what Labour will actually do but the atmosphere their election has engendered, an atmosphere of increased confidence and 'now its our turn' after eighteen years of Thatcherism. In particular Labour's plans for compulsory union recognition (following successful ballots) have made a difference in that a focus has been provided around which activity can be organised; building and maintaining union membership and proving the union's worth in the run up to the implementation of the legislation in 1998–9. While resistance can be expected from some newspaper groups, others are showing signs of ambivalence. Such a situation can help allow the stronger chapels to create momentum which may allow the weaker chapels to follow in their slip-stream. While the struggle to reassert the rights of labour may not be an easy one, there are good grounds for optimism as we approach the millennium.

ACKNOWLEDGEMENTS

Thanks are due to the NUJ provincial organisers for their help in providing material. Unfortunately Trinity, Johnston and Newsquest declined requests for interviews.

NOTE

1 Source: June 1997 meeting with Johnston group, recounted by provincial organiser (Interview, June 1997).

REFERENCES

Bourne, C. (1995) 'Papers Before Profits', *The Journalist*, December, pp. 18–19.

Ecclestone, J. (1997) 'What We Want from Tony Blair', *Press Gazette*, 25 April.

Gall, G. (1992) 'The NUJ: A Union in Crisis', *Capital and Class*, no. 48, pp. 7–15.

—— (1993) 'The Employers' Offensive in the Provincial Newspaper Industry', *British Journal of Industrial Relations*, 31/4, pp. 615–24.

—— (1995) 'HRM in Practice: A Case Study Revisited', *Personnel Review*, 24/3, pp. 43–55.

Gall, G. and Murphy, D. (1996) 'Journalism in Changing Times: The Changing Relationship between Professionalism and Trade Unionism in the British Newspaper Industry', in Fincham, R. (ed.) *New Relationships in the Organised Professions*, Aldershot: Avebury.

Noon, M. (1991) 'Strategy and Circumstance: The Success of the NUJ's New Technology Policy', *British Journal of Industrial Relations*, 29/4, pp. 259–76.

—— (1992) 'New Technology in the Provincial Newspaper Industry: Reply', *British Journal of Industrial Relations*, 30/4, pp. 329–31.

Smith, P. and Morton, G. (1990) 'A Change of Heart: Union Exclusion in the Provincial Newspaper Sector', *Work, Employment and Society*, 4/1, pp. 105–24.

—— (1992) 'New Technology in the Provincial Newspaper Industry: A Comment', *British Journal of Industrial Relations*, 30/4, pp. 325–7.

Part III

Local newspapers: exploring the range

Chapter 8

There is no alternative: the demise of the alternative local newpaper

Tony Harcup

'Square eggs may be sensational – but the real news is in *Leeds Other Paper*.' So ran an early promotional poster for *Leeds Other Paper*, one of the longest lived of the alternative local newspapers which sprang up in the UK in the 1970s only to wither and die by the 1990s. Square eggs may not have been the slickest of advertising pitches – this was before any of us had heard of Saatchi and Saatchi – but the slogan addressed two of the fundamental questions posed by the rise of the alternative press. What is news? And whose news is it anyway?

A typical issue of an alternative newspaper from the late 1970s or early 1980s might feature a straight news report of tenants trying to get their damp homes repaired, a picket's eye view of a strike at a local factory, a preview of a feminist event such as a film show, a court report of a case involving some anti-fascist activists and a lengthy investigation into a housing development proposed by a councillor who was both a landowner and a member of the Planning Committee considering the application.

Those staples of traditional local newspapers such as showbusiness celeb-rities, weddings and the latest grip-and-grin picture of the mayor, were entirely absent from the alternative press. While the alternatives were being forged amid the fallout of the 1960s, for the traditional local press news remained what it had always been. News was what journalists were given by established news sources, such as the police and fire services, the courts, councils, health authorities, MPs, companies, organisations like the Rotary Club and those local charities or other groups which were deemed worthy of an entry in reporters' contacts books. As Brian Whitaker noted in his study of the *Liverpool Free Press*: 'What an examination of published stories and their sources reveals is that news – certainly the serious news – is mainly a one-way traffic. "Them" telling "us" what they want us to know' (Whitaker, 1981: 32). Ordinary members of the public, Whitaker claimed, were rou-tinely excluded as sources of news for the commercial press. After all, they did not have press officers on call twenty-four hours a day, they may not even have been on the telephone, and it took time to establish their bona fides. When compared to the organised news sources and the lists of established diary events, such as court cases and routine calls to the emergency services, it was little wonder that 'ordinary people' were often seen by newspapers as 'difficult, expensive and inefficient sources' (Whitaker, 1981: 38). It was as much the desire to challenge this exclusion, as to counter any overt political bias by the commercial press, that prompted the creation of an alternative news agenda by the alternative local press.

The 'alternative local press' is used here to include the host of local newspapers, such as *Leeds Other Paper* (*LOP*), *Liverpool Free Press*, and *Rochdale's Alternative Paper* (*RAP*), which were independently and usually co-operatively owned; geographically based; and defined themselves as providing 'ordinary people' with an alternative to the mainstream media. Although papers such as *Islington Gutter Press* sprang up in parts of London, the alternative press was never London-dominated. As Nigel Fountain observed: 'The papers emerged in far outposts, to the surprise and outrage of local dignitaries alike' (Fountain, 1988: 177). The hedonistic 'hippie' underground publications such as *Oz* and *IT*, and the plethora of red-topped party mouthpieces with variants of 'Socialist' and 'Worker' in their titles, are not the subjects of this chapter.

The non-aligned alternative local press developed out of the community politics of the late 1960s and early 1970s. Many of those involved were ex-students who found it possible to live on relatively small amounts of money such as social security giros. This was just as well, because wages were typically poor in the alternative press. Many journalists were the first members of their families to have the chance of higher education. Compared to the era of Thatcherite austerity which killed off most of these radical publications, the 1970s was a time of relative freedom, hope and activism. Alternative newspapers were just one product of this optimistic and participatory culture, along with a vast range of community-oriented initiatives including worker–writers' groups, agitprop theatre companies, and local photography projects.

A study for the Minority Press Group noted that alternative local newspapers pushed to the forefront 'the question of who benefits and who loses from any particular decision, whether a hospital closure or a housing scandal, and show what the effects and sufferings are to people in the area. They also provide local oppositional forces with an otherwise unavailable platform for their views' (Aubrey *et al.*, 1980: 16). Instead of covering the usual round of fires and crimes, or regurgitating the opinions of local bigwigs, the alternative local press reported the views and actions of people living on housing estates, of those involved in community groups, of rank-and-file trade union activists, unemployed people, and the views of those active within the women's and gay movements and the black communities. In the words of *Wilko's Weekly*, a BBC Radio Four series on local newspapers, the alternative local press became 'parish magazines of the dispossessed' (Harcup, 1994: 3).

What distinguished the alternative from the commercial press, as Bob Franklin and David Murphy noted in what was a rare academic examination of the subject, was that the former used 'as primary sources the contacts who are marginalised by the usual process of news production, and . . . gives coverage to the news for which these contacts provide the raw material' (Franklin and Murphy, 1991: 126). Beyond this, the likes of *LOP* published 'stories about the alleged corrupt or suspect activities of public figures who appeared as pillars of society or authoritative sources of truth in the traditional coverage of news' (ibid.: 114). By holding these 'spokespeople of authority' up for questioning, the alternative press challenged 'the system for which they speak' (ibid.: 125).

NEWS FROM EVERYWHERE

The best-known titles within the alternative local press included: *Aberdeen People's Press*, *Alarm* (Swansea), *Birmingham Free Press*, *Bradford Banner*, *Brighton Voice*, *Bristol Voice*, *Bush News* (Shepherds Bush), *Calder Valley Press*, *Cardiff People's Press*, *City Issues* (Sheffield), *City Wise* (Nottingham), *Coventry News*, *Durham Street Press*, *East End News* (London), *Exeter Flying Post*, *Hackney People's Press*, *Huddersfield Hammer*, *Islington Gutter Press*, *Leeds Other Paper*, *Liverpool Free Press*, *Manchester Free Press*, *Metro News* (Bury), *New Manchester Review*, *Nottingham Voice*, *Other Paper* (Burton-on-Trent), *The Post* (Hull), *Rochdale's Alternative Paper*, *Sheep Worrying*, *Sheffield Free Press*, *Spen Valley Spark*, *Styng* (Barnsley), *Tameside Eye* and *York Free Press*.

The Minority Press Group, a project set up to monitor the radical press in this country and overseas, identified approximately eighty local alternative newspapers published in the UK in 1980 (Whitaker, 1981: 169). Some of these newspapers published barely a handful of issues while others survived for more than a decade with sales ranging from a few hundred to occasional claims of 10,000 copies.

The majority were monthly, A4, offset-litho printed, and co-operatively run. Some, like the *Liverpool Free Press*, had been established by journalists working on the local newspaper who felt the need for an alternative outlet. Most, like *LOP*, were the product of people with no formal journalistic training or background. Yet, in the words of Tom Hopkinson, founder-director of the Centre for Journalism Studies at Cardiff: 'The strength of many minority papers is precisely that their reporting has been more true, more factual, more objective than that done by newspapers with fifty times their staff and fifty thousand times their resources' (Whitaker, 1981: 6).

It would be inaccurate, however, to present the alternative local press as a homogenous category. The Minority Press Group identified five distinctive types of publication. 'Left opposition papers' such as *LOP* and the *Bristol Voice* were distinguished by their preference for analysing news in terms of the issues involved rather than presenting news as a series of isolated events, while 'Community newspapers' such as the *Peckham Pulse* focused on a particular neighbourhood and emphasised participation in the production of the paper. 'Radical populist papers' such as *Rochdale Alternative Paper* used the techniques of popular journalism with an emphasis on news as opposed to issues while 'Counter-cultural papers' like the *Waveney Clarion* were based on reporting largely rural 'alternative societies'. Finally, 'Labour movement papers' such as *Hull News* and *Coventry Workshop Bulletin* were distinctive because they had been established by trades councils to provide a self-consciously oppositional point of view (Aubrey *et al.*, 1980: 25–8).

The usefulness of these distinctions is questionable, however, since most alternative local newspapers combined various of these elements, especially the first three features. With open editorial policies and a shifting population of contributors, an alternative newspaper could change its style and direction within a few weeks – and even within the same issue. What helped to make the alternative press alternative was its independence of the monolithic tendencies of the large conglomerates which at the time were buying up the remaining independent traditional local newspapers.

The guiding spirit behind the alternative local press was perhaps best expressed in 1984, when one of the occasional national conferences which brought together representatives of many of these titles came up with the following statement:

> An unambiguous definition of an 'alternative newspaper' is impossible, but there seem to be features common to all of them. They are: local, anti-racist, anti-sexist, politically on the left, overtly rather than covertly political, not produced for profit, editorially free of the influence of advertisers, run on broadly collective principles. ... Most alternative newspapers are small, their existence precarious. With one or two notable exceptions their circulations are in the hundreds rather than the thousands. But this tells us nothing about their influence nor their value. As virtually all the mass media are in the political centre or on the right, the voice of the local alternative newspaper is an important counterweight. Small need not mean insignificant.
>
> (National Conference of Alternative Papers, 1984: 1)

Anybody who doubted the potential significance of a small-circulation publication could have asked those councillors, council officials, businessmen and senior police officers whose allegedly corrupt activities were relentlessly pursued by the likes of *Liverpool Free Press* and *New Manchester Review* (Whitaker, 1981: 113–20; Franklin and Murphy, 1991: 114–24).

The alternative press was not successful, however, in breaking with all the traditions of the commercial media, as was demonstrated by the report of a workshop on sexism at the same national conference. Despite their best intentions, and a positive attitude towards the feminist movement, it seemed that most alternative newspapers were male-dominated. The conference proceedings expressed concern that alternative papers 'were still stereotyping women' and that

> women's skills, for example typing, might take them away from decision making. *York Free Press* described how they were trying to break from tradition when women recently went to interview miners. Although the miners had made blatantly sexist comments they decided not to comment on these remarks. However, we agreed that whenever officials and representatives were involved it was essential to expose discriminatory attitudes. ... Some papers found that feminists who were once involved were now choosing to work in women-only campaign groups and this had the effect of making the papers even more male dominated.
>
> (National Conference of Alternative Papers, 1984: 1)

The same conference also discussed how to cover industrial issues and to get away from what was described as the predictability of reporting 'one closure, two marches' in every issue. An industrial reporter from a commercial evening newspaper advised the alternative hacks: 'Capitalise on trade union suspicion of the straight press and spell out the links between job losses and their knock-on effect. ... Fill in the gaps the straight press leaves, and redress the imbalance by setting a broader context' (National Conference of Alternative Papers, 1984: 2).

One of the suggested ways of doing this was to compare what happened to the bosses and the workers when a firm closed. *Rochdale's Alternative Paper* was particularly adept at keeping tabs on local business chiefs and the powers-that-be and developed a microfiche and card index of all local limited companies and members of the 'local bourgeoisie'. This time-consuming research, conducted before ownership of computers and electronic databases became relatively commonplace, enabled the paper to put the spotlight on those who ran the town in which its readers lived and worked.

A deliberate decision was taken by the *RAP* collective to personalise stories as far as possible. They explained why:

> It is precisely that aspect which explains much of the appeal of the straight press. But the 'alternative' nature of our use of this technique lies in the fact that its targets come from a different social class to those typically attacked by the other press. This gives the paper its bite and provides figures that readers can recognise, while seeing them in a new perspective. An average issue of *RAP* will contain over 50 representatives of the local bourgeoisie. The basic recipe is then topped up with features or special investigations. We have covered in depth, and from the alternative angle, a wide range of local institutions: the Rotary Club – membership, connections, activities; the Magistrates Bench – names, ages, political affiliations and the names of the secret committee which chooses them;

the local churches ... the death industry; estate agents; bookmakers; the health service etc.

(Aubrey *et al.*, 1980: 71–3)

But innovative journalism was no guarantee of survival when these newspapers confronted the formidable problems of small circulations, the lack of money for promotion, the burn-out of key individuals, outdated technology, a declining market for activities such as commercial printing which helped subsidise many newspapers, and the fracturing of the community and radical politics which provided a bedrock for alternative newspapers. Consequently, life expectations were often short. *RAP*, for example, folded in 1983 despite maintaining higher-than-average sales figures of 7,500 each month. Co-op member David Bartlet explained:

We ran out of steam. The do-it-yourself, volunteer approach to print production seemed to be inappropriate, and the people who sustained it in the Seventies, who were all 'Sixties people', moved on. There were no Sixties people left, and the Seventies lot were different.

(Hobbs 1993: 20)

Some alternative newspapers turned to listings as their salvation, in the hope of emulating the commercial success of London's *Time Out*. None succeeded in the long term. The only survivor from the heydey of the alternative local press is the *West Highland Free Press*, a weekly published since 1972 on the Isle of Skye, where there was a gap for a traditional local paper. Although it remains independent of the major newspaper publishing groups in Scotland, it is more akin to a traditional commercial newspaper than to alternative papers like *LOP* and *RAP*.

In their analysis of radical failure, Charles Landry and others blamed the demise of the alternative press and other left-wing projects on a lack of professionalism and business sense. While their argument was overly simplistic and faintly patronising, there was some truth in their description of why alternative newspapers tended eventually to lose their 'best talents' to other jobs:

Because working in the radical political economy is low-paid and requires an idealistic commitment over and above material considerations, in the long term it can only sustain employment for those who are young, single, without major financial commitments, or extremely principled, to the point of being prepared to engage in radical forms of self-exploitation.

(Landry *et al.* 1985: 98)

It will be helpful to consider in more detail one of the longest-running alternative local newspapers, which began publication in the 1970s, survived the 1980s, but finally died in the 1990s.

LEEDS OTHER PAPER BECOMES *NORTHERN STAR*

The first issue of *Leeds Other Paper* hit the streets in January 1974, during the State of Emergency and Three-Day Week imposed by Conservative Prime Minister Edward Heath in his losing battle with the miners. Declaring itself unequivocally the 'Leeds libertarian socialist newspaper' and selling at 4p, *LOP*'s stance could be gauged from the front-page headlines: 'Don't let the bastards carve us up. Hit the bosses where it hurts (in their pockets).' Readers were informed in that portentous debut:

> *Leeds Other Paper* exists to provide an alternative newspaper in Leeds, i.e. a newspaper not controlled by big business and other vested interests. It is our intention to support all groups active in struggle in industry and elsewhere for greater control of their own lives. The production will be intermittent at first – we are not professionals and we are few in number. We hope to grow, however, into a regular newspaper. If you wish to help in any way – articles, contacts, distribution etc. – your assistance will be greatly appreciated.
>
> (*Leeds Other Paper*, January 1974: 4)

Despite these uncertainties, the paper went on to be published 820 times, first monthly, then fortnightly and later weekly, before closing down exactly twenty years later in January 1994.

Established by a group of mostly ex-students who were active in community and anarchist/libertarian politics, *LOP* was made possible by the cheap and relatively easy to run offset litho printing presses that became available from the late 1960s (Aubrey *et al.*, 1980: 6). The £150 required to buy its first press was raised by jumble sales, benefit events and a 6p a week levy paid by supporters anxious to challenge the local newspaper monopoly of the city's notoriously pro-Conservative Yorkshire Post Newspapers.

Important decisions were taken in the early days that if *LOP* was to be regarded by its readers as a 'proper paper' it had to be published regularly, and that people should be able to buy it where they expected to buy newspapers – in newsagent shops. Throughout its history, the bulk of *LOP*'s sales were through newsagents. Folding and delivering bundles of papers to shops were just two of the uninspiring but essential contributions usually undertaken by the many unpaid volunteers who were crucial to *LOP*'s continued existence.

Initially staffed by people signing on the dole and others giving up much of their spare time, *LOP* was from 1978 run by a formal workers' co-operative with (low) paid staff funded by income from sales, advertising, commercial printing and typesetting, and (briefly) creative use of the Callaghan Labour government's Job Creation Scheme. Voluntary labour continued to play an important role throughout most of the paper's life. There was no editor, and until its final few years editorial meetings were open to staff, contributors and readers alike.

The overtly propagandistic tone of the first issue was quickly dropped in favour of a more journalistic style, although the underlying independent politics remained. As an internal style guide commented: 'A good story is one that reinforces the ability of the mass of people to do things for themselves . . .' (Harcup, 1994: 5). *LOP*'s news agenda was in opposition to what the paper's workers saw as the mainstream media's shallow, limited and often downright lazy approach to stories. Where traditional reporters too often seemed content to get a 'line' or an 'angle' on an event, *LOP* contributors were encouraged to cover issues in depth as well as breadth. Sometimes this could result in thousands of predictable words about yet another damp house, accompanied by a blurred photograph of a tenant pointing to an indiscernible dark patch in the corner of a room. And it could certainly be a grim read at times. One respondent to a readers' questionnaire in 1986 commented: 'My mum finds it so depressing she barely looks at it.' But at other times *LOP* could produce uplifting copy about a community initiative or a compelling exposé of a local scandal.

One example of the latter was *LOP*'s ground-breaking investigation into the use of carcinogenic chemicals at a local dyeworks. Whereas the mainstream media tended to take notice of health and safety stories only after the event, when there was a disaster or at least a body or two, *LOP* exposed the potential health risks before even the workers or their trade unions were aware of them. In his previous life the reporter had studied textile chemistry, and this enabled him to understand the implications of technical documentation that had been released in the United States but not publicised in the UK. So *LOP*'s investigation was helped by the fact that the reporter responsible had been trained not as a journalist, but as a scientist. *LOP* having done the hard work of providing breadth as well as depth, the story and the paper's research were three years later made the basis of a major Channel Four television documentary.

Other reporting coups for *LOP* included exposing the government's civil defence bunkers at the height of the Cold War; the paper was the first to publish details from the then secret *Protect and Survive* instructions on surviving nuclear attack (the scooped *Yorkshire Post* later paid *LOP* £15 for a photocopy); uncovering mortgage lenders who boycotted certain inner-city areas; and investigations into the mysterious death of nurse Helen Smith; land deals involving Freemasons; allegations of brutality in mental hospitals; fascist groups' claims to have built links with black Muslims; the secret training in the UK of military personnel from the Chilean dictatorship; local companies' use of the right-wing vetting agency the Economic League; conflicts of interest within the government-appointed Leeds Development Corporation; the antics of Eric Pickles's 'radical right' Tory administration at Bradford City Hall; and the asbestos contamination of hundreds of houses in the Armley area of Leeds.

In 1985 a ten-week study of media coverage of the multicultural Leeds area of Chapeltown found that while the *Yorkshire Evening Post* only mentioned the area in the context of prostitution, drugs, policing or rioting, *LOP* covered a far wider range of subjects, including plans for a recording studio, a court case, the opening of a multicultural centre, a Police Community Forum, a local woman's attempt to raise funds for her training as a dancer, and controversy over a proposed local dance centre (Harcup, 1994: 6).

At times *LOP* also played a more overtly campaigning role. The paper was involved in mobilising opposition to the transportation of nuclear waste through heavily populated areas of Leeds; in questioning the acceptance of a 'curfew on women' during the Yorkshire Ripper era; in challenging local authority plans to replace the historic (and inexpensive) Kirkgate Market with yet another shopping mall; and in aligning itself with Yorkshire's mining communities during the 1984–5 strike against pit closures, helping to collect food for miners' families and being one of the few media outlets to report from the strikers' side of the police lines.

Occasionally there would be a bit of journalistic licence in the creation of news. A reporter who had recently become a father got upset when he saw the number of toy guns on sale one Christmas. He decided the time had come for a campaign against war toys, so he formed a protest group and then reported on it copiously in the pages of *LOP*. He even paid a nocturnal visit to a children's playground and 'disarmed' a climbing frame which had been created in the shape of a tank – he removed the offending gun barrel with a hacksaw. Needless to say, he was back with a camera the next morning, and his swords-into-ploughshares escapade duly featured in the subsequent issue of *LOP*.

Even when it was rather less proactive, *LOP* could fulfil its self-proclaimed mission as an alternative newspaper simply by being an outlet for people to approach with stories which they felt the mainstream media had either ignored or distorted. Indeed, it was not unknown for frustrated members of staff from other local newspapers surreptitiously to pass on to *LOP* stories that had been spiked in their own organs. And, of course, *LOP* was the only newspaper in Leeds to report industrial disputes at the *Yorkshire Post* and *Yorkshire Evening Post*.

LOP's very existence as an alternative source of news and views challenged the hegemony of the local Establishment and the mainstream media in three important ways. First, because the paper demonstrated that there was more than one way of looking at the world. Second, because it contested the accepted notions of common sense and challenged spokespeople which other local media reported as authoritative sources. Third, because it illustrated how news and views relied on social construction as much as the reporting of any objective truth.

But despite its journalistic achievements, and its development of a comprehensive arts listings guide, sales of *LOP* rarely topped the 2,500 mark throughout its history. One street survey carried out by the paper's volunteers found that 70 per cent of those questioned in Leeds city centre had 'never heard of *LOP*' even though it was on sale in most newsagents in the area at the time. In 1991, in a failed bid to attract more readers in the rest of West Yorkshire, the Leeds tag was dropped and the name changed to *Northern Star* (after a nineteenth-century Chartist paper). In the quest for a younger, more postmodern readership, it gradually became more of a what's on guide with 'lifestyle' features and fewer hard news stories. Dwindling sales and mounting debts, combined with increasing staff turnover and burn-out, a declining number of contributors and chronic under-capitalisation, resulted in the paper publishing its final issue on 20 January 1994 (Wainwright, 1994: 9).

LOP had fallen victim to the political and economic forces that had already killed off most other radical publications. Perhaps the only surprise was that it had been able to survive so long in the hostile climate created by fifteen years of Conservative governments which proclaimed 'there is no alternative' and did their best to promote individualism at the expense of the community activism which *LOP* depended on for its subject matter, its readers and its continued production.

As one former *LOP* journalist commented at the time of its demise: 'It was only a grotty little thing produced on a few sheets of recycled paper that 2,000 people would buy, but that doesn't measure up to the impact it had over the years. It had a profound effect on Leeds in its small way' (Harcup, 1994: 30).

Certainly, experience of an alternative news agenda must have had some effect on those who were introduced to journalism by contributing to *LOP*. Working on the paper proved to be an unconventional entry route into journalism for many who have since gone on to work for media outlets as diverse as the *Yorkshire Evening Press*, the *Scotsman*, *Sounds*, *New Musical Express*, *New Statesman*, Granada TV, *Harrogate Advertiser*, *Derby Evening Telegraph*, *Scotland on Sunday*, the *Big Issue*, *Northern Echo* and others.

But if many of *LOP*'s journalists have remained in the media, it could be that a large proportion of *LOP*'s former readers now receive little local news of any sort. Readers' surveys consistently showed that *LOP* appealed to a section of the population that had rejected the mainstream media. A 1986 survey found that a third of *LOP*'s regular readers never read, watched or listened to any other local media; only a fifth regularly bought any other local paper; and half had no contact with other local media beyond picking up the occasional copy of the *Yorkshire Evening Post* or watching *Look North* on BBC TV's regional output. The 'dispossessed' have lost their 'parish magazine'.

CONCLUSION

Franklin and Murphy claimed that the brief flowering of the alternative local press illustrated, 'perhaps more poignantly than any other aspect of the local media, the power of the market in marginalising ideological debate' (Franklin and Murphy, 1991: 106). The discernible irony is that the demise of these newspapers coincided with the arrival of computers and desktop publishing technology which might have made their production cheaper, quicker and less labour-intensive.

Not that all alternative voices have been silenced, of course. The huge number of football fanzines launched in the late 1980s and early 1990s show that some 'ordinary people' can find ways of getting their views into print, even if only in an area of special interest. Other outlets include the dozens of community broadcasting groups lobbying for licences, the ubiquitous World Wide Web, and national alternative newsletters such as the Brighton-based *SchNEWS*. But the idea of a wide-ranging alternative local newspaper, available in newsagents and aimed at everyone who lived in a particular city or area, appears to have been a phenomenon of the 1970s and 1980s.

Perhaps the lasting legacy of the alternative local press is the challenge that these newspapers offered to complacent notions of what constituted news. Some of that has filtered through to the commercial press. As one former *LOP* reporter commented: 'The alternative press changed the established press, it forced it to start reporting community groups and all the rest of it' (Harcup, 1994: 29). Certainly, there are many people still working in journalism for whom a good story remains what it was in the alternative press – one that, in the words of the *LOP* style guide from all those years ago, reinforces the ability of the mass of people to do things for themselves.

REFERENCES

Aubrey, C., Landry C., and Morley, D. (1980) *Here Is the Other News*, London: Minority Press Group.

Berry, D., Cooper, L, and Landry, C. (1980) *Where Is the Other News?*, London: Minority Press Group.

Fountain, N. (1988) *Underground: The London Alternative Press 1966–74*, London: Comedia/Routledge.

Franklin, B. (1994a) *Packaging Politics: Political Communications in Britain's Media Democracy*, London: Edward Arnold.

—— (1994b) Letter published in *British Journalism Review*, vol. 5, no. 3, London: Cassell.

Franklin, B. and Murphy, D. (1991) *What News? The Market, Politics and the Local Press*, London: Routledge.

Harcup, T. (1994) *A Northern Star: Leeds Other Paper and the Alternative Press 1974–1994*, London and Pontefract: Campaign for Press and Broadcasting Freedom.

Hobbs, A. (1993) *Alternative Voices*, published in *GMB Direct*, Sept./Oct. 1993, London: GMB.

Landry, C., Morley, D., Southwood, R. and Wright, P. (1985) *What a Way to Run a Railroad*, London: Comedia.

Leeds Other Paper: bound copies are available for inspection at the Local History Library in Leeds.

National Conference of Alternative Papers (1984) *Editorial and Workshop Reports*, Spring 1984, Leeds.

Wainwright, M. (1994) 'Star of North Falls after 30 Years of Shoestring Scoops', *Guardian* 21 January, p. 9.

Whitaker, B. (1981) *News Ltd: Why You Can't Read All About It*, London: Minority Press Group.

Chapter 9

Looking at the world through the eyes of . . .: reporting the 'local' in daily, weekly and Sunday local newspapers

Mike Glover

In February 1997 the *Press Gazette*, the journalists' trade magazine, illustrated a silly item in its off-beat column 'dog' with a rag-out of the front page of the *South Wales Echo* from December 1934. The item was about the long-passed fashion of multiple headlines. There were no less than five over the front-page lead. They were (in descending order and size): GIRL'S COURAGE IN REMARKABLE AIR ACCIDENT; PLANE CRASHES THROUGH HOUSE AT CROYDON; Comes to a Standstill near the Gas Stove; BACON AND EGGS SPOILT; But Father Saved and Fire Danger Averted. But it was not the bizarre priorities, the haphazard use of capitals and lower case or even the quaint design which caught my eye. Rather it was the geography. Here was a Cardiff-based newspaper deciding to lead its front page with a story from London's suburbia. Closer examination showed that none of the four stories illustrated by the sample front page was from the principality. The others concerned a gun raid on a shop in Dublin, an Atlantic rescue drama and a general British weather story.

None of the stories seemed, by modern standards at least, particularly newsworthy. None was of national significance or such horror that they would have moved the hearts of the newspaper's Welsh customers. There was not even any hint that the people caught up in these relatively mundane dramas originated from the South Wales area. And yet this publication was quite content to dominate its front page with items that could, by no means, be described as local. I knew that the world and the market in which local newspapers operate had changed beyond recognition in the intervening sixty-three years. What I hadn't realised was just how this had affected basic news values. There is not a local evening or weekly newspaper editor today who would dare lead the front page with stories from the other corners of the British Isles, not unless there was some overriding significance not apparent in the 1934 examples quoted above. Sundays are a slightly different matter, as we shall see later in this chapter.

The most obvious difference between the early 1930s and the late 1990s is the competition. In 1934 there were fewer truly national newspapers, radio was in its infancy and restricted to the BBC, television was a gleam in a few scientists' eyes, free newspapers had not been thought of and as for the new media like the Internet, cable, teletext, audiotext et alia, they were not even possible. Social changes have been just as significant. Evening newspapers in particular used to be bought at the factory gate when the hooter sounded at 5.30 in the afternoon, by men, who probably read them on the bus or in the pub on the way home. The reader had probably not been exposed to any other media since they read their local newspaper the previous night. Today the local evening rag is more likely to be bought by mum, or dad, picking up the kids from school around 3.30 pm. If the purchaser is in full-time employment then he or she probably travels by car, finds it difficult to stop on the yellow lines outside the remaining newsagents, listens non-stop to the radio on the way home, and turns the television on as soon as the threshold is crossed. Instead of an evening of endless tedium in a dark room lit by a single bulb and a roaring fire, the modern family has an endless choice of evening entertainments inside and outside the home.

These scenarios are gross simplifications, of course, of the complex world in which we live, but are designed to illustrate how the combination of social change and the explosion of media has had a drastic and dramatic effect on the local newspaper industry. But despite these upheavals, and against the gloomy predictions of pundits, some local newspapers are thriving. Evening newspapers' sales have declined, roughly halving in the last twenty-five years. But it is far too early to write them off. In any conurbation they still outsell the nationals by far. In some they outsell all the nationals put together. Most have penetrations of between 40 and 60 per cent of the local households. The Sundays are having a real boom period with established ones increasing sale and new ones springing up across the United Kingdom. More than 90 per cent of the British population reads a local newspaper of some sort. So how have they done it? And what of the future?

Broadly they have done it by getting down their cost bases by investing heavily in modern technology and reducing production and editorial staffs, improving their distribution methods, being in the forefront of modern design and focusing their content on the changing market place. It is the last of these which is the concern here. There have been trends and fads which have been absorbed over the years. The use of design and more lifestyle content have addressed the increased influence of women particularly in purchasing decisions. There have been significant moves to make news-papers more useful to the readers, ranging from giving television programme details to what's on-type information. There has been the switch from small, stunted pictures of formal occasions to the use of bigger, brighter, human-interest photographs.

There was a period, particularly in the early 1980s, when many evening newspapers thought these were, in themselves, answers to the declining sales. They looked at the decline in local communities, the mobile work force and an increased tendency of households to make single newspaper purchases.

They noted the obsession with television, particularly the popularity of soaps from Hollywood and Australia as well as those closer to home, and concluded that readers were just as interested in the plots and the private lives of the actors as they were about their real-life neighbours. They even fell for propoganda from a government alarmed at the soaring crime rate who claimed that the real problem was fear of crime rather than its actuality. The result was that they tried to become all things to all readers: a locally published national newspaper which cut back on local crime and council coverage to make way for soap stars and lifestyle features. In effect they took on the popular national newspapers at their own game. Guess what? The sales decline accelerated.

Newspapers seemed to have forgotten what they do well and diverted limited resources into what they do less well. They ignored the fact that people who had less time to read accessed the national and international news that they wanted from television and radio. They did not want their local newspaper to take up valuable space with inferior, and in many cases out of date, national news. Every piece of market research ever conducted on behalf of a local newspaper has come up with the conclusion that what readers want is more local news. To use the marketing jargon local news is the Unique Selling Point of local newspapers. But that is not an answer in itself. What exactly does 'local' mean? Does it mean from the region, from the town or city in which the newspaper is based, or from down the street? And if you told the subject of your research that the newspaper could have more local news if you omitted the crossword or the TV programme listings, or if the cover price of the newspaper went up by 10p, then you might get a very different, not to say abusive, answer.

We are not dealing with rocket science here. There are no magic formulae which provide universal answers. It is up to each editor to look at the resources at his or her disposal and come up with a combination which suits the community the newspaper serves. Those communities vary enormously, both in their make-up and in their strength. Broadly the further a community is from London the stronger it is likely to be and the more likely to support a thriving local newspaper. It also has a direct affect on the way local news is interpreted. As if to torpedo this argument out of the water before it is launched, London itself has a very healthy evening newspaper, the *Evening Standard*. But it is a unique product. It hardly has any hard news at all, never mind local news. It has looked at its market and decided, very successfully, that it cannot hope to unite all the disparate communities of the capital. It has a veneer of hard news, of the type favoured by national newspapers, packs of features based on the lifestyle of the commuter, lots of comment, financial and business news and is jammed full of advertising columns which again are targeted at its market. The *Evening Standard* has gone for the community of interest, rather than the geographical community. It looks at the world through the eyes of the London commuter.

This phrase 'looking at the world through the eyes of . . . ' is the nearest I have been able to come to describing how the successful local newspaper selects its content. In the 1960s and 1970s there was an attempt to launch a series of evening papers in commuter towns round the fringes of London. Slough, Reading, Hemel Hempstead and Basildon were seen as areas of fast-expanding populations who would support such ventures; some like Bedford and Milton Keynes never even got off the ground. Slough and then Hemel Hempstead closed down. Reading and Basildon hang on by their fingertips. The people who moved in to these areas had neither the history that provided the traditional readership, nor the community spirit to provide the glue that binds an evening newspaper readership together. Of course Milton Keynes, along with other similar centres, has a thriving weekly newspaper market. It is as if the weekly newspaper's attractions can overcome a lack of tradition and community cohesiveness while an evening cannot.

Outside this ring of commuter towns, there are conurbations which also house the capital's workers, but in addition have a strong enough local community to give a local evening newspaper an identity of its own: Oxford, Swindon and Northampton are typical. They have managed to survive on daily circulations around the 30,000 mark. But it is when you come to the big regional centres that evening newspapers come into their own: from Portsmouth to Sunderland and Norwich to Wolverhampton, taking in such Metropolitan areas as Manchester, Birmingham, Leeds and Newcastle. By the time you get to Scotland, Wales or Ulster, the appeal of the national press has melted away. A view of the world through London eyes is not very appealing. Local newspapers thrive, whether they be evenings, weeklies, mornings or Sundays.

It is relatively easy to see the world through the eyes of the citizens of the cities. They have pride in their regions and a vested interest in knowing what is going on locally. Anything that goes on in them is potentially of interest. Even if the readers live in one leafy suburb, they are likely to know someone or work with someone who lives in another. The problems of the disadvantaged estates conjure up the perils lurking within stone-throwing distance. The escapades of the well-heeled local plutocracy have enough relevance for the aspirations of mere mortals to feel within reach. All human life is there and its minutiae can all be read about in the local rag. These are the conurbations where the evening papers thrive. Not so far away are the market towns which are the province of the weekly paid-for newspaper. Morpeth and Alnwick and Blyth may not be so far away from Newcastle. Indeed the *Newcastle Evening Chronicle* sells quite well in these places. But as well as a need to see the world through the regional eye, there is also the stronger need to see the world through the parochial eye of the town itself. Economics decree that there is not the critical mass necessary to support a newspaper devoted to such towns six nights a week, but a big weekly newspaper is just the ticket. Successful newspapers, however often and whenever in the week they come out, take their lead for their content by harnessing this community pride and vested interest.

Probably the single biggest reason newspapers continue to defy the gloom-merchants and survive all the other media competition is their right to be partisan. The broadcasters are manacled by laws and regulations which stem from legislators' fears of the power of the airwaves. Newspapers have remained largely unshackled, despite the recent efforts of some elements of Parliament. Thus a poor local newspaper may carry a couple of paragraphs about a child being knocked down by a lorry in the high street. That is probably what the local radio station would say also. A good local newspaper would carry an analysis of how many accidents there had been in the high street, what local traders and the authorities think about it and a history of their fight for a bypass. A picture of the child in happier times would help everyone to relate to the tragedy and would be essential, whatever the politic- ally correct would say about intrusion. A brilliant local newspaper would have all this, but scream from its front page: BUILD THIS BYPASS NOW! It would not only explain and interpret the background, putting the accident into context, it would campaign, fight for its readers and take sides in the debate. Of course there would have to be an element of common sense. If there was such an outcry every time someone fell off a bike or suffered a minor graze, the impact would be lost. The newspaper would be made to look ridiculous. But the principle holds good. Such an approach requires resources. Local radio, certainly the commercial ones, survive on three or four journalists if they are lucky. They have time to do little but ring up the dreaded spokesperson for public authorities and regurgitate what they wish to make public. Fate does not look kindly on newspapers with the same resources or attitudes. A weekly newspaper which researches and originates its own articles as well as producing them, probably needs between fifteen and twenty journalists, of which fewer than a handful will be in full-time production work. An evening newspaper with similar demands six days a week has any number from thirty to a hundred jour- nalists, but up to a half of them will be managing, designing or producing pages.

In the example of the high street accident, the reaction will depend on the time of the day or week that it happens. Imagine yourself in the newsroom of the local daily rag. The accident happens at 8.30 am as the child is on the way to school. This is a very convenient time for evening newspapers. The police reporter picks up a tip from a policeman concerned that people should know why the traffic was disrupted that morning. The reporter tells the newsdesk. Luckily the news editor that day is a long-standing resident of the town and an experienced journalist who instinctively knows that acci- dents are a burning issue in the high street. He sends the police reporter round to the police station to follow up the details. He convinces the editor this is the only issue that matters that day and he agrees to clear the front page. The newspaper prints at 11.30 am but the last deadline for material is 10.30 so he has less than two hours to gather all material.

A second reporter is sent into the newspaper library to research the history and identify local contacts with a view on this issue. A third reporter is put onto telephoning the council, the local MP, the local chamber of trade or anyone else with a known opinion on the subject. The chief photographer is alerted so a picture can be taken of the scene and file pictures of those people quoted can be dug out. The newspaper sales department is alerted so that poster bills can be prepared and supplies increased in the areas affected by the story. The editor meanwhile has been liaising with his designers to give the front page the feel and impact he thinks necessary. Probably a senior subeditor or someone similar has been cleared to rewrite all the copy coming from different sources in a way that the editor dictates. A leader writer has been briefed to wax lyrical in the comment column. Another reporter, who knows the local area well, has guessed which school the child is going to and has had the initiative to ring the headteacher, confirm the child's name and persuade the head to part with the latest school picture. The parents are being contacted by the school to confirm permission. A second photographer is dispatched to copy it. The police reporter, having confirmed the details of the accident has now come back to the office and is phoning the local hospital to get the latest condition of the injured child. Up to ten people are now involved. Most of them are writing furiously. Meanwhile other journalists are getting material for other pages finalised. The deadline is approaching fast.

Such scenarios do not develop every day. Some newspapers would not react in this way until the next day. Others would deem the accident unworthy of such treatment and dismiss it as one paragraph. All this activity could be going on in a newsroom when, at the same time, the Prime Minister announces her retirement. So the whole newspaper would have to lurch in another direction: the original team's efforts destined for page 5, while another equally strong team starts working on the political story for pages 1, 2 and 3. It is easy to see why newspapers need resources, not least highly motivated and skilled journalists.

It may be that there is no evening paper in the town where the high street accident happened, or that one does exist and does not recognise the significance of the story. In either case a local weekly newspaper should fulfil the same role. It may have a couple of days instead of a couple of hours. Because of the extra time available it may take two journalists instead of ten. But the essential attitudes would not differ.

But newspapers, however campaigning, work in strikingly different markets. For ten years or so I worked in Bradford, an urban sprawl in the foothills of the Pennines, which had a marvellously cosmopolitan feel, having absorbed waves of immigrants for a century. Scots, Irish, Germans, Poles, Ukrainians, Baltic peoples, West Indians and a variety from the Indian subcontinent had settled there. Consequently the inhabitants had an interest in all corners of the world. Looking at the world through the eyes of Bradford was very complex and stimulating. They wanted news of the latest election in Pakistan as well as scores from the Bradford cricket league. At the time of writing I am based in York, just thirty-six miles away, but on a different planet as far as attitudes are concerned. A walled city with no significant history of immigration, its people are comparatively insular and parochial. Each city has an evening paper and each has to wrestle with the task of reflecting the local community.

And what about the local Sunday newspaper? It would most likely cover a larger geographical area than the single town or city. (As always, there are exceptions. One of the most successful local Sunday newspapers is *Bedford on Sunday*, but since it is distributed as a free, perhaps I can be excused for dismissing it from this argument.) The Sunday would only cover the high street accident if there was a wider significance or a hidden angle not picked up by the weekly or evening, something it could label an exclusive: BANNED LORRY FIRM IN HIGH STREET DRAMA might do the job or how about TRAFFIC CAMPAIGNER'S SON FIGHTS FOR LIFE?

Regional Sunday newspapers are an interesting phenonemon. Long-standing publications in England include the *Sunday Sun* in Newcastle upon Tyne and the *Sunday Mercury* in Birmingham each of which sells around 130,000 copies per week, and probably outsell all the national Sundays other than the *News of the World* in their own areas. Scotland has several including the *Sunday Mail* and the *Sunday Post*, which also sell well in northern England, boosting their total circulation to near the million mark.

Since the late 1980s a new wave of Sundays has opened. In the vanguard was the old Thomson organisation, which has since sold its English, Ulster and Welsh newspaper interests to Trinity and its Scottish papers to the Barclay brothers (see chapter 6). It set up the *Scotland on Sunday* from its Edinburgh base, *Wales on Sunday* in Cardiff and *Sunday Life* in Belfast. They have all taken on different markets and shapes. As if to prove the argument that the further from London the better, the most successful has been *Sunday Life*, a bright and bold tabloid which already sells more than 100,000. *Scotland on Sunday* sells nearly as many, by being an upmarket broadsheet aimed at AB and C1 readers. *Wales on Sunday* has had a more chequered history, changing shape and direction several times, making loss for most of its history and selling more like 60,000 at best.

The regional Sunday idea was copied by Westminster Press, the regional newspaper group since sold by parent company Pearson to Newsquest. In 1992 it launched *Yorkshire on Sunday*, which lasted just three years, selling at most 70,000. It had broken even by 1994 but steep increases in newsprint costs the following year killed it off, especially as the parent group Pearson was preparing Westminster Press for sale. Its brief history is worth a chapter on its own, not least because I was its editor, but here I just have room to say that the regional identity of Yorkshire was less easy to capture than than of Ulster, Scotland or Wales. There may be a message there for a government that wants to develop regional parliaments.

So what future is there for local newspapers? Their ownership is in turmoil. But the pattern is consistent, with multinational groups like Thomson and Pearson selling off their regional newspaper interests to groups which specialise in them, like Trinity and Newsquest. The Henley Centre which specialises in social and marketing research believes there are signs of a return to community. People may be sick of sacrificing the wider family to chase careers all over the country. Local loyalties and pride are set to return. Whether this is optimistic and wishful thinking or not, there does seem to be a continuing demand for local information and a view of the world through the local perspective. There is no one better placed to capitalise on this than the local newspapers which have been gathering local information, in most cases, for a century or more. They may need to diversify into cable, do deals with local radio and get on to the Internet. But they look certain to defy the doom merchants for the foreseeable future. But however long they last, I don't expect the Cardiff newspaper to lead its front page with a non-fatal plane crash in Croydon again.

Chapter 10

No news isn't good news: the development of local free newspapers

Bob Franklin

Free newspapers express a double paradox. First, they are distributed free of charge and yet free newspapers remain the most lucrative and profitable sector within the local press. Second, they are *newspapers* but they report little if any *news*. Both apparent contradictions are resolved by reference to a third, but highly significant, characteristic of free newspapers; their income is derived wholly from advertising revenues. Consequently, it is not necessary to sell these newspapers to generate income nor, since the papers are given away, is it necessary to report news to attract readers.

During the 1970s and 1980s free newspapers expanded at a quite remarkable pace but, since the early 1990s, this growth of titles has been stalled and has even experienced a reversal. But free newspapers remain a highly significant element within the local press because of the large number of papers which exist, the substantial distribution figures they have achieved and the considerable advertising revenues they command. Equally significant has been the tendency of free newspapers to exacerbate the already dwindling fortunes of the traditional paid-for weekly local newspapers. Using new print technology, free papers radically lowered the cost base of local newspapers seducing advertisers, advertising revenues and, eventually, readers from the paid-for local press. Undoubtedly the most significant impact of free newspapers has been the extent to which their limited and consumer-focused editorial has tended to influence and diminish both the range and quality of the editorial content of the local weekly press more generally (Franklin and Murphy, 1997).

This chapter examines the development of the free newspaper industry as well as considering the distinctive editorial content of free newspapers. The chapter begins by analysing the unique economic structure of free newspapers which distinguishes them from the traditional local press.

READERS FOR SALE! THE ECONOMIC STRUCTURE OF FREE NEWSPAPERS

When free newspapers were first published in the mid-1970s, few pundits would have predicted their explosive growth during the subsequent decade.

Editorially they were unambitious. Based on the give-away American 'shoppers', the early free newspapers were devoted wholly to advertising. By the standards of conventional local newspapers they were undoubtedly unattractive. Journalists working on the traditional paid-for papers dismissed them as little more than a whimsical fad. Refusing to acknowledge them as newspapers, journalists preferred the abusive and disparaging term 'free sheet'. Despite such critical peer review, the expansion of free newspaper titles throughout the 1980s was unprecedented; the growth of free papers was especially striking because of the simultaneous decline in titles and circulations for paid-for newspapers (Collins and Scott, 1986: 10–11). These divergent fortunes were not the only feature distinguishing paid-for from free newspapers.

Free newspapers reversed the traditional 'logic' of newspaper economics. The conventional wisdom informing newspaper production was that quality news coverage (and lots of it), reporting a wide range of issues, but with a firm commitment to a local news agenda, was the vital ingredient necessary to persuade readers to buy a newspaper. If the newspaper could illustrate that it enjoyed a sufficient circulation among local readers, local companies and businesses would advertise their products in the paper. By these processes, the traditional local newspaper generated its twin sources of income from copy sales and advertising revenues. Newspapers sold two commodities: news to readers and space to advertisers.

But the economic imperatives informing free newspaper production renders this 'logic' not merely redundant, but irrelevant. Free newspapers redefine the identity of the 'buyers' and the 'sellers' as well as the nature of the 'product' for sale in the free newspaper market place. The 'buyers' are no longer 'readers' trying to purchase a 'product' called 'local news'. The 'buyers' (readers) are reified into nothing more than a 'product' which is itself on offer to advertisers who, in their turn, become the new 'buyers'. Because of this revised rationale, the quality of free newspapers' editorial has become largely inconsequential to the paper's success. Free distribution guarantees delivery to a closely defined readership regardless of the paper's editorial merit or even the homeowners' wishes; love it or hate it, the local free paper is pushed through letter boxes every week by a small army of school children, pensioners, 'housewives', unemployed people and other casual workers.

Editorial quality is not wholly irrelevant in this new market place, however, since it is not sufficient merely to deliver free newspapers to households; advertisers must be convinced that these newspapers are read rather than used to line the cat's litter tray. Consequently editorial must accomplish a difficult balancing act in which it is sufficiently interesting to attract readers' attention, without being so engaging that it risks diverting them from the adverts. In this sense, free newspapers are somewhat akin to the colourful seats in a 'Mc'Fast food' café which are consciously designed to entice customers in but also to become uncomfortable after ten minutes.

Most media (with the exception of the BBC) but certainly all newspapers are reliant, to a greater or lesser extent, on advertising; these revenues lower the cost of media to readers and audiences and make them accessible to greater numbers of people. But free newspapers' total reliance on advertising revenues is unique and occasions a number of significant consequences for their economic organisation, their staffing structures, their news gathering and reporting routines and the subsequent character of their editorial.

First, the balance between advertising and editorial is overwhelmingly in favour of the former in free newspapers. The front page and two or three other pages feature news; the remainder are devoted to advertising copy. Second, their reliance on advertising revenues makes free newspapers vulnerable to advertising interests where they conflict with editorial. One study, or example, illustrated the willingness of the *Newcastle Chronicle* to offer front-page prominence to an advertising feature for Tesco even though this involved relegating a story about a double murder to the paper's inside pages (Gall, 1993). Advertorial is rampant; for local journalists it is a curse. Certain sections in the papers – whether sport, travel, business or even local politics (but never consumer stories) – may be dropped, not because of any lack of reader interest, but because these topics fail to attract advertising. Third, it follows that free newspapers need to employ substantially fewer journalists than their paid sister papers because they report so little news. Journalists, moreover, are less significant to the paper's revenue base than the telephone sales staff; the latter directly generate income. Fourth, free newspapers enjoy a less responsive and interactive relationship with their readers. They are less accountable because they do not have to win a readership by publishing relevant and high-quality editorial; they are merely distributed to targeted audiences in compliance with advertisers' requirements.

Finally, free papers minimise their production costs in other ways which paid-for papers have been unable, or less willing, to follow. They are less likely to provide or sponsor training for new recruits to journalism. Since many of these papers were newly established, moreover, they were less willing to accept the collective bargaining agreements established between managements and the traditional print unions and, during the 1980s were able to impose regimes of industrial relations which would have been unacceptable in the unionised paid-for newspapers. Free newspapers also cut the costs of news gathering in ways which many journalists and editors in the paid-for papers considered unprofessional. They became increasingly editorially reliant on non-journalistic sources of news such as the press and public relations departments in nearby local authorities, local businesses and even the information service of central government (see chapters 12, 13, 18). The resulting copy was cheap and cheerful but wholly uncritical, articulating sectional rather than community interests. The public relations officers' task is to persuade rather than inform. Alternatively, free newspapers accessed news by employing cheaper, more 'casual' journalists such as freelances or the local news agencies. The implications of these cost-cutting strategies on the quality of editorial is analysed below. The following section charts the changing fortunes of free newspapers since their emergence in the mid-1960s.

THE DEVELOPING FREE NEWSPAPER INDUSTRY

During the 1970s and 1980s the rapid expansion of free newspapers constituted nothing less than a press phenomenon. The growth in titles, their total distribution figures and the advertising revenues they attracted were breathtaking. Table 10.1 reveals the speed with which these new papers found favour with advertisers and readers. Some of the figures for year-on-year growth are remarkable. Free newspapers grew from 325 in 1980 to 494 the following year; a rate of 52 per cent in a single year. Across the decade free newspapers registered more than a fourfold expansion from 201 to 882 newspapers. Distribution figures grew at similarly impressive rates from 15 million copies in 1981 to 35.5 million in 1985, peaking at 42 million copies in 1989 (Newspaper Society Database, 1997, see table 1.1).

Free newspapers' advertising revenues reflect the rapid expansion of titles and distribution. In 1970 free newspapers earned £2 million in advertising income which represented a 1.4 per cent share of the total regional/local newspaper advertising market. By 1980 those figures had reached £84 million (13.1 per cent) and by 1985 £263 million (26.2 per cent); a doubling of market share in five years (*UK Press Gazette*, 1986: 29). This growth in revenues continued throughout the 1990s although figures dipped in 1990 and

Table 10.1 Free newspaper growth across a decade

Year	Number of titles	Annual increase %
1977	201	19
1978	259	29
1979	315	22
1980	325	3
1981	494	52
1982	520	5
1983	653	26
1984	730	12
1985	845	16
1986	882	4

Source: Newspaper Society Database, 1997 and Collins and Scott, 1986

1991 because of the impact of a continuing recession on the advertising industry.

This expansion in free newspapers is perhaps more striking because it occurred at a time of general decline in the fortunes of the local press; these two events were of course connected. Between 1970 and 1985, daily newspapers' share of the local newspaper advertising market fell from 62.9 per cent to 50.4 per cent; for weekly paid-for papers the equivalent figures signal a fall from 35.7 per cent to 23.3 per cent. Significantly, free newspapers' share of advertising outstripped that of paid newspapers in 1984 and has remained ahead subsequently (*UK Press Gazette*, 1986: 29).

Recent trends in the American newspaper market show a continuing success for free newspapers. Income has doubled since 1992, largely reflecting the shift of alcohol and tobacco advertisers from paid-for to free newspapers. Mainstream newspapers such as the *Chicago Tribune*, attracted by these advertising revenues, have recently launched new free papers. The *New York Village Voice*, a pioneer alternative weekly, has moved from paid-for to free with distribution increasing from 130,000 to 231,000; an increase of 13 per cent (*Press Gazette*, 1997: 1).

The growth of free papers in the UK during the 1970s and 1980s is readily explained by three factors: the poor and deteriorating state of the existing local weekly newspapers; the advertising industry's desire for new local media outlets; and the development of the new print technology. The state of existing local newspapers undoubtedly offered a market niche which free papers sought eagerly to colonise (Cunningham, 1988: 23). Local weekly papers' circulations were declining and yet they were protected from competition because typically they enjoyed a monopoly within their circulation areas (Hartley *et al.*, 1977: 32–3). In the perception of free newspaper entrepreneurs, these overstaffed, over-unionised, traditional papers offered little more than boring and uncritical celebrations of the parochial concerns of a local community which were published using outdated and clapped-out equipment. The owner of the Derby Trader Group of free papers claimed:

> there were many ancient, ailing, weekly paid papers. We've all worked for them, each one run by one man and a boy, with loads of correspondents sending in antiquated copy from village fetes about Mrs Jones' home-made jam. They were started in 1750, they were not professional and quite frankly they were ripe for the taking.
>
> (Pickering, 1986)

But the traditional papers fostered the development of the free press in more direct ways. Fearing an 'invasion' by a 'hostile' free paper and the subsequent loss of advertising revenues, many weekly newspapers launched their own free newspapers as a defensive strategy to 'warn off predators'.

Free newspapers' growing presence also reflected the wishes and interests of the advertising industry. The consumer boom of the 1960s encouraged advertisers to develop new media outlets. Advertisers were increasingly hostile towards existing newspapers which, protected by local monopoly, charged ever increasing prices for advertising space while the continuous downturn in their circulations meant they delivered ever diminishing readerships. Free newspapers, moreover, undercut paid-for weeklies and offered advertising at approximately one-third of the cost. Their audience reach was also greater since they distributed to people who never purchased a newspaper. But they also guaranteed advertisers' messages would reach specially targeted audiences like the much sought after, high income, high consuming social groups A and B (Franklin and Murphy, 1991: 83).

Finally, free newspapers were able to introduce the new print technology; these were new, non-unionised and, at least initially, quite modest enterprises. The new technology allowed cuts in budget; there would be no highly paid and skilled printers, fewer journalists, no unions, lower wages and more 'flexible' working arrangements. To top all this, new technology offered free newspapers the prospect of colour pictures, sharper definition of print and photography, the chance to update stories close to the deadline (largely redundant in these 'newsless' papers) and a 'clean' paper which people could read without having to wash their hands afterwards.

The editor of *The Wilts and Gloucestershire Standard* summarised the propitious environment in which the free press was nurtured:

> The free newspaper revolution forced paid-for regionals to challenge the unions, bringing in the new technology which had been available for years. It also radically lowered their cost base. These newcomers had the advantage of lower costs at several points compared to the larger papers. They had less expensive or less extensive overheads: they needed fewer journalists; and they could get the printing done on contract, that is they did not have to invest in the major cost of printers or a press. As the cost of placing adverts with the larger papers rose, so the free sheets were able to pull in the new or small and the regular advertisers who were beguiled by the low costs.
>
> (Hayes, 1996: 195–6)

An important symbol and expression of the free newspaper industry's confidence was the decision to establish a free daily newspaper in the Birmingham area: the *Daily News* was launched on 2 October 1984. The paper distributed 276,000 copies, claimed a readership of 427,000 and a 25 per cent share of the newspapers' advertising market in the locale (Ward, 1987). Reed Regional Newspapers bought a 51 per cent stake in the paper in 1987, merged it with other local titles and confidently predicted a move to profit as well as the launch of similar titles in other metropolitan areas such as Manchester, Glasgow, Liverpool and London. Around this time, Bob Maxwell was preparing forty-eight-page dummies of the free daily paper the *Londoner*, although the paper was never launched (*UK Press Gazette*, 9 November 1987).

The free newspaper formula which had been so successful in its weekly format was floundering when applied to a daily paper. The logistical problems were enormous. To win sufficient advertising a daily paper must service a very large community and guarantee delivery across the patch within the time space of one hour; this triggers costly problems of distribution. In metropolitan areas, moreover, the established morning and evening papers dig in for a sustained competitive fight. To be successful, the *Daily News* had to confront the very successful Birmingham *Post* and *Evening Mail* which enjoyed support from a loyal readership and consequently from local and regional advertisers. It was a battle the *Daily News* seemed destined to lose; the paper changed its name to the *Metro News* and moved to weekly publication in May 1991. Reed claimed that advertisers' unwillingness 'to take space on more than one day a week' was the key reason for the decision to close (Slattery, 1991: 1 and Nicholson, 1995: 17). The failure of the *Daily News* seemed to symbolise free newspapers' changing fortunes.

Free newspaper titles and distributions have both dipped across the 1990s. Distributions peaked at 42 million in 1989 and by 1996 had reduced to 28 million; a fall of 33 per cent. The number of free titles fell from the 1986 peak of 882 to 630 in 1996; a reduction of more than 28 per cent. Advertising revenues have also been falling, but in 1996 they eventually regained their 1989 peak of £629 million; in 1991 they plummeted to £540 million; a 14 per cent drop over two years. But despite these recent reversals of the early trend of sustained growth, free newspapers remain the most vibrant sector within the local newspaper market. The continuing decline of weekly and daily local newspapers means that free newspapers' share of the local paper advertising cake has actually increased across the decade: from 24.5 per cent in 1987 to 30.6 per cent in 1996 (*Advertising Association, 1997*). But the spell is broken. Free newspapers' apparent ability to buck market trends has gone. Five reasons explain the downturn.

First, the sustained economic recession from 1989 to 1993 hit the advertising industry particularly hard. Advertising, of course, is the very life blood of free newspapers and consequently the effect of this unrelenting downturn in advertising spend was the closure of titles. Second, during 1994 and 1995, all newspaper publishers faced substantial rises in the cost of newsprint at a time when general levels of inflation were low; the cost base of free newspapers increased in consequence (Oakley, 1995: 24). Third, one often unacknowledged outcome of the national newspaper price war has been to cap the price of local paid-for papers. As a result, they have become more competitively priced and relatively more attractive both to readers and advertisers; again the free newspapers have been the losers as a result of such trends. Fourth, the increasing tendency of national papers to 'regionalise' editions and tailor their editorial to focus on stories of regional significance has attracted advertisers away from local newspapers, whether paid-for or free. The intention of the nationals has always been to 'cream off some of the substantial advertising revenues which are available' (McNair, 1994: 173).

Finally, but most significantly, the declining fortunes of the free press can be traced to the changing patterns of ownership of free newspapers since the late 1980s and the group strategies of the new owners. Free newspapers were established and owned initially by independent entrepreneurs, like Eddie Shah, who had little if any experience or history of involvement in local newspapers. They had little empathy with the traditions of local journalism and considered local newspapers as mere vehicles for investment with the hope of making a financial return. This lack of 'feel' for the local press explains much of the initial hostility of those working on traditional newspapers to these newcomers. But between 1988 and 1989, free newspapers effectively changed hands as the original owners sold their local newspaper empires for substantial sums of money to the large corporate newspaper groups like Reed Regional Newspapers and Thomson Regional Newspapers; 80 per cent of the free newspaper market promptly moved to conglomerate ownership (Nicholson, 1995: 17). It seemed as if free newspapers had eventually won a modicum of recognition and respectability.

But the group strategy of the new corporate owners has invariably been to use free newspapers to protect and promote their paid-for titles. Free newspapers are used 'to defend territories and re-establish monopoly positions for paid-for titles' (Fletcher, 1995: 14). There are three strands to this marketing strategy. First, group managers have tended to develop advertising rate cards which favour the paid-for newspaper titles. In some groups free newspapers are not allowed to compete for advertising in particularly profitable areas such as house and car sales (Cunningham, 1988: 23). Second, it is often group policy to ensure that the best writers, managers and sales people are promoted to paid-for newspapers. The fact that most journalists consider a transfer to a paid-for title to be promotion reflects a tenacious journalistic prejudice against free newspapers as 'second best'; rather like the reluctance of many lecturers in traditional universities to accept more senior or even better paid posts in a 'new' university. Finally, there is a growing perception among many paid-for newspaper publishers that free newspapers are a 'complementary medium'. According to the chief executive of one free newspaper group, there is:

among many proprietors and managers ... a most foolhardy determination to restrict the growth of free titles under the illusion that, by so doing, the fortunes of the paid sector will be restored.

(Fletcher, 1995: 14)

After their extraordinary success across more than a decade, it appears that free newspapers, now incorporated into the larger newspaper groups, have become little more than financial pit props to support an ever declining paid-for local newspaper industry. In truth, free newspapers have always fulfilled a similar role. The expansion of free newspapers during the 1980s could certainly not be explained by public demand for these papers. On the contrary, newspaper growth often reflected little more than the ambitions of traditional paid-for newspapers to construct a defensive bulwark against potential competitors trying to invade 'their' territory.

'FILLING THE SPACE BETWEEN THE ADVERTISEMENTS': THE EDITORIAL CONTENT OF FREE NEWSPAPERS

While the financial fortunes of free newspapers have varied with the economic climate, there have been persistent criticisms of their editorial content. The evidence available to support these criticisms has varied from the professional and anecdotal observations of journalists and editors to more systematic research-based studies conducted by academics. The criticism has been threefold.

First, free newspapers have been too willing to subordinate editorial to advertising. They report very little news, few features or local stories of any kind; their emphasis is overwhelmingly on advertising. Editors and journalists, whether working on paid-for or free newspapers, concede that editorial is much 'thinner' in the latter. The editor of an evening paper alleged 'the role of journalists on free newspapers is to fill the space between the advertisements. They try to give a scattering of coverage of the local scene and carry some local stories but their staffs are usually so small and 75 per cent of their content has to be devoted to advertising' (confidential interview, 1996).

Second, when free newspapers' content moves away from advertising and advertorial, it tends to focus on consumer and human-interest stories rather than reporting significant events within the local community or providing information which might be helpful to the community. The assumption which seems to inform the editorial content of free newspapers is that their readers are primarily consumers rather than citizens. The editor of both an evening paid-for and free weekly paper suggested that the latter 'simply mops up the stories that we want to rerun'. But he also argued that 'as an editor, you want a much lighter frothier feel on the free paper to attract any attention at all. . . . So we tend to use the frothier stories in the weekly. But we also then use some filler material that we don't have in the main paper, you know, some recipes, days out, consumer pieces and entertainment and general sorts of feature-type pieces that we wouldn't use in *the newspaper*' (confidential interview, August 1997; emphasis added). The editor's final few words are significant and suggest a clear distinction between 'free papers' and 'newspapers'.

Finally, when free newspapers do report stories of relevance and significance to the community – reports of local council and court proceedings which used to constitute the essential ingredients of local newspaper content – coverage is vicarious and derived from non-journalistic news sources in town hall public relations departments, regional offices of the government information services or the press office in the local chamber of commerce (see chapters 12 and 13). A study of local government public relations officers' (PROs) success in generating stories in the local press by issuing news releases revealed that free newspapers were more likely to publish these 'source-generated' stories than paid-for weekly and daily papers. Typically, the resulting stories were simply verbatim transcripts of the original news release without any additional information reflecting journalistic investigation (Franklin, 1986: 31–2). In a later study, PROs identified free newspapers as overwhelmingly more likely to publish their press releases than other local newspapers (Franklin, 1988: 82); 82 per cent of PRO respondents in the study claimed a strike rate of 75 per cent or more for their press releases. But free newspapers seem to use these press releases quite cynically. The same study revealed that only 9 per cent of PROs nominated free papers as the local medium most interested in local government affairs; the lowest ranking of any newspaper (Franklin, 1988: 69). The conclusion seems inescapable. In circumstances of scarce editorial resources, free papers will publish well-crafted press releases which are handed to them on a plate.

But what is perhaps most striking is the absence of any academic study of free newspapers' contents which might provide a base line of evidence to support those criticisms alleging an absence of news and a focus on consumer and entertainment stories in free newspapers' editorial. The data presented below are necessarily indicative rather than substantive because of the modest sample they analyse, but they do highlight some central features of free newspapers' content. An important caveat is necessary at the outset. Free newspapers make highly variable commitments to both the extent and quality of their editorial. The weekly *Manchester Metro News*, for example, averages ninety-six pages per issue of which approximately one-third is devoted to editorial. This is a substantial commitment but, given the economic logic of free newspaper production with its emphasis on advertising revenues, even a high-quality free newspaper like the *Metro News* will carry less editorial than a paid-for newspaper equivalent.

The editions of ten free newspapers for the week ending 12 April 1997 were analysed to construct a profile of their editorial contents. While the base number of newspapers seems modest, the sample represents approximately one-third of all free newspapers distributed within the Yorkshire region; the papers achieve an aggregate Verified Free Distribution (VFD) figure of 850,227 copies.

Table 10.2 reveals that free newspapers tend to allocate between 75 per cent and 85 per cent of their total space to advertising; the *Weekly Advertiser* commits a remarkable 98 per cent to advertisements. The remainder of the newspapers' space is divided between regular features and news. Most free papers include predictable items such as television listings, horoscopes, crossword puzzles and readers' letters as part of their regular weekly content.

Table 10.2 Free newspapers' allocations of space to news and advertising

Newspaper title	Space (sq. ins)	Adverts %	Regular features %	News %
Aire Valley Target	7,440	80	8	12
Bradford Star	8,184	80	7	13
Weekly Advertiser	3,720	98	–	2
East Leeds Weekly News	7,440	86	4	10
Huddersfield Weekly News	5,152	86	4	10
Leeds Skyrack Express	7,920	75	5	20
North Leeds Weekly News	7,440	86	4	10
Weekend Times	5,148	80	6	14
West Leeds Weekly News	7,440	86	4	10
Wharfe Valley Times	10,752	85	4	11

Particular papers feature distinctive 'regular items' although these tend invariably to focus on leisure and entertainment. 'Bar Talk', for example, assesses the merits of local pubs while 'Soundbite' reviews newly released albums. The 'A to Z of Churches and Chapels' presents a guide to local church architecture and 'Clean Up' offers tips on how to spring clean a house. Other features present a greater community focus. 'On the Beat' provides a weekly platform for the local police, 'Christian Comment' delivers the local weekly newspaper's version of Radio Four's 'Thought for the Day' and 'What Do You Think?' is a 'vox pop' inviting readers' views on a range of moral and social issues. In the copy of the *Aire Valley Target* analysed, the paper asked: 'What should we do with children who are disruptive at school?'; answers were usually characterised by a discernible lack of liberalism!

The news content of these free papers accounts for between 10 per cent and 20 per cent of their total contents. Table 10.3 reports the percentage of this news space which, in turn, is allocated to particular topics and issues. The table illustrates the centrality of items about 'leisure', 'sport', 'charity' and 'crime' to free newspapers' editorial content. These papers report a very narrow news agenda with virtually no reporting of politics (despite the fact that the sample date fell in the period prior to the 1997 general election), local government, education, health issues or local business. All these matters might be assumed to be important to the local community and would certainly win editorial space in paid-for newspapers. Only the *Wharfe Valley Times*, the *Weekend Times* and the *Leeds Skyrack Express* attempt to address a broader range of topics.

This limited news agenda is further restricted by papers' preoccupation with certain kinds of stories. Items about crime, for example, focus on 'youth crime' and emphasise vandalism and violent crime. The *Aire Valley Target*'s front-page headline 'Join Us in Crime Battle' is typical of coverage

Table 10.3 Editorial contents of free newspapers

News topic	Aire Valley Target	Bradford Star	Weekly Advertiser	East Leeds Weekly News	Huddersfield Weekly News	Leeds Skyrack Express	North Leeds Weekly News	Weekend Times	West Leeds Weekly News	Wharfe Valley Times
Crime	4.4	21.0	–	13.8	–	24.2	13.8	–	13.8	10.7
Politics	–	–	–	–	–	1.3	–	–	–	8.2
Business	3.6	17.1	–	–	18.7	1.8	–	13.7	1.8	–
Charity	17.6	–	26.3	–	–	0.3	–	2.1	–	2.4
Sport	20.5	20.0	–	34.5	13.2	39.3	34.5	20.4	34.5	32.1
Roads/environ.	1.7	6.9	–	7.4	7.0	13.4	7.4	4.2	7.4	11.9
Health	3.6	–	–	–	–	–	–	0.14	–	6.5
Education	–	–	–	–	–	6.6	–	6.2	–	–
Local govt	–	–	–	–	–	–	–	–	–	14.2
DIY/Home/Gdn	2.7	–	–	30.0	4.4	–	30.0	11.3	30.0	–
Leisure	46.0	35.0	47.4	14.3	41.2	9.5	14.3	34.8	14.3	6.3
Other	–	–	26.3	–	15.4	3.7	–	7.0	–	7.6
Total	100	100	100	100	100	100	100	100	100	100

(12 April 1997, p. 1). The *Bradford Star* warns of the 'Estate Wreckers' (p. 4) and reports 'The Battle to Control Vandals' (p. 19). Violent street crime is another favoured focus with *East Leeds Weekly News* reporting the story of a 'Teenager Attacked by Gang Despite Clampdown' (p. 27); the *Leeds Express* reported the 'Cruel Attack on 4ft 6ins Woman' (11 April, p. 3).

Many of these stories, whether classified as health, sport or business, lean heavily on a human interest content. Perhaps predictably, stories reporting charitable activities contain a strong human interest element and are invariably accompanied by a photograph of a group of young children, bed pushers, marathon runners, or men who have shaved off their beards for cash, presenting a larger-than-life cheque to the suitably delighted representative of a favoured charity. But other topic categories offer thinly disguised human interest stories. One of only three health stories published across all the ten papers, for example, reported (with accompanying photograph) the case of a 3-year-old girl suffering from Treacher Collins Syndrome which results in severe facial disfigurement (*Wharfe Valley Times*, p. 11). A second very quirky health story reported allergic reactions to the newly introduced perfumed bus tickets on certain Bradford bus services; the story was splendidly headlined 'Mum Kicks Up a Stink About Perfumed Bus Tickets' (*Bradford Star*, p. 2). Similarly, one of the few business stories, 'Businessman at 14', told of a teenager's 'hidden talent for business' and his rise to became 'boss' of his own computer business (*Leeds Express*, p. 3). Many of the sports stories reported human interest concerns from football matches in aid of charity and a newly established baseball team which needs funding, to a story about a local man who is cycling from John O'Groats to Lands End to raise cash for the Children's Society (*Weekend Times*, p. 26).

Stories classified in the general category 'other' are also largely human interest stories including reports about the growing dangers of 'dog smuggling' at Leeds/Bradford Airport, the retirement of a local nurse and the sad tale of Spike the hedgehog, a patient at Burley in Wharfedale Hedgehog Hospital: 'Tackling a Prickly Subject' (*Wharfe Valley Times*, p. 13).

Two final points are noteworthy. First, free newspapers report virtually no national or international news. The only two national/international stories which were published, reporting a Bradford campaign to support third world businesses ('Join Fight to Rid World of Poverty', *Bradford Star*, p. 5) and a bingo club's outing to Aintree on the day of a bomb scare ('Grand Day Out Ruined', *East Leeds Weekly News*, p. 3), constitute an incalculably tiny fraction of the ten newspapers' contents. The world beyond the parish pump is out of sight and out of journalists' and readers' minds. Second, both the story count and the word count in these newspapers are very low. At one end of the range, the *Aire Valley Target* published twenty-four stories; the *Weekly Advertiser* published six. News items are short and are typically considerably shorter than the television listings or the crossword. Stories will often be reported in features headed 'The News in Brief', but these items are not elaborated at other sites in the newspaper; this news remains 'in brief'. Much of what passes for news stories are simply the truncated staccato soundbites extracted from press releases received from local charities, sporting and other clubs.

This analysis confirms many of the criticisms levelled against free newspaper content which were noted above. Features and stories focus largely on entertainment with little coverage of the local community beyond its charitable, sporting and leisure activities. The world of local business, local government, local education and health services has disappeared from view; the world beyond the parish pump is likewise invisible. The analysis also confirms the free press's reliance on advertising. This emphasis follows inevitably from free newspapers' revenue base; they earn income by selling readers to advertisers. This is their essential function. They are not newspapers in any traditional understanding of what newspapers should provide for their readers or how newspapers should report and serve their local communities. Indeed their reliance on advertising revenues, which subordinates readers' interests to those of advertisers, may well be incompatible with the role which some have identified for the local press.

Free newspapers certainly fail to meet the brief envisaged by the Royal Commission on the Press in 1977 which argued that

> democratic society needs a clear and truthful account of events, of their background and their causes; a forum for discussion and informed criticism and a means whereby individuals and groups can express a point of view or advocate a cause ... the responsibility for fulfilling these needs unavoidably rests in large measure on the press.
>
> (Press Commission, 1977, para. 362–63)

Free newspapers do not meet these responsibilities. But that was never their purpose. A free newspaper executive claims distinctive editorial ambitions inform the free press; local newspapers have different 'product roles. The paid-for newspaper provides the reader with news. The free newspaper provides consumers with information' (Fletcher, 1995: 14). This is free newspapers' distinctive contribution. But free newspapers' success reflects more than this division of labour within the local press. Some editors claim they are popular with readers. The executive editor of one group of weekly local papers argues that

> the early free sheets proved that some readers liked them and were less interested in the detailed local news that most paid weeklies dished up for them than the editorial department supposed. These readers were more interested in the small ads.
>
> (Hayes, 1996: 196)

These views about readers' preferences are obviously contentious but, if readers are genuinely content to receive newspapers with such sparse editorial content, it seems as if *no* news might be judged to be *good* news after all; at least for those who publish free newspapers! But it is very bad news for journalists, editors and local communities who insist on believing that local newspapers have a crucial democratic role to fulfil by providing an open and public forum for debate within the local communities they report.

REFERENCES

Advertising Association (1997) *Advertising Statistics Yearbook 1997*, London: Advertising Society.

Blyth, J. (1997) 'Frees Taking Lead in US', *Press Gazette*, 8 August, p. 1.

Collins, W. and Scott, R. (1986) 'Frees and the Regional Press', *Marketing Week*, 25 April, pp. 10–11.

Cunningham, J. (1988) 'Frees Are Jolly Good Business', *Guardian*, 1 August, p. 23.

Fletcher, W. (1995) 'Born Free, Tamed by the Old School', *Press Gazette*, 18 December, p. 14.

Franklin, B. (1986) 'Public Relations, the Local Press and the Coverage of Local Government', *Local Government Studies*, July/August, pp. 25–33.

—— (1988) *Public Relations Activities in Local Government*, London: Charles Knight.

Franklin, B. and Murphy, D. (1991) *What News? The Market, Politics and the Local Press*, London: Routledge.

—— (1997) 'The Local Rag in Tatters' in Bromley, M. and O'Malley, T. (eds) *The Journalism Reader*, London: Routledge, pp. 214–29.

Gall, G. (1993) 'Journalism for Changing Times: The Impact of New Technology and Industrial Relations on the Editorial Content of the Regional Press', paper presented at the Annual Conference of the Political Studies Association, University of Leicester, 21 April.

Hartley, N., Gudgeon, P. and Crofts, R. (1977) 'Concentration of Ownership in the Local Press', a research paper for the Royal Commission on the Press, Cmnd 6810–5, London: HMSO.

Hayes, A. (1996) *Family in Print: The Bailey Newspaper Group, A History*, Gloucestershire: Bailey Newspapers Group.

McNair, B. (1994) *News and Journalism in the UK: A Text Book*, London: Routledge.

Nicholson, R. (1995) 'The Last Days of Empire', *Press Gazette*, 18 September, p. 17.

Oakley, R. (1995) 'The Root Cause', *Press Gazette*, 27 November, p. 24.

Pickering, L. (1986) quoted in BBC Radio 4 programme *The Free Press*, broadcast 15 July 1986, produced at Radio Stoke by John Abberley.

Slattery, J. (1991) 'Ward Goes as Dream Daily Goes Weekly', *UK Press Gazette*, 27 March, p. 1.

Ward, M. (1987) 'Daily News: Up and Running Well', *UK Press Gazette*, 5 October.

Chapter 11

The local newspaper in the age of multimedia

Richard Beamish

INTRODUCTION

Regional and local newspapers are finished! It's just a matter of time. Look at the year-on-year sales, advertising and the medium itself. They are old fashioned, fuddy-duddy and will never wake up to the future. A stuffy image has dogged the regional press for many years but the truth is as far away from those comments as it could be. Nine out of ten adults continue to read a local or regional newspaper each week with 1,400 newspaper titles circulating or distributing across the country as part of a £5 billion industry employing 35,000 people (TGI, 1996 and Newspaper Society, 1996a).

The local press remains the second biggest advertising medium in the country (after television) with a yearly investment of £1.9 billion (Advertising Association, 1997). Detailed examination of many local newspapers reveals how carefully they are geared to the needs of their local communities – both in content and style. And as for the future – well this is where the story really begins!

Many local and regional newspapers now have their own Internet World Wide Web sites, carrying a variety of news content and advertising. They are attractive, regularly updated and well used. They complement the printed product for advertisers and readers alike. But this is not all. Audiotex, cable television, teletext, fax-back and e-mail services are among the wide variety of alternative media sources tried by newspaper publishers as part of the drive of moving from the world of 'print on paper' to a world of content. It is in this area that regional newspaper publishers have the greatest strength. No one can match the regional press when it comes to its brand (trusted within its circulation area), its ability to gather, sort and reissue information, and its advertising effectiveness as a medium. The way to protect this franchise is to ensure these newspapers stay ahead of the game; if regional publishers with their considerable information-gathering resources can offer electronic services, nobody else will get a look in.

So, far from being left behind in the rush towards new sources of information which are interactive and based on personal rather than local issues, the regional press is geared up and ready for the so-called 'killer-application'. It is experimenting but at the same time offering services of genuine value which will, in turn, attract new customers to electronic services and new readers to the paper. But how did all this begin? What were the deciding factors that plunged so many publishers into an area in which most had little experience and the number of users remained small?

LOCAL NEWSPAPERS AND NEW MEDIA: A BRIEF HISTORY

The key year was 1993. A number of chief executives of newspaper groups were expressing concern that the Internet presented itself either as a huge opportunity or a real threat, but no one knew enough to decide which. At the same time the European Commission published a report on new media (Commission of the European Communities, 1993) which argued that reading a newspaper would no longer be regarded as an indicator of intellectual activity by the year 2000. The newspaper industry evidently needed to know more, and soon. Was this a real threat or a fad which would go away and was best ignored?

The Newspaper Society formed a steering group chaired by Michael Toulmin, then Chief Executive of United Provincial Newspapers (UPN). A research fund of over £100,000 was raised from a levy on members and consultants, Meta-Generics, were appointed. A small group of chief executives also visited a number of newspaper publishers with their own Internet sites in the United States. In August 1994 the consultants' first report was published. *The Multimedia Revolution* attempted to provide an overview of new media development, including forecasts for the future, and sought to identify the way forward for publishers. At the same time the first Internet web sites were appearing for UK newspapers, with the *Bucks Free Press* pages (edited by Alan Cleaver) usually credited as comprising the first, regularly updated site.

The report argued that the way forward lay with Video-on-Demand, a concept being piloted in the US and later by British Telecom (BT) in Colchester. At its heart lay the ability to send video and audio signals along traditional copper twisted pair cable, something previously thought impossible. Home shopping, local, regional, national and international news, specialist documentaries, sport and films could all be sent to the individual home by ordinary telephone to be downloaded onto a set top box. Its major disadvantage, that information could only be sent over relatively short distances, was seen as a strength for local publishers who could capitalise on this by providing local content. The BT trial established that the technology worked well enough (you could still make a telephone call while a programme was running), but the key question of whether and how much people were prepared to pay for the set top box and for individual services remained unresolved.

A second report, *The Multimedia Revolution* (second edition), published in 1995 was essentially an update although it arrived at some very different conclusions. It argued that Video-on-Demand had not made the anticipated progress in the previous year and it was becoming clear that the Internet was both the short- and medium-term way forward. It argued that success in the future depended on:

- building on existing strengths in terms of content generation, local knowledge and understanding the customer's needs;
- continuously monitoring changes in markets, the competition and technologies;
- mastering skills relevant to new media including technology, editorial, advertising, design and marketing;
- understanding the costs and revenue probabilities for new ventures and the levels and trends in installed technology bases, both within and beyond their communities;
- prioritising opportunities based on their customers, the competition, technology and the resources available;
- developing an action plan for investment, including experimental but relevant technology.

(Newspaper Society, 1995a: 49–50)

Because regional newspaper companies are comparatively small (and, indeed, the sector as a whole compared with global media players) the possibility of alliances was discussed. This might involve two or more regional newspapers, cross-media agreements (working with cable, perhaps), or expansion (newspapers choosing to develop new products and services themselves).

A significant achievement of both reports was their success in removing the mystique (and, therefore, the fear of the unknown) where new media developments were concerned. Publishers were aware of the threats posed by alternative sources of information but they were also aware of the tremendous opportunities available if sufficient expertise could be harnessed to a detailed knowledge of local and regional requirements, and the trusted brand of the local newspaper.

For the Newspaper Society the next stage of the strategy involved providing ongoing information and support to the industry, acting as a catalyst rather than co-ordinating any single project. To this end an additional report was produced in 1995 entitled *On-Line Publishing Feasibility Study* (1995c), which offered an explanation of what is involved in providing an Internet service.

In addition Meta-Generics produced a software tool complete with manual designed to help senior managers within the industry to determine the commercial merits of various potential new media initiatives (Newspaper Society, 1995b). This somewhat unlikely utility was intended to be used with a board of directors or, at the very least, a group of senior managers. The idea was that an initiative or new media concept title was entered into a PC and the program would then ask a series of searching questions about it, from information on the company, its staffing expertise, readership, rivals and potential rivals, to capital equipment and other costs involved. Much of this information required considerable research and discussion before an accurate response could be supplied. The end result was an assessment score which rated the likelihood of that particular initiative becoming a commercial success. The work could also be completed by hand from a question bank but the complicated formulae designed to weigh the various factors made it a difficult and cumbersome exercise.

Trials suggested the decision-making tool would be highly successful in terms of helping senior managers decide whether to invest in a particular new media initiative such as, for example, an Internet pub guide. But the main reason for this lay not so much with the formulae involved as with the fact that the software generated considerable research and intense discussion.

Follow-up surveys of the use made of the software (which was circulated to all chief executives) showed that, of those who had actually tried it, some 90 per cent considered it useful or very useful. The problem was that fewer than 20 per cent of chief executives appeared to have used it at all.

At the same time more local newspaper World Wide Web pages were appearing, of which a surprising number were from small independent publishers such as the *Newbury Weekly News* (*www.newburynews.co.uk*).

Publishers were beginning to realise the potential of the Internet for searchable classified and display advertising which could go beyond their circulation areas as required. A number of classified advertising initiatives were discussed in 1996, including a proposed liaison between the Press Association and News International. The regional industry response was to develop its own classified database, which became known as ADHunter (*www.autohunter.co.uk* and others) and is described more fully in the case study later in this chapter. One by one the other proposals fell by the wayside, realising that a true regional newspaper industry consortium encompassing all of the major groups was ultimately too strong a group to compete with in a limited marketplace.

There were other initiatives taking place. Midland Independent Newspapers (MIN) established its own new media division and formed an alliance with Mirror Group Newspapers (MGN), owners of L!ve TV, the cable channel which broadcasts from Canary Wharf. A studio was built in the newspaper offices in Birmingham and local broadcasting began in November 1995 under the title *Birmingham Live*. During daytime hours the first thirty minutes of every hour of L!ve TV in the Birmingham area was provided by *Birmingham Live*, complete with local advertising. By June 1997, the breakfast slot was extended so that the period from 7.00 am to 9.30 am each weekday was exclusively local (see chapter 4). The company also supplied radio news services in the form of live bulletins throughout the day to local radio stations and, of course, is now part of Mirror Group Newspapers itself.

The largest newspaper group, Trinity International, established Channel One Liverpool at the offices of the *Liverpool Daily Post* and *Liverpool Echo*.

Channel One, a subsidiary of Associated Newspapers and based in London, shared output with the Liverpool outlet in a similar way to that of L!ve TV but the approach was different. Instead of being based on a separate floor the television studio was placed adjacent to the editorial floor, with a gauze screen providing a backdrop which clearly showed the newsroom to viewers. This posed difficulties for the Independent Television Commission who initially argued that a *Liverpool Daily Post* and *Liverpool Echo* banner in the newsroom constituted advertising.

The technology in Liverpool is unique in the UK in that programming is rarely live. Each news item (including links) is recorded and digitised ready for broadcasting. Thus items can be altered and changed just by changing the order of programming or adding additional pre-recorded links. The hardware and software involved enables programmes to appear as if the newsreader is live.

Both L!ve TV and Channel One Liverpool offer teletext services.

THE ALTERNATIVES

There are now a large variety of ways in which local and regional newspaper publishers offer new media services to customers. The largest by far is the Internet, with target audiences ranging from ex-pats to advertising agencies. But there are other areas of activity, combinations and alliances, summarised for publishers in a further report, commissioned from Electronic Publishing Services, entitled *A Guide to Electronic Publishing* and published by the Newspaper Society in 1996.

Teletext

Teletext as a method of disseminating information together with broadcast television pictures (irrespective of whether terrestrial, satellite or cable television technology is employed) will be revolutionised with the advent of digital television in 1998. While it will clearly take some time before consumers purchase new televisions or set-top boxes in sufficient numbers, digital television will present numerous opportunities for new media developers. New-style teletext will be almost indistinguishable from Internet pages in look and feel in many cases, with quality images and true interactivity if accessed by cable or there is a telephone link.

Newspaper publishers employing teletext services at present include the *Liverpool Daily Post* and *Liverpool Echo* (see above) and Portsmouth Publishing and Printing (see the case study which follows). Some publishers offer some of their classified advertising on Teletext, the teletext service operating via the terrestrial commercial television channels. MIN also operated its own more advanced teletext service via cable in Milton Keynes for a time but found it uneconomic to continue.

Audiotex

Also known as audiotext, this is hardly a new media format and comprises a wide range of information and entertainment services delivered via the telephone. The most popular aspect of audiotex for newspaper publishers is dating services, but audiotex has been put to extensive and successful use for a whole range of consumer services at a number of publishing centres.

Internet services

These are by far the most common of all new media services for local newspapers. They are not expensive to set up and potentially have a wider reach than other new media formats. Newspaper sites vary from the straightforward provision of information for advertisers and agencies to highly sophisticated services providing editorial and advertising, linking in to a classified database such as ADHunter (*www.jobhunter.co.uk* and others).

It is worth looking at the *Hinckley Times* (*www.hinckley-times.co.uk*) as a good example of a small newspaper centre (although now taken over by MIN) establishing a web site which provides useful information for its users without detracting from sales of the newspaper itself. The *Surrey Advertiser* includes a link to the main Internet search engines (the pages which enable users to locate sites of interest by using key word searches). The *Irish Times* pages (*www.irish-times.ie*) are designed to appeal to ex-pats and have been successful in doing so.

The main problem with Internet services is finding ways of achieving a return on the investment. If the action in developing the site is purely defensive (i.e. to keep predators away) then perhaps this is not so important, but more publishers are looking for a return as part of the process of moving from a print-based medium to one focusing on content.

Subscription services, even for ex-pats who have difficulty obtaining copies of the paper, have yet to be successful and the prognosis is not good. In general terms people do not appear to want to pay for news and information. Newspapers are cheap, television apparently free and there is, as yet, no adequate system for making micropayments (paying small amounts via a small card similar to a BT Phonecard). The solution almost certainly lies with advertising revenue although the size of current audiences (about 2 million people in the UK currently have Internet access) is as yet insufficient for real money to be earned unless there is a coherent package on offer (see the Portsmouth Publishing and Printing case study below).

The advent of digital television will revolutionise Internet accessibility because much higher transmission speeds will be available via cable or even low level satellite. This 'moving away' from the computer to the entertainment console will mean many more people will be able to read World Wide

Web pages using nothing more than their remote control and the ubiquitous set-top box.

CD-ROM

The standard CD-ROM is a 12-cm laser-read optical disc, which is essentially the same as an audio CD. CD-ROM is now almost universal in domestic PCs and provides opportunities for all kinds of information services, including local information and entertainment, and substantial databases.

The use made of CD-ROMs by regional newspapers has been limited, because their very nature means that they are not easily updated. Some early experiments involved the use of CD-ROM as support material for an Internet service. Users would receive a new CD at the appropriate interval which would contain layout information, photographs and feature material which did not date quickly. The latest information would then be downloaded from the Internet to form a coherent whole for the user.

With increasing access speeds for the Internet this technology was always going to date quickly but there remains a substantial market for CD-ROM for special interest material. A number of newspaper publishers, including *The Scotsman*, have produced CDs containing special interest material (including video footage).

One of the most interesting uses of CD-ROM is to be found in Newspapers in Education, the programme founded by the Newspaper Society in 1984 to develop and encourage stronger links between local newspapers and schools. Pupils at Fulston Manor School in Sittingbourne, for instance, produced their own CD-ROM as part of their Advanced GCSE project work, focusing on their local newspaper, the *East Kent Gazette*, its history and activity.

Fax-back

A popular service within the business community, fax-back services have been little used within the regional press. The idea is that a request for specific information is responded to by the sending of a fax by return. The *Yorkshire Post* has operated such a service successfully for the business community for some years.

CASE STUDIES

The following case studies provide a better feel for what local and regional newspapers can achieve when a content-based approach to publishing is adopted which combines the search for profitability with a defensive approach to media information in the local community.

Case study 1: Portsmouth Publishing and Printing's Info 2000 programme

Portsmouth Publishing and Printing Ltd (PPP) is a medium-sized regional newspaper business in the UK, publishing an evening paper, *The News* (with a circulation of 75,000 copies), three paid-for weekly titles (totalling 80,000 copies) and four free newspapers (totalling 450,000 copies). Its main market is a mixed urban and rural area of around 24,000 homes within a radius of about 25 kilometres from the main offices. There is a strong emphasis in the area on high-tech industries while Portsmouth has the UK's principal naval base.

Although *The News* reaches 64 per cent of the local population in its core area, PPP faces intense competition from radio, television and national daily newspapers (which together have a local penetration of 62 per cent), direct marketing operations and a cable franchise (NYNEX CableComms), which offers over fifty television channels. There is, therefore, saturation coverage of media offering national and international information as well as fierce competition for local advertising revenues.

The company accepts that it cannot compete with the intense coverage of national and international information supplied by other media. Its new media objectives are, therefore, focused on the needs of the community for local information that only its newspaper-based infrastructure is able to supply. No other organisation supplies anywhere near as many people to gather information in this area and PPP aims to secure its position as the region's principal provider of local information.

To achieve this the company looked beyond disseminating information by printed products alone. Its new media strategy embraces a mix of cable, audiotex and Internet products as additional ways of distributing the information it gathers and publishes in its newspapers. PPP's key assets are its very strong newspaper brands. The new media services are being developed as an integrated part of those brands, designed to extend their media coverage.

PPP's own market research (1997) has shown that its audiotex services have succeeded in reaching around 22 per cent of the local market, the Internet has a 13 per cent penetration in the area (considerably above the national average) and 22 per cent of the local market subscribes to cable, of which 72 per cent have teletext capable television sets (i.e. 16 per cent of the local population can access cable teletext services).

Although local markets for new media may seem very small at present they are likely to grow significantly over the next few years. By extending its current brands into new forms of delivery, PPP can reach a wider audience, offer greater value to its advertisers and develop local new media markets before outside competitors can obtain a foothold.

PPP does not regard each of its new media product lines as new separate businesses with dedicated sales teams. This approach is unlikely to be profitable for some time, even if it were advisable. Instead the company treats its *NewsText*, audiotex and Internet services as part of its existing branded business, communicating the same news, information and classified advertising.

Products and services

Audiotex

PPP's audiotex services give consumers searchable access via the telephone to motors and property, and will soon be introducing recruitment and other categories of classified advertising. PPP has around 4,000 cars and 450 homes on the system at any one time. Revenue is generated from fees charged to advertisers. Response and specialist advertising services will also be added over the coming months to the developing range of information services.

NewsText

NewsText carries continually updated local news and information, and is broadcast on Channel 8 in NYNEX CableComm's Solent franchise, which covers some 218,000 homes geographically, including the Portsmouth region. Test transmission of *NewsText* pages began in February 1997, culminating in a full service later in the year.

Consumers are able to access up to 3,000 teletext pages, covering local news and weather, sport, entertainment, travel, council and community information, as well as classified advertising for motors, property, recruitment, dating and private ads. Cross-promotion back to *The News* is carried on *NewsText* pages. The name *NewsText* was chosen to reinforce the brand name of *The News*.

All classified advertisements carried in Portsmouth Publishing and Printing newspaper titles are automatically included in the *NewsText* service. The classified rate includes an allowance for this. Advertisers wishing to buy a full *NewsText* page for display advertising may do so at an additional cost.

News stories are updated during the day as PPP's journalists receive and edit new reports. It is part of their routine to provide a brief summary of each story for the *NewsText* service.

NewsText is a joint venture between Portsmouth Publishing and Printing Ltd and NYNEX CableComms. All news gathering, subediting, advertising sales and page input is supplied by PPP, within editorial guidelines agreed with NYNEX. PPP's sales team has also begun selling NYNEX's 'avails', the commercial airtime available between programming, on thirteen of NYNEX's cable television channels. PPP receives commission for all 'avails' sold, including keeping its unique expertise in selling advertising in the area intact.

Internet services

PPP launched its first web site, for the *Chichester Observer* (*www.chiobserver.co.uk*), on 1 January 1997, and is progressively introducing separately branded sites for all of its titles, although all carry the same classified advertising. The company aims to develop its sites as the main on-line access points for information about the local area. As with the *NewsText* service, the web sites carry local news and information, and searchable classified advertising for motors, property, recruitment, dating and bargains. PPP provides constant updates to the news that is on these sites. As the news is already being updated for the *NewsText* service, it is a relatively simple procedure to lift it across and use it again on the web sites.

PPP's approach to producing the new services is to use the output from its current newspaper systems to re-purpose the published material as automatically as possible. The raw text is extracted from the front-end system and dropped into *NewsText* and web page templates which produce the new services automatically. The templates are specially designed so that the unique features of each medium are properly exploited. Some human intervention is currently necessary to extract text from display advertisements and to edit recruitment advertisements and news stories, but most classified lineage is transferable without human involvement.

A classified advertisement carried in *The News* and then repeated in audiotex, *NewsText* and the Internet (*www.thenews.co.uk*), increases audience reach from 64 per cent to around 83 per cent, a gain of nearly a third. Opportunities to see the advertisement, however, almost double (Newspaper Society, 1997).

Instead of charging classified advertisers an add-on rate for these new media services, the company has added a small percentage increase to its newspaper rate cards and classified advertisements are automatically included in all four media.

PPP aims to continue with this policy as the penetration of its total package improves and it can show advertisers the gains in the market reached by their advertisements. To date, advertisers seems relatively amenable to this approach but they are resistant to spending the amounts PPP would need to charge if it was selling these extra services as stand-alone new products.

All of the services are driven by one transaction in one sales call. One of the company's short-term challenges is to get its sales staff to understand and sell effectively the benefits of the additional services. Another has been to organise the editorial function so that these new services are built into processing routines. In addition to its classifieds, PPP is developing a range of new revenue opportunities, including display advertising, sponsorship and web design services.

Portsmouth Printing and Publishing Ltd believes that its approach to integrating new media with its core business gives it a better route to profit and to the future; it develops PPP's most powerful asset – the influence of its newspaper brands and gives its core assets a longer and healthier life. It is one of the few companies to look at the issue of content rather than print on paper as the great strength of the local publisher, and is seeking to ensure that all staff think the same way. The days of new media departments being separated from the rest of the publishing centre and inhabited by expensive loss-making nerds are over.

Case study 2: ADHunter

The company ADHunter UK Ltd was formed in February 1997 by shareholders Trinity International Holdings, Newsquest Media Group, Northcliffe Newspapers Group, Johnston Press, United Provincial Newspapers, Bristol United Press and the Guardian Media Group. The consortium represents some 60 per cent of the circulation of the regional press in the UK, a massive 38 million newspapers weekly through 560 daily, weekly paid-for and weekly free titles. It also handles 70 per cent of all advertising volume appearing in the regional press (ADHunter PR material, June 1997).

The unique feature of ADHunter, however, is not that it covers all of the largest regional newspaper groups, or that it represents such a high proportion of the market. It is that the consortium is an open one, one of the basic principals being that additional members of the regional press are invited to share the benefits of ADHunter as subscribers.

Already ADHunter has become the UK's largest classified database with a potential advertising content of up to 1 million advertisements within twelve months. Auto Hunter was launched on 24 March 1997 and, of the 500,000 car advertisements placed in consortium titles each week, just over 400,000 appear on the Auto Hunter database.

The programme is set for fast expansion. Job Hunter (*www.jobhunter.co.uk*) was launched on 30 June 1997 and Property Hunter (*www.propertyhunter.co.uk*) the following September.

Each 'Hunter' product uses Intelligent Agent software, giving the site a 'smart search' facility. This enables someone looking for a car to complete a profile form detailing the specification and cost of the vehicle they wish to find. When a car matching the description comes up for sale they are contacted by e-mail, advising them accordingly.

The Auto Hunter site (*www.autohunter.co.uk*) includes information provided by experts from the motor industry. For example, Auto Hunter offers over 1,000 new and used road tests to those searching for information about their next car, on-line quotations for insurance and personal finance, and up-to-date facts and information about the car market.

The seriousness with which the consortium members viewed the ADHunter opportunity is illustrated by the fact that the initial publicity campaign was worth over £1 million. This included a major regional newspapers advertising campaign appearing in-paper and classified sections, magazine advertisements, press releases, Internet banner advertising, and attendance at major media conferences and motoring events.

Technically ADHunter is one of a new generation of web sites. In the past users were called 'surfers' because the information and sites were passive. The latest generation of web sites are interactive and Auto Hunter aims for a high degree of interactivity linked to the database, and also to the additional information and services it will provide.

Because ADHunter is owned by the regional press all ADHunter Internet services have the capability to be integrated into any regional newspaper's own web site. The Auto Hunter logos at the top of each page on the site can be used on the local site also to provide a more coherent image to the user. This helps local sales teams add value and increase market share by selling their own individual Internet services enhanced by the increased functionality that products such as ADHunter give the sites. In this respect ADHunter tries to make selling as easy as possible on a local basis by providing templates of web pages, created at no extra charge for local newspapers without specialist staff to use and to sell an Internet presence to local businesses.

BENEFITS

Revenue protection

The Internet provides a cost-of-entry factor which is far lower that that of newspapers, however small. Thus categories of advertising such as Motors, Property and Recruitment (60 per cent of classified income) are at risk from entrepreneurs who create niche market services. There are already over sixty Internet sites in the UK offering recruitment advertisers a platform. Sites such as Microsoft's Auto Locate could offer alternatives to the traditional classified advertising base if the predicted upsurge in Internet use accompanies the advent of digital television in the UK. Newspapers in the US have suggested that up to 10 per cent of advertising income has moved from newspapers to the Internet. The figure for the UK is not known but will not be as high. But if on-line usage takes off newspapers will become vulnerable to a form of advertising which is easily searched and cheap to access and set up.

Regional and local newspapers have an advantage over all other media within their own circulation areas. They represent trusted brands with considerable experience in selling advertising space and obtaining results. But all this will count for nothing if loopholes are left in the market for newcomers to exploit with a minimal cost base. It is for the same reason that Portsmouth Publishing and Printing Ltd sells 'avails' for NYNEX. The publisher retains the expertise, the goodwill and the trust.

Revenue generation

ADHunter can be used to generate increased revenue by:

- increasing income from private and trade advertisers as a result of adding value by placing their advertisements on to the Internet;
- selling pre-prepared templates to car dealers, recruitment and property service providers, or by developing Internet page design services;
- creating a telephone service to enable non-Internet users to access the database (similar to the Portsmouth Publishing and Printing approach above).

ADHunter is a good example of the regional press working together in its own interests, recognising that the real opposition is not from rival titles but from alternative media with lower start-up costs who seek to nibble away at their franchises. The non-executive chairman (David Worlock of Electronic Publishing Services) has his own consultancy and is not directly employed by any of the participants, ensuring a degree of neutrality.

The presence of comprehensive, easily searched local and national classified advertising supported in future by some display and editorial may yet result in a evolutionary path which takes the regional press towards a multimedia future.

CONCLUSIONS

The regional press in the UK has been preparing itself for some time for a possible future whereby print on paper is just one of a number of ways in which it communicates with its target audiences. Focusing on alternative ways of reaching those audiences, developing new products (some for niche markets) and forming alliances represent some of the more obvious strategies.

Perhaps more significant in the longer term will be the infrastructure required to move publishers (and their employees) away from the traditional newspaper culture to one where content, whether editorial, advertising or a mix of the two, is king. A number of publishers, including Portsmouth, have been looking at this seriously but so far none has succeeded in this most difficult of areas.

And there is still further to go. It may be that the local newspaper can offer itself as the Internet Service Provider (ISP) for the community it serves. In some cases working in tandem with a larger provider such as Unipalm Pipex or BT it could use its trusted brand to encourage Internet access in the home. It could provide software and sell modems so that the user will see the publisher's home page as she or he goes onto the World Wide Web. The publisher would collect the monthly rental as the dummy server, sharing the proceeds with the larger background service provider.

Perhaps this is the way towards a truly integrated service in which local publishers, working within a national consortium, can use their brands to ensure their future, and the future of a truly local yet personalised two-way information service.

REFERENCES

Advertising Association (1997) *Advertising Association Yearbook*, Henley-on-Thames: NTC Publications.

Commission of the European Communities (1993) *New Opportunities for Publishers in the Information Services Market*, Luxembourg.

European Commission/Andersen Consulting (1996) *Electronic Publishing: Strategic Developments for the European Publishing Industry towards the Year 2000*, Luxembourg.

Fulston Manor School (1995) *Investigating Newspapers* (CD-ROM), Sittingbourne.

The Newspaper Society (1994) *The Multimedia Revolution*, London: Newspaper Society.

—— (1995a) *The Multimedia Revolution* (2nd edn), London: Newspaper Society.

—— (1995b) *Opportunities Evaluation Workbench*, London: Newspaper Society.

—— (1995c) *On-Line Publishing Feasibility Study*, London: Newspaper Society.

—— (1996a) *Employment and Other Confidential Surveys*, London: Newspaper Society.

—— (1996b) *A Guide to Electronic Publishing*, London: Newspaper Society.

—— (1997) *Marketing Update*, London: Newspaper Society, February.

Target Group Index (TGI) (1996) London: BMRB.

Part IV

Constructing the local news agenda

Chapter 12

The local government agenda: news from the town hall

Shirley Harrison

SETTING THE AGENDA

It has been argued that the public sees the world, not as it is, but through the filter of the media (Tuchman, 1978: 210–11, McCombs and Gilbert, 1986: 4). While this may hold good for the public's view of events occurring on the other side of the world, of which the ordinary person will have little or no knowledge, it is not so straightforward a proposition when applied to the local media. Certainly journalists working in the local media select their material from a variety of sources, and present it from their respective editorial standpoints. But their readers can on the whole be expected to have a more intimate knowledge and understanding of that world than is reported in the local press. Hence local newspapers have to pay particular attention to the concerns and sensitivities of the community in which they circulate. Local journalists need to consider the sources from which they draw their material with equal care.

There have been a number of studies of the ways in which journalists and newspaper editors act as gatekeepers (Gandy, 1982: 1–18). One study which analysed the influence of government public information officers (PIOs) in America and Britain on the content of local newspapers found that about half the material provided by PIOs was used by the Louisiana newspapers, whereas in a sample of newspapers from Northumberland the figure was more than 90 per cent (Franklin and Van Slyke Turk, 1988: 29–41). These 'information subsidies', however, did not constitute the major source of information for the stories on government agencies: in both settings, journalists used other information sources.

This chapter explores the various ways in which local government public relations officers (PROs) interact with the local press, and provides some insight into the way in which they influence the reporting of the local council.

THE ROLE OF THE LOCAL GOVERNMENT PUBLIC RELATIONS OFFICER

The local council has a role in shaping the agenda of the local press. A brief look at how local government has evolved will help to explain why.

The changing face of local government

Once, the city fathers were just that – aldermen and councillors who looked after their domain in paternalistic fashion. As more and more people became eligible to vote, those who were seeking election found they needed to communicate with the electorate. So councillors announced their policies and the local newspaper reported their speeches. In the first half of the twentieth century all the cities, most small towns and rural communities were informed by their local paper, which was probably locally owned, about the doings of their local parish, district or county council.

Although there have always been policy differences between the political parties represented on local councils, a pragmatic consensus existed until relatively recently. Councillors tended to be senior, respected members of the community, probably over 60 years of age and tending to serve for lengthy periods. The 1964 general election created something of a revolution among the traditional constituencies, however. The mood of the times, together with the Labour party's apparently unassailable position nationally, led to a resurgence of interest in politics and many young people joined the main political parties as active and energetic members. By the late 1960s some were standing as local councillors (Wigfield, 1988: 9). This change opened the door to committed, full-time councillors, many of whom have since gone on to become members of parliament, ministers of state and, in the case of former Lambeth councillor John Major, Prime Minister.

But elected councillors are simply the public face of local government. Town halls are full of local government officers, the employees who carry out the policies of the council. The increasing complexity of local authority functions led in the 1960s to an expansion in employee numbers, with large departments such as education, housing and social services each employing perhaps a thousand or more staff. The chief officers of such departments wielded great power and had charge of large budgets, leading sometimes to conflicts between them. In 1971 a group of chief officers met under the chairmanship of Malcolm Bains, former county clerk of Kent, to consider the management of local authorities. The Bains report, published the following year, recommended that councils adopt corporate management, with a senior management team and a chief executive working jointly for the good of the whole authority, a model which was gradually adopted throughout local government. Bains also recommended the appointment of press and information officers (Smith, 1986: 32 and Franklin, 1988a: 1–59).

The 1970s also saw large-scale local government reorganisation with the creation of the large metropolitan shire counties in 1974 (abolished in 1986) and the creation of a two-tier county-district structure for everywhere else except London and the major cities (reconsidered by the Local Government Commission in the 1990s and largely reorganised from 1996 in Scotland and Wales and 1997 in England). At the time of writing there are five types of councils in England, each with different functions, and unitary authorities in Scotland and Wales. There are proposals for regional government in parts of England and a strategic authority for London; national referenda conducted in 1997 endorsed the new Labour government's proposals to establish a Scottish parliament and a Welsh assembly.

So over the past quarter of a century there have been three major developments, which have led naturally to the establishment of the public relations function in local councils. These are first, a greater politicisation of local government; second, a move towards more corporate and professional management in local councils; and third, substantial changes in the names, identities and functions of local authorities in all parts of the country. Before the local government reorganisation of 1974 there was a handful of press and public relations officers working for the counties and two London boroughs. By the mid 1990s, however, all counties, London boroughs and metropolitan districts employed one or more public relations specialists, and the smaller districts were rapidly catching up (Audit Commission, 1995: 9).

THE LOCAL GOVERNMENT PUBLIC RELATIONS OFFICER TODAY

The day-to-day work of a local government PRO varies depending on the type of authority, the status of the public relations function within the authority, the size of the PR department or unit and the character of the authority itself. Most local councils, however, expect their PRO to be involved as a minimum in the following four areas of activity.

Media relations

Local government PROs are employed under a variety of names. A recent survey (Audit Commission, 1995: 15) found that terms used included public relations, communications, information, marketing and press/media. Two-thirds of the PROs taking part in the survey said that media relations was the most important aspect of their role, although in the larger authorities and the London boroughs this emphasis on media work was greater (Franklin, 1988a: 63); in some types of local authority more than half the PROs had previously worked as journalists (ibid.: 87). This has traditionally been seen as an advantage in a job where it was very important for the council to get favourable coverage in the local paper. An ex-hack with good connections would understand the needs of local journalists and be able to satisfy them with material designed to give a good impression of the council. Issuing news releases, providing briefing material, arranging interviews and photo opportunities, placing feature articles and acting as an acceptable buffer between the newspaper and the council have comprised the major parts of a local government press officer's job.

To some extent these are still the activities which form the day-to-day routine of a council press office. In interviews with current local government PROs, however, the issue of de-skilling in local journalism has been raised regularly. It means that the PRO has to provide more material and, in effect, lead the reporter to sources and stories. PROs from local government and the emergency services comment increasingly that they have to explain the workings of their organisations to young reporters, which puts the press officer in greater control. The situation a decade ago when a PRO complained that he was 'effectively writing the front page lead in the local paper' has changed only in ways which further increase local newspapers' vulnerability to public relations activity (Franklin, 1986: 26). Sheila Williams, press officer for Milton Keynes unitary authority, claimed:

> I am pro-active with the media. I don't wait for the phone to ring. I fax releases to all my media contacts following the Council meetings. . . . Journalists don't generally come to meetings, so they tend to get their information about what has been discussed from me. I make it easy for local papers to get their copy. They don't go out and look for stuff like they used to – newspapers have to pick up what they can get. But journalists usually go straight to the councillors for quotes. The vast majority of my work is with local media. Training for journalists is not as good as it used to be. They don't know the difference between a county and a district, what the different departments of a local authority do and where responsibilities lie.
>
> (Interview, 25 February 1997)

In addition to their media liaison role, many PROs are involved in their council's newspaper, writing for it, laying it out, subbing and dealing with the production process. It is a major source of local news. Some papers enjoy very high distribution figures. A study revealed that most municipal papers distributed more than 100,000 copies while some like the *Strathclyde Reporter* reached 935,000 homes with each issue (Franklin, 1988a: 38). In Milton Keynes the authority 'publishes its own paper, the *Messenger*, once a month. A MORI survey showed that most people like to get their local news from the *Messenger* as a first preference' (ibid.).

Campaigns

Local authority PROs can and do run campaigns to target specific groups and to try to encourage them to do – or desist from doing – something, such as pay their council tax on time. The London Borough of Brent for example has conducted annual campaigns around the payment of local taxes since 1991, when it collected only 61 per cent of the local tax it was due (Walker, 1996: 2). In Easington District Council a different campaign tried to convince dog owners of the need to 'clean up' after their pets. A poster showed a man in a suit, with his trousers around his ankles, squatting next to a children's playground, with the headline 'So why let your dog do it?' The campaign became news, appearing in local newspapers and on national television (Harrison, 1995: 152–3).

Press officers' freedom to run party-political campaigns is severely limited by legislation. They are prevented by the Local Government Acts of 1986 and 1988, with their associated codes of practice, from running campaigns which might affect support for one or other political party. This legislation does not unduly constrain PROs in their day-to-day work, but it does provide a political context for their work which requires them to be conscious of political sensitivities; especially in the weeks running up to a local or general election. There are occasions when the legislation has been censorial as well as a little foolish. The government auditor for Scotland declared illegal £117,000 publicity expenditure by Edinburgh when the District Council produced a letterhead with the slogan 'Edinburgh – Improving Services, Creating Jobs'. The auditor pronounced the slogan party political and declared the expenditure illegal (Franklin, 1987: 28).

Crises, disasters and emergencies

Local authorities must have an emergency plan to deal with any disaster or emergency which affects their area, such as major accidents on the rail or road network, chemical spills, explosions, floods, multiple shootings or other murderous attacks. Such plans detail the organisational steps which should be taken in the event of an emergency and include details on the evacuation of residents, emergency contact numbers and so on. The way in which the council deals with media interest, which is often overwhelming at a time of crisis or disaster, is not as a matter of course dealt with in the council's emergency plan. Some councils have developed their own crisis public relations plan, often in the wake of a disaster in their area. There are moves to bring together the lessons learned from such disasters and to create a national model of best practice in dealing with the media at such times (Wade, 1996: 10). Hundreds of local government PROs have attended courses run at the Home Office Emergency Planning College on dealing with the media at a time of disaster. These courses make clear the special relationship a council has with its local media, a point which is also made by Tom Fox, head of public relations with North Lanarkshire Council. Commenting on press interest in the *E. Coli* outbreak in early 1997, which at that time had resulted in over 700 media calls to the council, he gave this advice to his fellow PROs:

> Remember the local press. When more glamorous characters from the national media appear it is easy to forget relationships with the local press are of paramount importance – they will still be there long after the rest of the media have left town.

(Fox, 1997: 4)

Strategy

Local government PROs are also responsible for internal communications within the authority, either in a technical sense – producing and distributing staff newsletters, videos and recruitment packs – or strategically, as part of the council's overall communications strategy.

Increasingly PROs are becoming strategists and there is some evidence that PR departments are becoming smaller but more senior. In the 1980s it was not unusual for there to be twenty, thirty or more staff in a county or metropolitan district PR department. The reduction in size to single figures in most authorities is partly due to council cuts in central support services. But this 'downsizing' has occurred in tandem with the increasing status demanded by and given to the public relations function in local councils. Some of those who started their careers in local government public relations as press officers have now reached the top of the tree, with the firm conviction that public relations in local government has a core strategic role. John Raine, chief executive of Derbyshire County Council, started work as a cub reporter at the age of 16 and joined Derbyshire as head of its PR unit following a job as a PRO with East Midlands Gas. He believes that PROs should have :

> direct access to the chief executive, chief officers and leading members, and a place at the table in the boardroom or chief officer group. In that way the PRO not only knows what's going on but has the clout to promote PR strategies first hand and to give advice and influence decisions before they become irrevocable.

(Raine, 1996: 2)

Among authorities which have elevated public relations to assistant chief executive level are the Metropolitan Borough of Knowsley, the London Borough of Hackney, and the county councils of Cambridgeshire and Hertfordshire, but an increasing number employ public relations professionals at director level.

THE RELATIONSHIP BETWEEN THE LOCAL GOVERNMENT PRO AND THE LOCAL PRESS

The heightened status and increasing professionalisation of the public relations function in local government has in many ways changed the relationship between the council and the local paper. According to the authors of *Public Relations for Local Government*, who were all at that time practising local government PROs:

> The role of the PR professional is not to act as the mouthpiece or gatekeeper, but to work to create and maintain that [open and honest] climate among chief officers and committee chairmen. At the end of the day, it is they who are accountable to the general public, and it is they not the public relations officer who should be ready and willing to be active in promoting the authority's messages through the media. The PR practitioner is the professional who can help create the effective channels and means, and as far as possible ensure that opportunities are planned and followed up.
>
> (Fedorcio *et al.*, 1991: 33)

PROs' relationships with the different elements of the local press are highly variegated reflecting newspapers' 'free' or 'paid-for' status. In Wolverhampton, the local paper, the *Express and Star*, is highly regarded by the local community. It is a traditional local newspaper which covers local council business in a way which few local papers are any longer able to do; although, as its editor concedes, the burgeoning complexity of local government means the paper is unable to match its own council reporting of a decade ago (see chapter 14). A survey conducted for the council in 1994 concluded that 75 per cent of the borough's residents preferred to get their local news and information from the *Express and Star* and consequently the council considers it important to have a good relationship with the newspaper and its municipal reporter (Kownacki, 1997), even though it risks attracting the criticism that the relationship is too collaborative or cosy. Kownacki suggests:

> The *Express and Star* is highly unusual in that it employs a municipal reporter – one of the old school who has been with the paper for over twenty years, and who is very well informed about local government in general and Wolverhampton council in particular. There is a very good relationship at all levels. We work closely on queries and complaints – I ensure that the journalist's queries on behalf of readers are dealt with properly. If the journalist gets hold of anything he always tips me off first, knowing that I will tell the council to come clean. Similarly, if I tell the journalist 'you're being led up the garden path on this one' the journalist will tend to believe me. It's a relationship of mutual trust. The paper and the council also co-operate on training.
>
> (Interview, 25 February 1997)

There is clear evidence, however, for the view prevalent among many local government PROs that free newspapers will print just about anything sent to them (Franklin, 1988a: 82). A typical edition of the *Sheffield Weekly Gazette*, for example, dated Thursday 17 April 1997, carried only two stories on its front page, both emanating from the council's press officers. The lead, headlined 'What to Do about a Bad Neighbour', describes in glowing terms a leaflet launched by the council's housing department, while the other story, 'Town Gun Moved to Museum Home', accompanied by a colour photograph, reports on the arts and museums department's decision to move a gun from one museum in the city to another.

In most areas there is a mixture of paid-for and free newspapers, but Milton Keynes is something of an exception. There are five local weekly papers circulating within the Milton Keynes area. All are free newspapers. One explanation for this may be that people in Milton Keynes have never been in the habit of buying a paper from the news-stand on the way home – the geography and pattern of travel to and from work militate against it (Williams, 1997; see also chapter 9). The papers are published on Wednesday, Thursday, Friday and Sunday. Two are part of the *Citizen* group owned by Johnston Press of Aberdeen, two are part of the *Herald* group, while the fifth is a newcomer, *MK on Sunday*, and part of the small *Bedford on Sunday* group, which first began distributing in Milton Keynes in January 1997. The first four papers will publish virtually anything which the council's press officer sends them; including quotes from councillors and photographs. *MK on Sunday* is different. It positions itself as an anti-establishment paper, pledging to look for trouble, especially corruption in local public services. 'It's like the *News of the World* without the sleaze. Councillors are rather nervous of it' (Kownacki, 1997).

The point here is that local newspapers' susceptibility to press releases issued by local government PROs reflects the resource base of the newspaper with free newspapers typically being unable to match the editorial and journalistic resources of their paid-for sister papers. Cost cutting occurs, of course, on paid-for papers and municipal correspondents are not always replaced. Fran Collingham, PRO at Wychavon District Council in Wiltshire, formerly a local newspaper reporter, recalls the time when the local paper used to have a specialist reporter who covered council business:

> The paper didn't just take material in the press releases sent by the council as read. He [the municipal reporter] would ring up the director of housing or one of his other contacts and find out for himself. Now the papers are all downsized and have hardly any staff reporters – no council specialists – so if the council sends out a press release it's just used as it is. As a former hack, I'm sorry that local papers have lost their investigative, questioning role. But their readers have changed as well. Shifting

populations mean that the paper doesn't have the same relationship with the local community that it used to have.

(Interview, 6 February 1997)

Peter Kay, news editor of the *Sheffield Telegraph*, has worked on local newspapers for twenty years, six of those as the municipal reporter on the *Telegraph*'s sister paper, the *Star*. In his view the relationship between the local paper and the council has changed enormously since the late 1970s, when the council used simply to send out a single sheet of paper with the agenda for council meetings. Now the agenda is accompanied by copies of the papers to be discussed, together with summaries of the technical detail in press releases, opportunities for interviews and photographs and substantial amounts of further information. He has also detected a change in the attitude of the council to the local press: councils are much more likely to be forthcoming about what they are doing and are not only willing to answer questions, but are active in getting their message across. It is clearly in their interests to get their story out first rather than wait for it to be found out. But some councils are still very nervous about talking to the press:

> I rang North East Derbyshire [District Council] the other day to check a detail on a planning matter and their planning department wouldn't speak to me – they insisted I went through their press office, although there was nothing controversial about what I wanted to know.
>
> (Interview, 19 May 1997)

This view echoes the advice given by Fedorcio *et al.* (1991: 34) that a reporter with an enquiry about a hole in the road should be able to talk directly to the person in the highways department responsible for putting it right, rather than to the 'gatekeeper or official mouthpiece'.

Sheffield council's press officer is another former hack and was a colleague of Peter Kay on the *Star*. Kay claims:

> We trust each other but that would not stop me running a story that was embarrassing to the council. Of course I'd give them the chance to comment. The relationship between a council and a newspaper is, in my experience, much more dependent on the individuals concerned than anything else. I've worked for editors who have had very different attitudes, from being generally supportive of what the council stands for and what it is doing, to being very distrustful and trying to catch them out. Clearly that affects the climate in which stories are shaped.
>
> (Interview, 19 May 1997)

NEWS MANAGEMENT

Setting the agenda

While most local authorities employ one or more press officers to handle calls from the media, councils are increasingly concerned to set the agenda by being pro-active, not reactive. As some of the comments quoted in this chapter indicate, press officers are well aware that the local paper may be understaffed and the local journalist underinformed.

Newspapers, morning, evening or weekly, are published according to a regular and pre-arranged timetable, with daily 'evening' papers running to several editions from the midday racing version to the late-night (actually late-afternoon) final. But newsworthy events do not conform to this time-table, or indeed any timetable at all. If the newspaper is not to appear with blank spaces in it, sufficient news must be found to fill the pages. Enter the local authority press officer, bearing stories. The press officer whose job entails producing ten news releases a week can ensure that the paper is regularly supplied with what Tiffen (1989: 4–5) refers to as an 'irregular and unpredictable commodity'.

Local authority press officers can, and do, prove helpful to journalists by providing material to fill the pages of their newspapers. Journalists may be grateful or resentful of this 'help', depending on the relationship between the press officer and the journalist, the type of material supplied and the spin put upon it, and not least the imminence of the paper's copy deadline.

We can divide the type of material provided by press officers into two categories: the positive stories showing what a good job the council is doing and which the authority wants the local paper to run; and information which the council has, and which the local paper is very keen to get hold of. The press officer can act as a news manager in issuing both types of material. But it is in the timing of the release of the latter material that the press officer has greater power. Where the local authority has sole ownership of the source of material, it is in a position of great power over those who want to find it out, and press officers sometimes use this power to ensure that the journalist uses the council-generated favourable story before the other material is released. As Hitchins, a former hack turned lecturer in public relations, notes in another context:

> When there is only one source of the information, interviews or pictures that the media want, then the potential to manage that information is absolute. The fact that Greenpeace were aboard the Brent Spar oil rig – and thus the only source of up-to-date pictures – allowed them to shape news coverage of the issue, to the subsequent embarrassment of the broadcasters.
>
> (Hitchins, 1997: 8)

Who is in control?

Pritchard is forthright in discussing the diminishing importance of the local press *vis-à-vis* other information sources, describing regional newspaper journalism as 'a town centre after the construction of a new ring road. Every year more and more readers take the by-pass' (1994: 55). A number of factors contribute to the increasing irrelevance of local newspapers within local media networks: the decline of local newspapers' circulations; the standards of their journalism; the growth of free newspapers, local radio, television stations, and dedicated news channels; the reduction in editorial autonomy and similarity in look and content between titles resulting from the concentration of ownership; and the lack of training for journalists.

Local newspapers' editorial consists of less news and more in the way of features, such as leisure items on hobbies and holidays (ideal vehicles for attracting associated advertising), and so-called 'infotainment', such as What's On supplements and syndicated interviews with the stars. Some papers have gone a stage further, clothing themselves completely in advertising, as the *Sheffield Journal* did in January 1997, appearing in succeeding weeks wrapped inside four-page ads for Sainsbury's and Tesco respectively. Each four-pager was designed to look like the front and back pages of the paper itself.

Local newspapers are ceasing to fulfil their former role as guardians of the truth, and keepers of the public record. Their journalists, in many cases hard pressed, de-unionised, demoralised and poorly paid, are increasingly reliant on press releases and promotional material provided for them by vested interests. Peter Kay described the problem in the following way:

> As staff numbers have diminished there is less time to spend on stories. For example, twenty years ago each reporter was allocated an area of the city and he would spend one day a week out of the office, knocking on doors in his patch, then filing reports. Now no one has the luxury of a day out of the office looking for material – you have to do it over the phone. You lose something if you haven't been there – taking it down the phone is no substitute. And it's easier to use a press release, more convenient if the relevant information is summarised than if you have to go out and find it out yourself. But whether or not it is used, and how it is used, is still dictated by rules of impartiality and balance.
>
> (Interview, 19 May 1997)

In such circumstances, the role of the local authority press officer may be to halt the decline. The professional local authority PRO, often a fully trained and experienced former journalist, is a more reliable source of news for the local community than many local reporters acting on their own. The PRO may be a member of his or her professional body, the Institute of Public Relations, and thus bound by its code of practice. Furthermore, council

PROs work in an environment where employees' rights still tend to be well protected and enforced by their trade union, so they are more comfortable about advising the council to be open, and to come clean about its misdemeanours. Newspapers, on the other hand, have rushed to de-recognise unions and reporters justifiably feel vulnerable if they try to take issue with editors or proprietors about the news values adopted by their paper.

One could argue that the town hall is becoming the last bastion of good municipal journalism. Without the carefully prepared material provided by professional local government PROs, local newspapers are unlikely to be able to perform their role as 'principal institutions of the public sphere' (Curran, 1991: 29)

REFERENCES

Audit Commission (1995) *Talk Back: Local Authority Communication with Citizens*, London: HMSO.
Barnett, N. and Harrison, S. (1996) 'The Citizen's Charter in Local Government' in Chandler, J. (ed.) *The Citizen's Charter*, Aldershot: Dartmouth.
Collingham, F. (1997) Interview with the author, 6 February.
Curran, J. (1991) 'Re-thinking the Media as a Public Sphere' in Dahlgren, P. and Sparks, C. (eds) *Communication and Citizenship: Journalism and the Public Sphere*, London: Routledge.
Department of the Environment (1988) *Code of Recommended Practice on Local Authority Publicity*, London: HMSO.
Fedorcio, D., Heaton, P. and Madden, K. (1991) *Public Relations for Local Government*, Harlow: Longman.
Fox, T. (1997) 'The Long Haul', *PR News*, February.
Franklin, B. (1986) 'Public Relations, the Local Press and the Coverage of Local Government', *Local Government Studies*, July/August, pp. 25–33.
—— (1987) 'Local Government Public Relations: The Changing Institutional and Statutory Environment 1974–1988', *Public Relations*, Winter, pp. 26–30.
—— (1988a) *Public Relations Activities in Local Government*, London: Charles Knight.
—— (1988b) 'Civic Free Newspapers: Propaganda on the Rates?', *Local Government Studies*, May/June, pp. 35–57.
Franklin, B. and Van Slyke Turk, J. (1988) 'Information Subsidies: Agenda Setting Traditions', *Public Relations Review*, Spring, pp. 29–41.
Gandy Jnr, O. (1982) *Beyond Agenda-Setting: Information Subsidies and Public Policy*, Norwood, NJ: Ablex.
Harlow, R. (1976) 'Building a Public Relations Definition', *Public Relations Review* 2.
Harrison, S. (1995) *Public Relations: An Introduction*, London: Routledge.
Hitchins, J. (1997) 'Swampy, Animal and Bernard Ingham: Locating "News Management" in Public Relations Education', paper presented at Public Relations Education Forum (PREF), Leeds, 3–5 April.
Johns, C. (1997) 'Driven by a Low Budget', *PR News*, April.
Kay, P. (1997) Interview with the author, 19 May.
Kownacki, J. (1997) Interview with the author, 25 February.
McCombs, M. and Gilbert, S. (1986) 'News Influence on our Pictures of the World' in Bryant, J. and Zillman, D. (eds) *Perspectives on Media Effects*, Hillsdale NJ: Lawrence Erlbaum.

Pritchard, C. (1994) 'The Cuddlies and the Junkies Wrestle for the Regionals', *British Journalism Review* 4 (4), pp. 55–8.

Raine, J. (1996) 'Proactivity Beats Reactivity', *PR News*, June.

Smith, G. (1986) *Local Government for Journalists*, London: LGC Communications.

Tiffen, R. (1989) *News and Power*, Sydney: Allen & Unwin.

Tuchman, G. (1978) *Making News: A Study in the Construction of Reality*, New York: The Free Press.

Wade, B. (1996) 'Hard Lessons Learned', *PR News*, June.

Walker, J. (1996) 'Cashing Up: A Turnaround on Income Collection in Brent', *PR News*, August.

Wigfield, A. (1988) quoted in an interview with the author in Lanstone, S. 'Improving Service Delivery in a Local Authority', MBA thesis, University of Sheffield.

Williams, S. (1997) Interview with the author, 25 February.

Chapter 13

Hungry media need fast food: the role of the Central Office of Information

Brent Garner and John Short

> The citizen has the right to be told and the Government has a clear duty to tell him what it is doing in his name, and with his money, and why.
>
> Sir Henry French, *Report of the Committee on the Cost of the Home Information Services*, 1949

In theory what Sir Henry asks for is straightforward: the people in a democracy have a right to know, the government a duty to inform, and the media a duty to deliver this information after proper scrutiny. In practice it is more complicated. Most writers on politics and the media have concentrated on how politicians, especially those in government, manipulate the media; a few have written on how the media manipulate the politicians; virtually none on how a third player fits into this relationship, namely, the £24 billion public relations industry. This burgeoning industry has generated considerable consequences, not only for the national media but also for the regional news gatherers who might consider themselves less susceptible.

Day-to-day government activity is routinely channelled to the public through the Parliamentary Press Corps, a media village at the heart of Westminster in which all regional newspaper and broadcasting groups have residents. These 'villagers' are also well placed to report the peculiarities of MPs from their region, the local relevance of parliamentary activities, even spice it all up with gossip. In this they find most MPs more than willing collaborators since they believe that appearances in the local media could translate into votes at an election. But even the combination of the press corps and co-operative MPs could not hope to cope with the level of activity generated at Westminster if policies were to be explained and citizens adequately informed.

The Government Information Service, the collective name for the press and publicity officers employed throughout the Civil Service, known as the Government Information and Communication Service (GICS) since November 1997, was set up to bridge this information gap and the Central

Office of Information (COI), which succeeded the wartime Ministry of Information, is the part of the GICS that has a regional network of offices in eleven English cities.

Prime Minister Clement Attlee told parliament of the COI's foundation in words inscribed in pokerwork over government information officers' desks:

> It is essential to good administration under a democratic system that the public shall be adequately informed about the matters in which Government action directly impinges on their daily lives. . . .
>
> (*HC Debs*, December 1945)

Initially the public were informed about fairly innocent matters like how to cook dried eggs or save fuel but even from the start there were rumours of other kinds of 'cooking'. The *Daily Express* and the *Daily Mail* (Scammell, 1995: 167) with typical British understatement called the COI 'propaganda agents for the Party in power' and a 'direct menace to one of our fundamental freedoms', while the 1948 publicity bill for Attlee's government, 'unprecedented in peacetime' and in real terms rivalling the Thatcher government's controversial spend in the 1980s (Scammell, l995: 166), was attacked by the Conservative opposition. Sir Fife Clarke, the third Director General, had good reason to write in 1970 that the COI had been 'born in an atmosphere of suspicion on the part of the press and the Parliamentary Opposition' (Clarke, 1970: 155).

It was the Thatcher years, however, that saw a quantum leap in this 'atmosphere of suspicion'. Since Lord Young's big budget campaigns in the mid 1980s, first in the Manpower Services Commission and then at the Department of Employment, critics have claimed that the practice of government information has radically changed.

> The increased use of advertising was part of a broader but radical shift in government communication strategy during the 1980s, reflecting successive administrations' concerns to manage political communications by and about government and its activities.
>
> (Franklin, 1994: 96)

> The peaks in employment advertising, the timing of general election (and the involvement of Saatchi and Saatchi) seem more than mere coincidence, a fact not lost on critics of government publicity.
>
> (Scammell, 1995: 208)

These criticisms peaked at the end of the 1980s when two quality broadsheets within a couple of months devoted entire pages to 'public concern' over official government information. The *Guardian* on 15 March 1989 questioned the quality of government statistics and the *Independent* on 10 May claimed that the government had 'become increasingly sophisticated in managing the news'.

At the centre of this criticism was the appointment, on 9 February 1989, of Bernard Ingham, Mrs Thatcher's Chief Press Secretary, to the position of Head of Profession, putting him according to one critic 'effectively in sole charge of the Government's propaganda machine' (Harris, 1990). Previously the Head of Profession had been the Director General of the COI, which, though accountable to the Chancellor of the Duchy of Lancaster, was not attached to a Departmental Information Division.

But criticism of alleged government propaganda did not extend generally to the regional COI because of the nature of its core work. An official pamphlet (COI, 1984) said: 'Export publicity for industry is one of the regional officers' main functions. They supply to headquarters articles, photographs, radio tapes and other material for overseas, and are responsible for tours by official visitors from overseas and for the resultant publicity.' The most high profile of the other duties was making press arrangements for royal visits. It would take a truly dedicated conspiracy theorist to interpret most of this work as political manipulation.

In fact during a survey for this chapter a senior political reporter in a major commercial regional television centre said that in the past (that reference to 'in the past' is significant) the COI seemed to have only two functions, 'to allocate rota passes for royal visits; the second to bombard us with incomprehensible and irrelevant press releases which ended up in the bin'.

There was more than a grain of truth in this criticism but for reasons with which the local media were not concerned. They quite reasonably thought that the COI should be a local contact point for all government information. The reality was more complex. The COI regional offices only dealt with those government departments that chose to use their service – and pay for it out of their budgets. In effect this limited the COI regional service to four main departments – Employment, Environment, Transport and Trade and Industry. The rest only used the service infrequently if at all. The results were twofold: a patchy service and an often irate local media.

Two examples of the latter arose during a survey for this chapter. A BBC TV specialist correspondent told us:

> I've had a good relationship with the COI in the regions. My criticism is of some of the Whitehall departments who have been more than unhelpful to regional correspondents.

A sentiment echoed by the news editor of a local Independent Local Radio (ILR) station:

> My concern is reserved for the departmental press officers who show almost universal disregard for regional media. They've never heard of us (despite listing in the Radio Authority handbook and innumerable media guides) and, more to the point, make little attempt to hide 'their distaste for handling a request from a little pop music station in the north'.

To put things in perspective, one main Whitehall press desk – and not the busiest – has to answer 100,000 media enquiries a year. To deal with this number they have to prioritise and the local media are generally low on the list. The choice between putting up a minister for News at Ten or a local FM station on the borders of Scotland looks straightforward from a Whitehall desk. The importance, however, of the regional media in informing the citizen and forming public opinion is a case of the whole being greater than the sum of the parts.

Whitehall press officers are aware of this and advances in technology have eased their ability to present ministers on local television and radio stations. The Home Office, for example, has a fibre optic link with Westminster Television studios at Millbank which means interviews or even remote on-camera statements are fed frequently to live television programmes throughout the country. Head of News Brian Butler commented, 'We constantly tell ministers and senior policy officials about the importance of getting the message across locally. Let's not forget, as ministers don't forget, that they all have constituencies in the regions, and often have developed good links with their particular local media – so they know its value' (interview with author).

The simple fact is that 88 per cent of all adults (44 million people) read a regional newspaper and in all regions more people read the local paper than any national paper, giving it a unique role in setting the agenda for the formation of public opinion. Add to this the facts that seven out of ten people listen to local radio on an average day and more people watch regional TV news programmes than national news programmes and there is some support for the argument that the 1997 election was won for Labour by the local media.

A senior Whitehall insider commented:

> I was speaking to somebody in the press office of the Labour Party who actually said they thought that Labour won the election through the local media. They admitted that they came to it a bit late but thought it had been enormously influential. You got a lot of space, or you can get a lot of space, if you've got a message and they run it unadulterated.

It is interesting that the previous Conservative government had also begun to pay more attention to the regional media in their final eighteen months. Their political motives may have been the same but their action grew out of the way the COI's regional service had developed since inception and the change in relationship between the regional service and Whitehall departments that had been brought about when the COI became one of the Thatcher government's executive agencies in 1990. As indicated earlier, the regional offices had never served all government departments, only those that budgeted for it and requested a service. After 1990, this meant only those willing to buy the service direct from the agency. When the government turned its attention to the regional media it discovered that they were not receiving the full output that they sought.

A number of steps were taken to fill these gaps and the latest one in 1996 was the establishment of the Senior Press Officer (SPO) system. Eleven SPO posts were created in the COI Regional Network, paid for by the Cabinet Office on the direction of the then Deputy Prime Minister, Michael Heseltine. The SPOs' remit was to fill the areas where a gap was perceived in the service the COI delivers to the regional media and to act in a co-ordinating role alongside government offices in the regions.

Some criticism has been made of these posts along the lines that they were propaganda posts created by the Tory Party in the run-up to the general election. The setting up of the posts in the year before an election certainly fuelled suspicion but in fact they were set up as permanent posts in part in response to regional editors who had campaigned for better intelligence over the range of government activity and they remain after the change of government.

It is more accurate to see the establishment of the new posts as an integral part of a dramatic change in the COI in the regions. From being a small and not often regarded part of the COI – only 100 staff out of a total of 1,500 – the regional COI has become the biggest division and the only part to increase its staff during an extensive period of general 'downsizing'.

Way back at the beginning of the COI, Lord Radcliffe, Director General of its predecessor, the Ministry of Information, said governments 'always tend to want not really a free press but a managed or well-conducted press. I do not blame them. It is part of their job.' (Hennessy, 1989: 364). He pointed out that governments were not 'powerless or ill-equipped in this issue' since they 'have all the resources of modern public relations at their beck and call'. In fact, they have two sets of resources, their party machine and the government information and communication service, with proprieties that divide the tasks between the two.

The divide that most people are aware of is that overtly party-political messages will not be handled by information officers who are civil servants. One recent classic example was the unease of the Scottish Office to allow the then Scottish Secretary Michael Forsyth to use the term 'Tartan Tax' in official speeches (and press releases) when referring to the Labour Party's plans to give tax-raising power to a Scottish Assembly (*Guardian*, 27 May 1997).

But this guardianship of propriety does not prevent the GICS servicing the elected government of the day in the best way that it can. In fact like all other parts of the machinery of government it is there to be used and to be used well.

The GICS handbook states: 'Information officers and other public resources are provided to help Ministers explain the Government's policies in a positive light.' But adds:

Government Information Officers are not used for image-making which is the province of the Party political machine. Ministers must be

protected from accusations of using public resources for political purposes, and they in turn have a duty to protect the integrity of civil
servants.

(GICS Handbook, 1997)

A forerunner guide (Green Book, 1980: 9–12) said that even where there was
'bitter political controversy' and furthering departmental policies would further the political party in office, 'this is perfectly proper'. Getting the 'best
possible press' could properly involve advising a minister to be 'softer' in the
way he deals with sensitive subjects like hospital waiting lists when he might
believe he had the statistics to win an argument or not to praise the new oil-
fired heating system in the hospital he was opening in a desolate mining area.

Again nothing new. This is much the same point that the archetypal spin
doctor, Niccolo Machiavelli, was making when he advised his political mas-
ters to appear 'merciful, trustworthy, humane, upright and devout'. And he
spells out clearly that it is appearing to have these qualities, not necessarily
having them, that counts: 'Everyone can see what you appear to be, whereas
few have direct experience of what you really are' (Machiavelli, 1988: 62–63).

Media advisers still nod approvingly in this direction. Pat Cadell, President
Carter's political adviser, lamenting his chief's defeat by President Reagan,
said: 'Too many good people have been defeated because they tried to substi-
tute substance for style' (Scammell, 1995: 20). Of course that is the view of a
political adviser in the USA. But even here in Britain politicians prefer media
events such as an eye-catching photo opportunity compared to a relatively
dull press conference convened in a local hotel; British politicians have also
learned what it takes to persuade the local media to turn out and give him
coverage.

Journalists and academics queue up to criticise this 'new' black art of
political marketing, laying the blame at the door of politicians, especially
those in government, and their co-conspirators. Just twenty-one years short
of the 500th anniversary of the first printing of *The Prince*, one of the most
respected commentators wrote: 'The belief of politicians that half of
politics is image making and the other half the art of making people believe
the imagery whatever "the facts", is rampant' (Keane, 1991: 101). He argued
that 'lying in politics' was one of five interlocking types of political censor-
ship in the new era.

But just as Machiavelli's advice has been simplistically misinterpreted,
giving him a not entirely deserved bad press, what Keane calls 'lying'
is a rather disingenuous description of what modern communications are
about. The remark Lord Tyrrell, Permanent Under Secretary at the Foreign
Office, made to a reporter is perhaps a richer description more worthy of
consideration: 'You think we lie to you. But we don't lie, really we don't.
However when you discover that, you make an even greater error, you think
we tell you the truth' (Sigal, 1973: 131).

To talk of information being true or false is questionable at best: without borrowing a phrase from *Yes Minister's* Sir Humphrey, information can perhaps be more meaningfully categorised as accurate or inaccurate. The distinction between information and knowledge is at least as broad and useful as that between 'law' and 'justice'. Where law and justice coincide can be, and quite often is, coincidental as good lawyers and bad judges regularly prove. Or between news and truth. It was a reporter who first spelled out this distinction:

> news and truth are not the same thing, and must be clearly distinguished. The function of news is to signalise an event, the function of truth is to bring to light hidden facts, to set them in relation to each other, and make a picture of reality on which men can act.
>
> (Lippmann, 1965: 226)

The same is true of the distinction between information, which is the commodity the government information officer deals in, and knowledge, which is what the reporter should turn this information into through judicious reflection. There are clearly occasions when 'official sources' are 'economical with their information'. The leaked memo written by the present shadow health spokesman when he was a backbencher suggesting that 'the best result for the next 12 months would be zero media coverage' (*Observer*, 22 June 1997) is not unique and the inconvenient (for the media) timing of a news release (*Independent*, 10 May 1989) certainly happens. But they are exceptions and can easily mislead a critic into thinking the exception is the rule and fail to see things that should be more obvious and are certainly more significant.

A former head of the Department of Employment Information Division, for whom the regional staff of the COI issue monthly unemployment statistics, put it this way:

> In my book there is no such thing as a pure statistic. A statistic's in the eye of the beholder. A fall in unemployment of 14,800 to one journalist will be good news, because it is a fall. To another it will be fiddling because of all the changes. To an economic journalist who will compare that fall with the previous month's fall of 60,000 it will be an indication that the scene is beginning to change. Now there are three interpretations of one figure.
>
> (Sutlieff, 1997)

On the alleged twenty-four changes (Clement and Hague, *Independent*, 10 May 1989) in ways of calculating the unemployment figures between 1979 and 1989, he said:

> All these changes, actually there weren't 24 that affected the count, there were many fewer than that although the figure 24 got into the language, were fully explained to the journalists at the time. There was nothing

hidden about them. OK, it's up to the journalist to call them fiddling the figures but what we had to do was put out the figures the Government provided and the best possible explanation of them. I remember that some of those changes were because the collection system had led to double counting. The Government said take them off. That was their prerogative. We told the journalists both the figures and the reasons for arriving at them. It was up to them what they did with those figures.

In the last set of unemployment figures published before the 1997 election, the Leeds office of the COI collected cuttings that showed that the official figures from the Office of National Statistics had been used but all with suggestions of 'fiddling', either quoting Opposition sources, or Sheffield Hallam University. Even the Conservative-supporting *Yorkshire Post* carried a news story with the 'fraud' claim for the figures though in an editorial it described it as a 'cheap shot fuelled by a dubious leak from the militant public sector union'. In the end the information staff put out the figures which the government, any government, has stamped with approval.

Clearly, the government information machine influences the contents of the news media but this is a finding that cannot be accepted in isolation. Structural changes in the media world offer a better explanation of why this is so than theories of political conspiracy or politicisation of the civil service – though this argument will tend to disappoint, lacking as it does the sexiness of conspiracy! An editor of the *Standard* in the tranquil years of the 1970s said that news management was the most difficult of all pressures for an editor to withstand: 'In a sense, most Government announcements and political activities involve an element of news management. This is related to presentation and timing if nothing else' (Wintour, 1972: 44). More recently Tony Bevins, political editor of the *Independent* wrote (*Independent*, 10 May 1989): 'So much of news the public reads, sees, and hears is manipulated by someone, somewhere; that manipulation has become commonplace in modern journalism.'

These opinions are shared by regional journalists. A specialist correspondent on a Yorkshire evening newspaper said of COI regional press officers:

It would be impossible for them not to be political because they are in a political job and it offers them all kinds of ways of manipulating the news agenda. With the best will in the world it is pretty well inevitable. Take just one example: Ministers come out into the regions for a working breakfast and announce a project or a policy. This is good copy. I'm not sure whether anybody could be precise in drawing a clear dividing line between what is strictly a departmental matter and what gives party political advantage. Choosing the event and to some extent setting the agenda seems to be a perk for whoever is in the driving seat.

And yet the introduction of the new SPOs which moved towards ensuring management of more ministerial visits than the traditional users of the COI regional network was apparently universally welcomed by the media. Eight months after they were set up a survey of the regional media produced the following comments:

> My eyes lit up when I heard of the SPO initiative as it's something we've been pressing for. At last we have a one-stop contact point for all Government business.
>
> (Will Rayner, *London Today/Tonight*)

> The SPO system has been very useful for leads and an effective early warning on initiatives of local interest. Keep it up.
>
> (Luke Collinson, Channel One TV)

> I hope the positive attitude of the past year or two will be sustained under the next Government. It is refreshing.
>
> (Jack Foster, Westminster Press/UK News)

> The COI is now more selective in the ministers it offers for interview, and is aware of the need to tie their visits into a good peg, an event of real relevance to the region.
>
> (News Desk, YTV)

What for one set of people, the regional editors, is an 'improved' service, for another set could be seen as more efficient government propaganda. The two do not, of course, necessarily contradict each other and indeed should complement one another. We would argue, however, neither originally nor particularly controversially, that public relations generally, of which the Government Information and Communication Service is part, subsidises the media with 'free information' and that helps shape the news agenda.

There is a dimension to the 'information subsidy' which influences the nature of the local news agenda even more than the national one. As staff on local media are reduced – a forty-two page free newspaper may be put together by a single journalist – the public relations officers by tailoring information to the media's requirement can make this subsidised information even more valuable. The packaging of politics (Franklin, 1994) is unquestionable (even if the effects of this packaging are questionable) but there is a persuasive argument that government information officers were following tabloid trends in the local media rather than setting them.

A study of the media and the poll tax referred to the 'rise of the public relations state' and quoted the American critic Gandy's claim that at every level of government there are information specialists who make sure that the government's message is reported the way it wants it to be reported. It was Gandy who claimed that these information specialists operate 'information subsidies':

These are not bribes or material handouts, but measures to reduce the cost to information seekers of obtaining information they need to construct the news. By making life easy for the news seekers, information managers can influence and even determine the flow and character of coverage about their activities in the news media. That is, obviously, the basis on which all public relations and publicity work rests.

(Deacon and Golding, 1994: 415)

The old brigade of provincial editors would have snorted at this interpretation but there are few regional journalists today who do not recognise the reality. A local radio news editor said there was 'no doubt COI press releases put items on the agenda which, given enough time and resources, we would ignore' (Horsman, 1997). And a study (Franklin and Van Slyke Turk, 1988) of the take up of local government press releases showed a remarkably high rate of 96 per cent. One of the authors of that study (Franklin, 1994: 116) later explained the economic reason for the high 'strike rate' with which few journalists would quarrel. The local media have space which has to be filled quickly and cheaply. A press release written by former journalists – as most government, national and local information officers (and most regional COI staff) are – takes less editing than Mrs Pickle's local village notes or Mr Pickle's 2,000-word report on the village cricket game.

The growth of what Franklin calls the fifth estate – 'if media constitute a fourth estate, public relations professionals undoubtedly form a fifth' (Franklin, 1994: 116) – has clearly accelerated over the last few decades. But it is not a new phenomenon. An eighteenth-century play had a Mr Puff, 'professor in the art of puffing', identifying different types which include 'as the circumstances require, the various forms of letter to the editor, occasional anecdote, impartial critique, observation from correspondent, or advertisement from the party' (Sheridan, *The Critic*, 1779).

A century and a half later the journalist and critic, Walter Lippmann, argued that the development of the publicity man:

is a clear sign that the facts of modern life do not spontaneously take a shape in which they can be known. They must be given shape by somebody, and since in the daily routine reporters cannot give a shape to facts, and since there is little disinterested organisation of intelligence, the need for some formulation is being met by interested parties.

(Lippmann, 1965: 218)

The obvious consequences of this persuaded every sizable organisation – a New York press survey had found 1,200 press agents regularly active before the First World War – that it was 'safer to hire a press agent who stands between the group and the newspapers'. Today, churches, charities, pressure groups as well as big businesses have a press office. In May 1997 a world congress on PR held in Helsinki revealed that their business was worth £24 billion.

Baistow had estimated that there were about 10,000 press officers in the UK in 1985 and that 'their numbers were increasing by as much as 30 per cent a year' (Baistow, 1985: 69). In a recent survey, Delano and Henningham estimated that there were 15,175 news journalists across all British media (Delano and Henningham, 1995: 6). Today there are more press officers than news journalists (Franklin, 1997: 23).

The fight for control of news agendas is not between journalists and 'press agents' but just between 'press agents'. What the journalists largely do – especially in the regions but even in the national media to a large extent – is choose between what organisations offer them through public relations: a motor manufacturer launching a new model in Spain; a multinational tobacco company sponsoring research; an anti-smoking lobby dressing up as skeletons outside the building in which the research is being announced; a pop group releasing a new album, a rival group accusing them of stealing one of their tunes; Swampy protesting against a bypass: the COI organising the opening by a government minister of a new road, a group of mothers sitting down in the road as a protest; a report from an anti-drug group in an inner city, a pro-cannabis group issuing their own report; the COI organising a royal visit, councillors refusing to attend a royal civic dinner; a briefing by a government department or a counter briefing by the Opposition. The list is virtually endless and easily demonstrated by reading, listening or watching the news any day with care.

And if one of these organisations wants to improve its chance of getting its message in the news, or even getting itself off the agenda, it hires a professional. Lippmann saw this in the USA seventy years ago: 'So if the publicity man wishes free publicity he, speaking quite accurately, has to start something. He arranges a stunt: obstructs the traffic, teases the police, somehow manages to entangle his client with an event that is already news' (Lippmann, 1965: 218).

In one of the first studies of politics and the local press, two Liverpool academics noted: 'Politicians are apt to complain the journalists too often prefer to cover the gossipy showman politician than the less publicity conscious, but worthy local party man who is doing a good job' (Cox and Morgan, 1973: 58). This is something the COI has known for some time. It is no coincidence, for example, that Mrs Thatcher was seen to kick off a Department of Employment scheme called Employment Training, using a football at Scunthorpe football stadium. Far from some political conspiracy, here was an enterprising COI man who arranged for a 'sexy' group involved – Football in the Community with soccer stars – to teach Mrs Thatcher to kick off the scheme. Hardly surprising that the rather drier formal announcement of the scheme in London by the Secretary of State was eclipsed.

The same Secretary of State may have been surprised to have seen photographs around the world of his hands round his leader's throat! In fact he was placing the head on a waxwork model of Mrs Thatcher at York Waxworks Museum where one of the ET trainees was working and secured massive attention for the scheme. It takes little reflection to decide whether the Secretary of State would have preferred the space to be filled with a measured defence of the programme with statistical evidence of its success. It takes even less reflection to decide whether he would have got any space at all for such an approach.

In a world that is tabloid, politicians have learned they have to swallow the pill however bitter or disappear. One current Labour minister, when in opposition, confessed:

> To be in the media is to exist as a politician. Politicians now see themselves as another consumer product and anxiously ask: 'Are they still buying me?' In other words, there is a temptation for my whole political existence to be determined by media coverage, constantly living in a world of the immediate, superficial and easily consumable concepts.
>
> (Battle, 1995)

The media, financially neutered, have to be fed an easily digested if colourful diet of fast food. This has tended to turn politicians, who cannot live without them, into showmen. It has also elevated some simple presentational ideas into big political ones. We do not just live in a public relations state, we live in a public relations world. And that glaringly obvious fact explains better, if less sensationally than plots in corridors of power, the shape of the news agenda, including the political news agenda.

REFERENCES

Baistow, T. (1985) *Fourth Rate Estate*, London: Comedia.
Battle, J. (1995) *The Catholic Post*, RC Diocese of Leeds newspaper, October.
Central Office of Information (1980) *The Government Information Officer* (Green Book), London: COI.
—— (1984) *Government Communicates: The Work of the Central Office of Information*, London: HMSO.
Clarke, Sir Fife (1970) *The Central Office of Information*, London: George Allen and Unwin.
Cox, H. and Morgan, D. (1973) *City Politics and the Press*, Cambridge: Cambridge University Press.
Deacon, D. and Golding, P. (1994) *Taxation and Representation: The Media, Political Communication and the Poll Tax*, Academia Research Monography 11, Luton: John Libbey.
Delano, A. and Henningham, J. (1995) *The News Breed: British Journalism in the 1990s*, London: The London Institute.
Franklin, B. (1994) *Packaging Politics: Political Communications in Britain's Media Democracy*, London: Edward Arnold.
—— (1997) *Newszak and News Media*, London: Edward Arnold.
Franklin, B. and Van Slyke Turk, J. (1988) 'Information Subsidies: Agenda Setting Traditions', *Public Relations Review*, Spring, pp. 29–41.

French, Sir Henry (1949) *Report of the Committee on the Cost of the Home Information Services*, Cmnd 7836, London, HMSO.

Gandy, O. (1982) *Beyond Agenda Setting: Information Subsidies and Public Policies*, Norwood, NJ: Ablex Publishing.

Government Information and Communication Service (1997) *A Working Guide for Government Information Officers*, London: GICS.

Harris, R. (1990) *Good and Faithful Servant*, London: Faber and Faber.

Hennessy, P. (1989) *Whitehall*, London: Secker and Warburg.

Horsman, R. (1997) Interview with the author.

Keane, J. (1991) *The Media and Democracy*, London: Polity Press.

Lippmann, W. (1965) *Public Opinion*, New York: The Free Press.

Machiavelli, N. (1988) *The Prince*, ed. Quentin Skinner and Russell Price, Cambridge: Cambridge University Press.

Scammell, M. (1995) *Designer Politics*, London: Macmillan.

Sheridan, R. S. (1779) *The Critic*, London: S. French.

Sigal, L. V. (1973) *Reporters and Officials: The Organisation and Politics of Newsmaking*, Lexington: D. C. Heath and Co.

Sutlieff, B. (1997) In private communication.

Wintour, C. (1972) *Pressures on the Press: An Editor Looks at Fleet Street*, London: Deutsch.

Chapter 14

The changing role of the local journalist: from faithful chronicler of the parish pump to multiskilled compiler of an electronic database

Rod Pilling

It might well be possible to write off one remarkable action of a local newspaper executive in the 1990s to eccentricity – but it did illustrate the plight of paid-for local papers as they struggle to enter the twenty-first century. Ben Stoneham, the managing director of the *Portsmouth News*, offered his journalists a £5-a-year pay rise, provided they agree to purchase every issue of the paper at a special rate of 1p per copy. If they did this, then those copies could be included in the audit of circulation, which would then rise. This extraordinary pay offer, which was reported in the trade weekly *Press Gazette* on 28 March 1997, no doubt gave many local journalists a wry smile but it also underlined the kind of pressures that were being exerted on newsrooms. The £5-a-year pay rise was an extreme example of the relentless downward pressure on costs that characterises the industry. That pressure has typically been directed toward editorial costs and been strongly felt by journalists in newsrooms. The second aspect of this strange offer – the desperate attempt to boost circulation – was an indication of how challenging many paid-for newspapers have found it to retain readers.

This chapter explores the changing role of the local print journalist as the local press faces the millennium, with increased competition from other media both for the attention of its audience and for the patronage of its advertisers. The chapter examines the impact of the contraction in the local press on the newsrooms and journalists; analyses the extent to which the attitude of local journalists to local public life – the parish pump – is changing; questions whether the local 'fourth estate' is scrutinising and investigating; and, finally, interrogates a new concept – the local press as electronic database ripe for multimedia exploitation.

THE SHRINKING LOCAL NEWSROOM

National Union of Journalists' newspaper organiser Bernie Corbett is in no doubt about the predicament of the local press: 'Local newspapers have a diminishing role. They are part of a contracting industry' (Corbett, 1997).

Corbett (1997) recalls vividly the kind of weekly newspaper on which he began his career:

> Twenty-five years ago your average local weekly newspaper had pages the size of bed blankets absolutely crammed with all kinds of parish pump news. A paper of the same name now will in many cases be a tacky sort of tabloid, that hopeless ideal of being the local version of the *Sun* or the *Daily Mail*. There is a lot less space to fill with news. Far fewer stories are covered. The parish pump, street-level stuff is not considered newsworthy. Local courts and local government have dropped out of coverage to a large extent. The local weekly has become useless as a conduit of information for local communities and local democracies – even the good local papers. They don't have enough people and they don't think it is interesting enough.

Jock Gallagher, executive director of the Association of British Editors, agrees: 'We became involved in a study of the magistrates' courts and discovered an awful lot of local papers were simply not covering them' (Gallagher, 1997).

ENTER THE NEWSROOM 'SWEATSHOP'

These are strong charges, which, if true, amount to a major change in the role of the local journalist. To what extent are they rejected or qualified by the keepers of the parish pump, the local journalists and editors? One might expect a more sanguine picture to emerge from the Guild of Editors, which surveyed 420 local editors and 600 trainees in 1995, as part of an initiative to reform training to provide 'Tomorrow's Journalist'. The publications to emerge from this exercise, however, make pessimistic reading. A picture emerges of a local press largely staffed at reporter level by trainees – middle-class graduates paid low salaries and expected to work long hours and produce numerous stories. The executive summary of the survey results puts one of the major concerns of trainees baldly: 'Trainees want . . . change in the sweatshop culture of some newsrooms.' (Guild of Editors, 1995: 1). The survey found that 80 per cent of trainees, who were predominantly graduates who had paid for their own pre-entry training, started on less than £10,000 a year in 1995, less than two-thirds of the average wage and well below the typical starting point for graduates. One editor puts it emotively in his quoted response to the survey: 'The abiding shame is that the salaries offered on local papers – especially bearing in mind the profits made – are pitiful' (ibid.: 5). Another is quoted as stressing the 'stronger downward pressure upon staff costs' (ibid.: 3) Editors in turn complain that the trainees 'lack local knowledge' and that too few are 'working class' (ibid.: 1). What has rather cruelly become known as the 'Samantha syndrome' among editors is being described. Middle-class graduates keen for a career in the media take up the

trainee jobs on local papers as a means to a media career. The survey overview expresses the trainees' predicament plainly: 'Trainees complain that
starting salaries are so low . . . the only way to survive is to go into debt
or lean heavily on their families for financial help' (ibid.: 2). Most of the
trainees move on quickly – so the local commitment of the staffing, one of
Kleinsteuber's five tests of localism, along with local access, control of
content, technology, finance and legal licence, is low (Kleinsteuber, 1992).

Trainees, of course, are not alone in 'the sweatshop culture'. During
advertising recessions newspapers generally cut back on editorial staffing and
when advertising returned and the number of pages increased they were
reluctant to increase staffing. Some twenty-five of the forty-five journalists at
the Exeter *Express and Echo*, a part of the large Northcliffe group, sent a
petition to their editor in May 1997 asking him to take on more staff to 'ease
exceptionally long – sometimes twelve-hour – shift patterns' (Morgan,
1997a). The journalists were 'shell-shocked' by the editor's reply, which, they
said, was to read them the riot act (ibid.).

Editors too are feeling the strain and their role is changing. They are
spending more time on management, marketing and promotion; fewer local
editors enter the annual competition which was set up to award a prize for
their writing: 'The reason given by editors is that they no longer have time to
write' (Guild of Editors, 1996: 2).

Trainees, who do much of the reporting for the local press, typically
conduct the greater part of that work in the office. One is quoted as remark-
ing: 'Being tied to an office because there aren't enough staff for you to go
out is the antithesis of what reporting should be.' (Guild of Editors, 1995: 5).
And a large part of the trainees' life is devoted to the press releases which are
supplied to them by organisations keen to invest in self-promotion: 'Editors
listed hand-out rewriting as the most essential competence required of trainees of six months standing' (ibid.: 7). The dangers of this reliance on press
releases have been well rehearsed elsewhere. They skew the local news
agenda and give a promotional advantage to those organisations with sufficient resources to provide them. Rewritten, or worse, merely inserted
verbatim, they threaten – even eliminate – journalistic independence. They
do, however, fill space quickly and cheaply and represent an informational
subsidy to the local press – mainly from public and corporate bodies keen
to 'manage' the news about themselves (see chapters 12 and 13).

There is also a move to introduce a new lower tier of copy producers – the
editorial assistant. This move is reflected in the responses to the Guild of
Editors. One editor envisaged: 'A two-tier system of journalists. Top quality
reporters engaged on complex and important newsgatherings and a lower
tier of editorial assistants who can deal with rewrites, obits, wedding reports'
(Guild of Editors, 1995: 6). These assistants type up page-filling copy from
the 'armies of amateur correspondents' encouraged by some local weekly
papers (Guild of Editors, 1996: 2). Mike Woods, regional editor for Southern

Newspapers and a member of the Guild's training committee, speaks enthusiastically of this development: 'We have three editorial assistants re-typing wedding and club reports. You have to ask "Do you need to train all journalists to exactly the same level?"' (Woods, 1997). In 1996 the Guild proposed a three-tier scheme for training with the lowest tier covering the skills relevant to an editorial assistant.

INFORMATION OVERLOAD AT THE PARISH PUMP

One of Britain's most successful regional journalists, Keith Parker, led the Wolverhampton *Express and Star* during its growth into England's highest-circulation evening paper. He achieved this by putting resources into report-ing, by producing papers with high story counts and with strongly local editions. Parker, who started in weekly papers in 1957, recognises many changes in local news coverage in the late 1990s: 'In the late 50s you covered everything that moved – every council meeting, every court case. You could argue that that was great for local democracy' (Parker, 1997). He argues that this would be impossible today – that public life has changed and grown rapidly: 'There are so many courts that no newspaper on earth could possibly cover them all. There has also been growth in the number of public bodies. Newspapers have to be selective' (ibid.). This has made life more complex for the local journalist and has led to ethical problems: 'The amount of crime has soared. One of the great problems of any daily newspaper is how many do you cover and what do you cover. You have to be selective. This can be unfair on individuals and . . . a lot of serious crime goes unreported' (ibid.).

He acknowledged that three developments have accentuated the reduction in coverage of local public affairs – the rise of free newspapers, the fashion among editors for the tabloid values so scorned by Corbett, and a rise in secrecy and suppression in public bodies.

Like many industry commentators, Parker believes 'it's a tragedy for local democracy that newspapers have closed or gone free' since 'we all know free newspapers generally are aimed at advertising and have a small editorial staff. They're just not able to cover all the things that need to be covered in a local area'(ibid.) (see chapter 10).

Second, he believed the aping of the national tabloids was both a serious error and a disservice to the community, especially in the city evening papers which have introduced 'metro' editions: 'So-called large city newspapers have failed miserably simply in my view because they haven't followed their people out of the city centres. . . . The papers have rather arrogantly remained big city newspapers and have failed to follow the people out' (ibid.). He instanced massive circulation declines for newspapers at Man-chester and Birmingham as evidence of the error. He contrasted this with the steady increase in circulation of his paper, the *Express and Star*, which has concentrated on local editions for its area of local boroughs.

Third, Parker pointed to the unwillingness of many public bodies to be reported: 'There's a whole raft of these sort of bodies that do not even admit the press to any of their discussions.' Worse, this public evasiveness has been accentuated by the growth of public relations: 'A lot of local authorities are not permitting newspapers to go direct to the Director of Housing or the various heads of department. Everything must go through the press department so you get this sanitised version of what is happening. That's sad' (ibid.).

FROM PUBLIC INTEREST TO INTERESTING THE PUBLIC

Parker stressed a fourth major reason for the reduction in the coverage of local public affairs. There was, he said, a much greater need to interest readers which was driving local journalists to concentrate less on public life:

> Forty years ago, thirty years ago, papers covered a lot of local politics, and national politics, with columns and columns of discussion between local councillors. These days you find very little of that, unless there's a twist to it simply because it's a turn-off for readers, by and large. . . . Newspapers are tending to concentrate these days more on what they think their readership will be interested in rather than what they think their readers should be interested in.

> (Ibid.; see chapter 16)

Alison Hastings, the young editor of the Newcastle *Evening Chronicle*, is at least a journalistic generation away from Parker and has a very different approach, but she too stressed this need to interest the reader. She and her editor-in-chief, Neil Benson, have labelled their approach 'human interest with a hard edge'. It has involved training reporters to look for colour and to follow-up for reactions rather than be content with filing straight court or council reports. The newsroom in Newcastle begins with the premise: 'court and council are a turn-off' (Marks, 1997b). A new 'family desk' has been given a central role in the newsroom with a brief to cover health, education, family, consumer and employment stories.

It is quite clear – from both the newspaper veteran, Parker, and the new generation editor, Hastings – that the local journalist has undergone a fundamental shift in role away from faithful, unselective chronicler of local public life. Competition for attention from other, newer media has, in some respects, driven the local press away from the parish pump. As Benson says: 'There's a lot of media around and it's slack for a big newspaper like this to be turning out dire court and council stories' (ibid.).

And yet, a belief in the efficacy of the local is an enduring faith of journalists. Parker, whose faith has led to remarkable circulation success in the Black Country, puts it well. Readers' tastes have changed, he says, but he is in little doubt about what local newspapers can offer them that they still want: 'People generally want to feel part of a community; they want to have some allegiance' (Parker, 1997). He would argue that where local papers were successful – and in the mid-1990s there was some resurgence among week-lies – they were providing this. The Guild of Editors agrees: in a rapidly changing world there is one certainty 'that local news and pictures still sell newspapers – something that most weekly editors have known all along – and that even in the brave new electronic world of the Internet the parish pump connection remains exclusive to the provincial press' (Guild of Editors, 1996: 2). And it offers evidence for this faith: 'those evenings which had the best sales performance over the previous decade were ... those which had stuck to the basics of newsgathering and remained closely involved with their local communities' (ibid.).

Tunstall in his study of newspapers over a thirty-year period from the 1960s noted an increase in emphasis on local news in the 1990s. He reports 'a relentless pursuit of the local' which he terms 'super-local' (Tunstall, 1996: 70). He remarks on a change in the editors of evening newspapers that he interviewed: 'Every editor, interviewed in 1994, said that their concerns were now overwhelmingly local' (ibid.: 62). He notes an increasing divergence from national newspapers: ' 'Newspaper' has come to mean for most British adults either a super-local freesheet or a super-national London tabloid' (ibid.: 75). But he also notes a change in the pattern of ownership which may, in my view, impact on the future role of evening papers. Confidence in these has been dented: 'It is undoubtedly the decline in sales of evening papers which has spread alarm' (Guild of Editors, 1996: 2). The evening paper editors that Tunstall interviewed in the 1970s were part of monopolies which took in the city and its suburbs; those that Tunstall was interviewing in 1994 were part of regional monopolies that incorporated adjacent daily papers. Given the regional reorganisation of production by some of these groups the concept of the regional – rather than local – evening paper may not be far away. Corbett, of the NUJ, is wary of such a trend: 'The logical development is one paper covering several towns or cities editorialised for each of them. Effectively you may well get a regional paper with local bits' (Corbett, 1997).

LIFE IN THE OLD WATCH-DOG?

Local journalists have clearly reinterpreted their role as chroniclers of local life – but do they still operate as a fourth estate, a watchdog, that subjects local public life to scrutiny? Past studies have suggested that such a role may well have been exaggerated. Murphy characterised the local press in the 1970s as quiescent; Whitaker in the early 1980s debunked it for being the unquestioning mouthpiece of a very narrow range of establishment sources offering little access to oppositional views. Franklin and Murphy, while recognising that the larger evenings in particular were capable of interrogating institutions, depicted the local press as a reinforcer of the local establishment: 'The general disposition of the traditional local press, both weekly and evening, is towards news coverage which appears to uphold the local establishment and to celebrate the values of a stable, orderly and conflict-free local community' (Franklin and Murphy, 1991: 74).

An interesting recent piece of research by journalist Andrew Head throws light on this question. Head's study intended to find out how much investigative reporting is going on in the regional press. It involved a survey of thirty-five regional daily or evening papers, an analysis of the published work which they regarded as 'investigative' and a comparison of the content of six months of the *Northern Echo* in 1963, during the editorship of 'the most famous investigative editor' Harold Evans, with a similar period thirty years later. Head's study concludes that there is investigative reporting taking place but far less than is claimed. All thirty-five papers claimed to be active investigators but only 'a handful' met Head's criteria. Most had submitted 'straightforward news reports or feature articles' rather than genuine investigation. The regional fourth estate – that oft-vaunted 'watchdog' – was underperforming. Head comments:

> Asking journalists about investigative reporting is like asking the general public about sex. Muckraking has macho appeal and so answers inevitably veer toward the five-times a night variety. But ask reporters about the techniques and sources they use, and ask them for copies of their work, and a less virile picture emerges. While each of the 35 regional papers claimed to be doing investigative work, only a handful were truly performing.
>
> (Head, 1995)

Head's study, however, had little comfort for the notion of some golden era of investigative reporting in the 1960s: 'A search through six months of the Evans' paper failed to yield a single investigative article' (ibid.). By comparison, two major investigations were published during the corresponding period in 1993.

Interestingly, Head's study found a marked shift in journalistic attitude to the major figures in local public life between the 1960s and the 1990s:

> The 1963 *Echo* was filled with studiously covered meetings, court cases and official reports. Coroners, headmasters, businessmen and the police were given acres of newsprint to lecture and pontificate. And their views were treated with reverence – hardly a critical voice interrupted the smooth flow of information and propaganda from the establishment to the masses.
>
> (Ibid.)

Deference and reliance on the same sources, so trenchantly analysed by Hall in 1978 and vigorously debunked by Whitaker in 1984, were the order of the day.

However, Head's content analysis of its contemporary equivalent points to a change for the better: 'The *Northern Echo* 30 years later shines by comparison. Alternative voices cry out from every page and there are in-depth features and independent analyses of events every day' (ibid.). Reporting in one daily paper had become more questioning and analytical – and this was probably typical of a general change. He concludes: 'Local newspapers have traditionally been dull, parochial and establishment-led. Today, they are generally less so' (ibid.). Parker agrees and believes the modern young journalist is more likely to challenge authority:

> I cannot imagine when I was a reporter standing up in court and objecting to an order being placed forbidding a name and address (or something like this). I suppose I would have done it, but it has happened on this newspaper a dozen times over the last year or so where reporters have stood their ground and had a go at the bench in open court. I think that's great. It warms the cockles of your heart.
>
> (Ibid.)

MULTISKILLING: RE-SKILLING OR DE-SKILLING?

One of the major engines for change in the role of local journalists is the introduction of new computer technology. This is having three particular impacts on the role of the local journalist. First, it is changing the production process by eliminating certain tasks and merging others. Just as computers replaced the craft skills of printers in the late 1970s and 1980s they can likewise be used to automate some of the traditional skills of journalists. Within the print production process two particular functions are changing – those of subbing and page layout. Subeditors have traditionally checked copy, allocated it to a typeface and size, cast the story off to an appropriate length and then added a headline. Page layout editors have organised stories, headlines and pictures onto a page of their own design. New systems can now simplify this. The new systems can both automatically set body copy and 'design' pages. Pages can be set up as templates, with 'slots' for headlines, copy and pictures, which can be electronically pasted in. If the reporter writes to length, his copy will fit the available slot, with no need for subbing. The page-planner, whose page is planned by the machine eliminating time spent on design, can add the headlines. This can make the process cheaper by automating certain subediting functions, and it can be used to restructure newsrooms by largely eliminating subeditors. David Montgomery, chief executive of Mirror Group, has been quick to hail 'the death of the sub' (Morgan, 1997b). But does the new production necessarily deliver quality in terms of news values or design? Bernie Corbett, of the National Union of

Journalists and a subeditor with considerable experience on local, regional and national newspapers, is highly sceptical:

> The new technology is very user friendly and can produce very high quality results. The problem is that the newspaper companies are using this technology to replace people by machinery. A potentially high quality production system is producing low quality output because too small a number of people are given too many functions. Typically a reporter will write a story to go onto a standardised template page. I picked up an evening paper the other day and three of the pages had identical layouts. A page planner or subeditor could put such a page together very quickly but have they read the copy? Is there any prospect of them saying 'this story is not worth 400 words'? Of course not. The design is inflexible and they do not have time to adjust it to take account of the material. They are just required to do a very mechanical job of shoe-horning the copy into preordained spaces. This is the misapplication of technology to cut costs rather than maintain or improve standards.
>
> (Corbett, 1997)

The second way in which new technology is putting a gleam in the eye of cost-conscious finance controllers is through the opportunities that it offers for 'multiskilling'. As the technology which captures words, images and sounds converges on a digital format based on the personal computer, there is much advocacy of people combining jobs that previously were done by separate people. A good example is the way local reporters are already encouraged to carry automatic cameras. For those in control, this is only the beginning. The Guild of Editors has already asked: 'When will hand-held video cameras become standard equipment for reporters and photographers?' (Guild of Editors, 1996: 2). A central part of its proposals to reform training was to broaden the programme to prepare journalists to contribute to other media in recognition of 'the growing influence of broadcasting and global electronic communications on the traditional print media' (Guild of Editors, 1996: 8). There is some concern within the Guild that these moves mean 'a dilution of skills' (Marks, 1997a). Corbett agrees: 'There is undoubtedly an element of de-skilling in this. Traditional craft skills are being lost.' However, the potential capacity of digital broadcasting distribution systems, cable systems and the burgeoning Internet to offer local publishing is likely to increase this desire of the local press to exploit multiskilling (see chapters 4 and 11).

EXPLOITING THE ELECTRONIC DATABASE

Changes to the way pages are produced only account for part of the fiendish gleam in the eyes of newspaper executives like Mirror Group's David Montgomery, who proclaimed his 'vision' to the 1997 World Newspaper

Congress. Apart from the 'death of subeditors' and the multiskilling of journalists, Montgomery's reforms will eliminate 'a culture of waste and duplication' that he believes also embraces the gathering of newspaper content (Montgomery, 1997). In large media companies like the Mirror Group a story will only be reported once: it will then be relayed to different publications, be they the *News Letter*, Belfast, or *Birmingham Post* or even cable television. The reporter is no longer keeping an eye on the parish pump with his particular readers in mind, he is contributing to an electronic database and his digital contribution can be re-used and re-sold through different publishing arms of the new multimedia corporations. The Guild of Editors, believers in 'the parish pump connection', are also betting on this development: 'the electronic database which now rests at the heart of most modern newsrooms contains a mass of marketable information' (Guild of Editors, 1996: 2; see also chapter 11). Montgomery has announced the introduction of an 'Academy of Excellence to retrain and multiskill every journalist in our organisation' (ibid.). Not surprisingly, some journalists were sceptical that Montgomery's 'vision' would liberate them as he claimed; they suspected another round of cost-cutting. His plans for changes in the role of reporters have also met with some more serious and sustained critiques. Former Mirror editor, Roy Greenslade, responded in a lengthy article that Montgomery's vision was a profound misunderstanding of newspaper journalism which would undermine it if implemented. He warned: 'Every journalist should read the following words from . . . Montgomery . . . and despair' (Greenslade, 1997). The words to which he was referring were: 'An organisation like ours with many titles in its stable should cover a story only once, but use it many times in its different products' (Montgomery, 1997).

In his lengthy article, Greenslade explained that the act of reporting is crucially an act of interpretation for a particular newspaper's audience by the reporter, who is typically guided and urged along by a news editor with a specific kind of article in mind. The relationship with the particular newspaper and its readers is imperative: 'In a sense, the reporter is the newspaper. He or she must have the paper in mind when researching and writing, possessing an instinctive grasp of what is and what is not important' (Greenslade, 1997: 10).

That is why, he argues, newspapers send their own staff reporters to cover stories of particular importance to them rather than rely on news agencies. They aim to get extra information, different information, even 'the scoops that are the lifeblood of journalism. This is the reason we exist' (Greenslade, 1997). He illustrates his point with a lengthy comparison of the way two different newspapers covered the same story and argues the impossibility of one reporter supplying both stories. He dismisses Montgomery's plans and scornfully concludes: 'The best papers all have the largest reporting staffs' (Greenslade, 1997). Greenslade makes no reference to the fact that the national titles under Montgomery's control have all consistently lost circulation as he has cut back on staff, but many journalists would make that connection. In the new vertical 'Fleet Street' that is Canary Wharf there is a grim joke that Montgomery will be the first newspaper executive to bring out a national newspaper without journalists . . . and this usually brings the reply that it will also be the first without readers.

Montgomery's plan to recycle content would also cause alarm to Mike Jempson, whose Presswise organisation aims to help people who feel they have suffered an injustice at the hands of the press. Jempson comments:

> Generally the local media are better at handling their sources than the national media. We tend to receive complaints when the national publication has picked up on the local story. An example involving a surrogate mother illustrates the point. The local paper ran an authoritative story preserving the women's anonymity in line with her wishes; but a national paper picked up the story and identified the woman and caused a great deal of difficulty. We are concerned that stories generated by local journalists can go into the system and be recycled by people with far less direct contact with the sources.
>
> (Jempson, 1997)

CONCLUSION

This examination of the role of the local journalist began with an example of eccentricity – Ben Stoneham's bizarre pay offer to his journalists. It could have included far more examples that demonstrated the diversity of the local press. Many of these examples would have illustrated enduring journalistic values as well as quirky ones. In the weeks around the strange pay offer, *Press Gazette* reported a successful one-year newspaper campaign to establish intensive paediatric care facilities in a local hospital, a murder case report that was out on the street within twenty-five minutes of the verdict, and a paean of praise from a politician for an election special issue which took up almost all the news pages of a free newspaper in west London. Elsewhere journalists in Maidenhead walked out when a four-page special was cancelled at short notice. Challenges by local journalists to 'news blackouts' ran regularly. These reports and the daily commitment of many hard-working local journalists are a reminder of what is enduring in the local press. The members of the Guild of Editors have faith in this: 'According to editors the essentials of reporting . . . will remain unchanged into the next century' (Guild of Editors, 1995: 7).

This analysis, however, has found that significant changes are taking place in the role of the local print journalist. First, on most local newspapers fewer journalists are working harder and being far more selective in their coverage of local affairs than they were a generation ago. With a keen eye on the interest of their readers as well as their staffing, they are covering courts and councils far less. This could be leading to what Corbett called 'a deficit in democracy' as the newer local – radio and cable – fail to fill the gap. The 'sweatshop' journalists are aided in their need to fill space by the press releases of resource-rich organisations and by the notes of amateur correspondents. In response to these, the editorial assistant is emerging as a new role in the newsroom. Second, the local fourth estate is still in operation; the 'watchdog' is still barking. Few journalists actually investigate – twelve of forty-two evening papers had specialists in 1995 – but this may be no fewer, and could well be more than in the recent past. Encouragingly, the general tone and structure of news reporting is far more questioning, though less thorough, than it was thirty years ago. Establishment figures are still very prominent in editorial columns but they are treated with far less deference and, today, a wider range of voices gains access to the same columns. Third, the large corporations which established regional monopolies in the 1980s and 1990s, are introducing technology with which they intend to revolutionise the role of the local journalist. If they are successful some production jobs are likely to go in the electronic newsroom, and a new structure will emerge, without traditional subeditors. Reporters are likely to become multiskilled 'content gatherers' for their multimedia database. Organisations will work to exploit that database by publishing its contents in as many ways as they can across as many media as they can. As a consequence of regional monopolies, independent local evening papers may find themselves replaced by editionised regional papers. The faithful chronicler of the parish pump on evening papers, perhaps, is to become the compiler of an electronic database in a regional newsroom; but, if he does, he might well remember his readers' taste for the local, for allegiance and community, and he should remember their ability to detect and reject fake localism.

REFERENCES

Corbett, B. (1997) Interview, 4 July.
Franklin, B. and Murphy, D. (1991) *What News? The Market, Politics and the Local Press*, London: Routledge.
Gallagher, J. (1997) Interview, 9 June.
Greenslade, R. (1997) 'Hack of All Trades', *Guardian*, 23 June, pp. 10–11.
Guild of Editors (1995) *Survey of Editorial Training Needs*, London: Guild of Editors.
—— (1996) *Tomorrow's Journalists – A Green Paper on Editorial Training*, London: Guild of Editors.
Hall, S., Critcher, C., Jefferson, T. and Roberts, B. (1978) *Policing the Crisis*, London: Macmillan.
Head, A. (1995) 'Investigating the Investigators', *Press Gazette*, 3 April, pp. 18–19.
Jempson, M. (1997) Interview, 12 June.
Kleinsteuber, H. (1992) 'The Global Village Stays Local' in Siune, K. and Truetzchler, W. (eds) *Dynamics of Media Politics: Broadcast and Electronic Media in Western Europe*, London: Sage.

Marks, N. (1997a) 'Support for Industry Wide Qualification for Journalists', *Press Gazette*, 2 May, p. 14.
—— (1997b) 'Inside Evening Chronicle, Newscastle', *Press Gazette*, 9 May, p. 14.
Montgomery, D. (1997) 'My Mission: The Full Monty', *Press Gazette*, 13 June, p. 14.
Morgan, J. (1997a) 'Staff Petition for Shorter Hours', *Press Gazette*, 23 May, p. 7.
—— (1997b) 'Monty Plans Journalistic Elite', *Press Gazette*, 6 June, p. 1.
Murphy, D. (1976) *The Silent Watchdog: The Press in Local Politics*, London: Constable.
Parker, K. (1997) Interview, 18 June.
Tunstall, J. (1996) *Newspaper Power – The New National Press in Britain*, Oxford: Clarendon.
Whitaker, B. (1984) *News Limited: Why You Can't Read All About It*, London: Comedia.
Woods, M. (1997) Interview, 13 June.

Chapter 15

The business of freelance journalism: some advice from an old hand

Peta Van den Bergh

A freelance according to the *Oxford Dictionary* is a person working for no fixed employer. It is still the best description around of what the life of a freelance is like. A freelance must be someone capable of doing many different things for different people from which if they are lucky they will be able to eak out a living. It's a life of hard work, often for little reward and without any security.

Journalists become freelances for a number of reasons. In the past it was often by choice as staff bored with life on the same paper opted for what they thought would be more lucrative and exciting work. But nowadays it's far more likely to be because there is no other choice available. The reasons for becoming a freelance have changed as has the way in which the industry organises its workforce. Changes in employment law, the advent of cross-media and new technology plus restructuring of many famous and well-established newspaper groups mean less staff jobs and freelance opportunities are becoming available. Redundancies and the advent of 'short-term contracts' have turned staffers into freelances; as a result there are more freelances than ever before working in the industry and it's a trend that is on the increase (see chapter 1).

True there may still be journalists who seeing no chance of promotion or change will opt to freelance, and those who hope by making an impact as a freelance to pick up a staff job on a leading national or regional paper. But the chances are that those coming in to the freelance world will be journalists newly trained, just out of college who faced by a dearth in available jobs have no other choice than to try and build up experience by becoming one.

Over the last ten years the shape of the media has changed irrevocably. Large chains of provincial papers, previously the main provider of work for freelances, have been broken up or sold. Local radio stations, expected to generate new jobs and work for freelances, have pulled back, cutting down on costs by relying on central news gathering or deals with local papers for their news. Commercial television companies operating as publishing houses employ less staff and commission independents to produce programmes. They have followed the BBC example of dumping factual programmes for entertainment. There is, moreover, less news space available as tabloid and television wars lead to increases in advertising, lottery and bingo. There is now less work than ever before available for staff and freelances.

THE FREELANCE LIFE: GETTING ORGANISED

To survive as a freelance, a journalist must be so good that people want to use them rather than someone else. The 'perfect freelance' is a 'jack of all trades', someone who can report and sub, at the same time as being able to work for newspapers, magazines, TV and radio. They will also be able to do PR. On top of that they will also have some specialisation that will make commissioning editors rely on them for material.

Most media courses give their graduates a grounding in basic skills looking towards giving them a chance of working in all sections of the media. Unfortunately, being taught how to film with a video camera at the same time as being able to interview means that the quality of journalism is suffering along with the skills that the freelance can offer.

Most freelances find that much of the day-to-day work such as building up contacts, chasing up stories and finding work can only come with experience. New freelances find themselves caught up in a familiar Catch 22 situation, that it's only by experience that you will build up your contacts, the first prequisite that every freelance needs either in terms of getting stories or for getting work, and you cannot get the work unless you have the experience.

In the past freelances could buy a typewriter or camera and expect to be able to provide a service. The days of a freelance standing around, note book in hand, cigarette in mouth, listening to conversations, ready to leap off to a phone to beat everyone to the story are long gone. Nowadays a freelance is expected to buy and maintain vital equipment such as computers, faxes and digital cameras. It takes a lot of money for a journalist to become established in business, and freelancing even if it is for the local newspaper is a business. Access to direct input and super information highways linking providers and users may open up new avenues but unfortunately it's the freelance and not the management who pays for changes in working practices and keeping up to date with new systems. The freelance has to keep on top, if not ahead, of what is happening in new technology as well as what is going on in the market place. And that is on top of paying for somewhere to work.

Not only do freelances have to spend a lot of money to establish themselves but unlike staff journalists they also have to be 'businessmen' acting as their own agents, bookkeepers, offices managers, debt collectors and lawyers, and now self-assessors of their tax.

A freelance has to deal with taxation, copyright, insurance, invoicing, chase up late payers, pay their own bills, fund their own pensions, and insurance schemes in case they are ill and cannot work, negotiate rates, organise travel, keep up to date and pay for new equipment and possibly for the training to be able to use it. The freelance also has to know what is going on in the market place, keeping in contact with commissioning editors. All this at the same time as working to earn a living. And without any of the resources or security that staff journalists have, no instant access to cuttings libraries or background information nor any form of income when they take a holiday. They will also have to face competition from other freelances some of whom will work for agencies.

A freelance has to overcome many prejudices. Many rightly complain that they receive cursory treatment and little financial reward from some editors and staffers who, in turn, point out that as a freelance works for more than one employer they cannot expect to be treated with the same consideration as staff.

These attitudes might seem simplistic but they lie at the very heart of how the profession views its freelances. Those freelances who may very well have started out as a staffer on a local paper, or those hoping to impress an editor and land a staff job, will work hard at building up good relationships with local staffs who in turn will respect them and to a certain extent encourage them, realising that it is more important to keep freelances in line with what the staff is doing than allowing them to be used by managements to undercut them.

Others look on freelances with a certain amount of suspicion and often 'contempt' as being 'shady characters' working on the periphery of journalism or as being 'lump labourers' shirking their responsibilities towards paying tax and, by getting paid less, posing a threat to staffing levels. Neither of the latter is of course true: 'shady characters' would never be trustworthy enough to get work and all freelances doing shifts get taxed at source. Unfortunately it's often management and staff, the latter regardless of the security of receiving a monthly pay cheque, who show little responsibility towards freelances, refusing to give them or back them in getting many of the same benefits awarded to staff whom they may often have worked alongside for many years.

A freelance's working life, by its very nature, has to be fairly flexible. It's very important to set up a strong, disciplined method of everyday working to give some form of stability. Planning how to work is one of the most important aspects of a freelance's life. Unlike a member of staff whose work pattern is to some extent mapped out by the employer, as a freelance you have to use a terrific amount of self discipline in planning how to carry out your work without wasting time. Most freelances work at home; although they have none of the problems of having to travel into work they do need to set up a rigid pattern to give a definitive line between working and 'being at home'.

The first thing a freelance should do is to step back from their work and plan it as an employer would do for a member of their staff. Map out a weekly or monthly chart, breaking down the hours in a day; using a basic daily plan set up a regime in which a certain period of time is allotted to what needs to be done. Work out how long each project is going to take, including the time that should be spent on the mundane work of running a freelance office, such as doing paperwork and invoices.

Set out the same starting time every day and keep to it; if working for more than one outlet mark down the deadlines and dates when the work is expected in. Write down any shifts, meetings or interviews that have to be covered, estimating how long they are going to take and how much time is going to have to be spent on travelling to and from them.

Once you know what your out-of-'office' commitments are going to be, you can then plan your creative day, and work out how much time you are going to spend on each project. You can also plan your work knowing for example that there is usually a specific time every day when, because of meetings or deadlines, it's impossible to get hold of people; that time can be spent on catching up on office or paper work.

Keep a 'day book' in which to make a note of meetings and what went on. It will help to record how well you are keeping to plans and for checking the accuracy of your estimates of how long you need to devote to your various tasks, and whether any amendments need to be made. It will not only help to assess how cost effective you are being in carrying out your work but will also help to calculate your fee. A detailed work chart has the additional bonus of enabling you to plan how to move work around if a sudden 'rush' job comes in. More importantly it acts as a useful reminder of how you might have got on with some people and can always be a useful refresher if you run in to disagreement on what might have been said or agreed upon.

RELATIONS WITH THE LOCAL NEWSPAPER

Many freelances start work in the same way as staff journalists by working for local papers. If you do decide to become a freelance sit down and analyse what you are good at and what you have got to offer that will make commissioning editors want to employ you as opposed to someone else.

Before even attempting to sell a story you must make sure it's the sort of copy that the paper would want to take. Buy copies of the paper so that you know what it is like and then ring the news or features editor and arrange an appointment to meet them to talk about the sort of things they would be interested in and what you might have to offer. Work out very carefully which is the right market for your material. You do not want to waste time or expense in sending it to people who are not going to use it and, more importantly, antagonising them. Find out when an editor is available for a chat; you do not want to contact them when they are busy and finding it difficult to concentrate on talking to you. Most commissioning editors, on local, regional and national papers will always find time to see the 'new' freelance, there's always the chance that the journalist might produce the 'big scoop' or turn out to be someone they might want to use.

Take in a portfolio of your work. If you have not had anything published take in copies of work that you might have done for your college or university. The commissioning editor wants to know if you are sufficiently 'on the ball' to find and produce the sort of stories which might interest the paper. The chances are that they will want to see what work you can do before actually commissioning or sending you out on a job. They will want to know if you have got good contacts, which if you work on a local paper is the most important way of getting hold of a story, and whether you can actually find something new and original for them. Having met the commissioning editor it is then up to you to produce the stories for them.

Unless a freelance is of such quality that he or she can demand and get the fee or contract that they want, they have to rely on the goodwill of the commissioning editor and the staff if they are going to get the proper rate for the work they have done. If you are worried about what you should charge, have a word with a member of staff and check whether they have an agreement which covers fees; they should have a good idea of what the usual payment should be. The house agreement should also cover what sort of expenses and insurance coverage a freelance might expect to get.

The rate for the job

Most local papers pay on a lineage basis, that means the freelance gets paid for the number of lines published. Under this scheme a line usually runs to four words in length. Advised minimum rates for weekly papers are £1.70 for up to and including ten lines with 17p for each additional line; daily, evening and Sunday regional and provincial papers pay £2.90 for up to and including ten lines and 29p for each additional line. These rates also apply to diary items and sports coverage. Feature payments on weekly papers run to £1.85 for up to and including ten lines; 19p for each additional line. Daily, evening and Sunday newspapers pay £3.24 for up to and including ten lines and 32p for each additional line.

The rates paid to photographers by local papers vary widely with weekly and free newspapers paying £14.50 for up to ten square inches and £17 for ten to fifty square inches; daily, evening and Sunday provincial and regional papers paying £20.50 for up to ten square inches and £26.50 for ten to fifty square inches.[1]

Unfortunately no freelance is ever going to make a living working solely for local papers as the rates are very low. Some freelances having spent a whole day covering a court receive only a few pounds, for a few lines, which might be all that they could get out of it or that the paper has decided to publish. It might be all they will get for the story as there are fewer places to sell it. Most follow the example set by some photographers in charging for a half day or day rate for covering a story exclusively. Some freelances insist on a minimum of about £25 for an ordered news story and to cover court cases. Papers will pay extra for leads, £45 for a page lead and £15 for a tip. They may also agree to on/off fees of around £35 for 300 words. A day rate is usually based on the staff agreement or the figure of £90.00. When it comes to doing a feature try and work out a fee which takes into consideration how much time might have been spent on research and background work; sometimes it's worth asking for a day rate as that is far more likely to reflect a fairer fee than that paid for lineage or wordage.

Getting commissioned

Editors will not commission anyone in advance unless they know the particular freelance's work or have been given a detailed description of what the story is about. They do not want to commission someone and then find out that the copy is unusable. They might suggest that the freelance should do the piece and send it in so they can decide whether or not they and use it.

Plan what shape the idea should take; remember that any editor's time is precious. Do your research thoroughly. If you haven't structured and thought through, to a reasonable extent, how you would proceed with the project you can hardly blame the editor for feeling that he or she would rather see what you would come up with than commit themselves there and then.

If you are contacting an editor for the first time send them a one-page synopsis with a working title; this shows you have given some thought to the direction in which you think the article or story should go. If you are worried about someone pinching your idea, something that does unfortunately happen, do not include your list of contacts. Send the editor some of your cuttings to provide him or her with more information upon which to decide whether or not to commission. If you do not have any cuttings an editor may ask you to submit the whole work before deciding whether to use it. Send it off giving them about a week to think about it and then give them a call. Remain persistent and polite. If they do decide to use it, they should write confirming acceptance and stating the fees to be paid, any arrangements about expenses and, in the case of written material, the length purchased. Any verbal agreement must be confirmed in writing.

It is important to speak to the editor beforehand to let him or her know that you are sending the material. Most newspapers and magazines are wary of being inundated with unwanted material and have a policy of refusing to accept unsolicited work. Give them a date by which they must let you know if they are going to use the material and put it in writing. You will be within your rights to charge them if they hold on to it beyond that date; this particularly applies to any material that has a news aspect to it.

Contracting in

A contract in law is entered into the moment that a commission has been given and accepted. It is normal practice to agree terms confirming them in writing before doing the work. Because of time pressures this is often difficult in various areas of the media, particularly in local papers where commissions are often given over the phone. If an editor does give such a commission, write a letter back confirming the agreement; unless they write back refuting the terms they are deemed as having accepted it. Make sure you always get the name of the person you have spoken to and who has commissioned you. It's not unheard of for a news desk assistant or secretary to get carried away with enthusiasm and commission work they had no right to commission.

Always ask for a by-line. This is particularly important for the young freelance as it is the only way that they can show what they have done to new editors from whom they want to get work. By-lines are every freelance's showcase. Most managements are fairly sympathetic although there are a few papers who, wanting to give an image of being 'staff only' papers, have a deliberate policy of not giving any by-lines to freelances. You can take action against a paper if another journalist's name appears on your work.

The contractual terms should include the minimum rate to be paid; a minimum length for written material; arrangements for expenses; an adequate specification of material to be published; a date by when payment should be made; and the deadline by which time the material should be delivered. A verbal agreement is also valid under law, but if there is a dispute it often comes down to the court having to decide whose case is valid; that is when your day book record of what was said will come in useful. If a commission has been cancelled before the work has been done, a cancellation or 'kill' fee of at least 50 per cent should be paid. Once work has been submitted it must be paid in full, whether it has been published or not. The commissioning paper or magazine is legally bound to fulfil its side of the contract once the freelance has delivered the material as specified.

Payment should be made within one month of the delivery of the material. Some editors pay on publication. It is important to stipulate in any letter or contract a date which relates to when the material is to be delivered, as that can be some weeks and even months before publication; if that happens freelances should negotiate either full payment or a percentage up front. Most freelances come to an arrangement with their local paper that instead of having to invoice for payment they will get paid under a self-billing arrangement. This means that the commissioning editor keeps a record of what you have supplied and automatically arranges payment. Some papers will not pay unless the story has got an ordered number. If an editor delays in paying, a freelance should look to charging an 'interest' premium and should add such a clause to any letter of confirmation that they send.

Expenses

If a commissioning editor agrees a fee that also covers expenses, the free-lance should carefully take into consideration what they expect to have to spend. Remember that fees will be taxed which means that expenses which normally would be exempted might get taxed as well. Keep all copies of receipts to prove how much has been spent on items such as travel. Expenses should normally be agreed in advance, as having done the work you do not want to put your expenses in to find out that they are not prepared to pay them or that they will only pay for certain items. They should be paid on the same basis as to staff, covering full subsistence, travel costs – including mileage as assessed by the AA – phone calls and entertainment. Most local papers have agreements with staff which will normally contain a paragraph giving details of what they will pay for expenses.

If a paper or magazine specifically rings up asking you to carry out an assignment on its behalf which means incurring extra costs, then you are perfectly within your rights to ask for payment for those expenses. The same applies if you have to do a project which requires doing specific research for which you might have to buy various documents. Some expenses should be paid in advance if you are carrying out an assignment which might entail you having to bear heavy costs.

When it comes to incurring debts that are outside the usually accepted format, you must check in advance whether the paper would be prepared to pay for them. You cannot expect a paper to pay for something that it has not calculated as being part of the 'contract'. On the same basis a paper cannot expect you to provide a service such as producing background material or even a 'tip off' without being reimbursed.

If you do decide that you are going to specialise the chances are that you will already be known to magazines or papers covering that area; if not, then you will have to market yourself in the same way as if you were newly into journalism. But with the additional bonus of being able to offer a special skill or knowledge that others might not have.

A freelance who wishes to specialise should join an association or organ-isation that looks after that area. Most groups such as travel writers and sports writers have their own associations. It's a good way of making con-tacts as editors will often be members; they organise trips, help make contacts and generally keep members up to date with what is going on. They will also be able to guide you on what are the going rates for work covering that particular area.

Copyright and moral rights

Freelances legally retain the rights on all their work, both copyright and moral rights. Copyright is the ownership of work both commissioned and non-commissioned. Copyright is automatic and can provide you with an income from the work for the rest of your life (and for your estate for seventy years after death). You only lose rights by signing or selling them away; freelances are strongly advised against doing so. An editor buys first right only. They must get your permission or pay an additional fee if they want to syndicate or use the material again. You may agree to license them the work.

Some local papers will run different editions and have slip sheets in some of the other papers in the same group. They may, and often do, argue wrongly that as they commissioned you or that as you are selling copy or pictures shared with other papers to whom you supply, one payment covers all use. Many papers try to insist on buying all rights or asking freelances to 'assign' rights on the grounds that they need to buy all rights to material because of the advent of electronic media. Again only agree to license the use of material and with it extra payments on the specific requirement that it can only be used in specific ways. Freelances can take legal action against anyone who goes ahead and uses their work without permission and without payments under the Copyrights, Designs and Patents Act 1988.

Ownership of copyright can also have an influence on a freelance's tax status. Courts will interpret ownership of copyright to mean that you are self-employed as a staff member's work is owned by their employer. Always add a clause at the end of your work stating that copyright belongs to you, inserting the date.

Moral rights are the 'rights' of a journalist to be given a by-line or credit for their work. It also safeguards them from having their work altered in a way that might be derogatory and which could damage the freelance's reputation. Although moral rights do not apply at the moment to newspapers and magazines they do in broadcasting and electronic publishing, an area which some local papers are now entering. Unlike copyright which automatically belongs to you, moral rights are only retained by asserting them in writing.

Taxing matters

As a self-employed person a freelance works under contracts for services, and is on Schedule D for tax purposes. Freelances are responsible for paying their own tax and National Insurance; companies should not tax freelances at sources. Freelances are allowed a range of expenses to be offset against earnings before their tax bill is calculated; these take in to consideration allowances that staff would not receive such as operating an office.

Although freelances are not supposed to be taxed for working shifts, many employers and in particular newspapers have bowed to pressure from the Inland Revenue and tax them under Schedule E or PAYE. This means that the freelance is treated as being a member of staff with tax being deducted from their freelance fee as well as a week's National Insurance contribution at the employee rate (class 1) for each shift worked.

In the past taxation at source mainly applied to freelances working as subeditors in house on shift but over the last few years the Inland Revenue has been attempting to re-apply this to cover anyone working in house, or out of an office, under direction from an editor. Despite freelances arguing that they receive none of the benefits that staff receive such as holiday payments, pensions or sick pay the Inland Revenue refuses to accept that a 'daily' or 'hourly' payment' means that there is any difference between the form of services offered by a freelance and that offered by a member of staff. As a result a series of test cases have been taken against the Inland Revenue to try and define how working conditions and practices affect the definition of what a freelance might be.

If you do find yourself being taxed at source, you are perfectly entitled to ask for a contract of employment. Unfortunately, unlike staff, freelances cannot receive any unemployment benefits if a 'shift' or contract is terminated.

Most freelances do not need an accountant when it comes to keeping a simple record of accounts. Most of the basic work can be done by yourself but an accountant can give you credibility when presenting your new self-assessment forms to the Inland Revenue. Recent changes to the tax system mean that in future freelances have to pay tax in any year on the income they expect (which is difficult for new freelances to calculate) to make that year. The payment for the following year will be adjusted to take in an over-estimate or shortfall that may have occurred the previous year.

Freelances tend to run into financial problems because they leave their tax problems to the last; earning a living takes over from finding time to deal with checking accounts and producing tax returns. Unfortunately you do not get paid for the hours you might spend working out your figures.

AND FINALLY ...

There can never be any security as a freelance, however well established you might think you are. Your work as a freelance with any outlet, however prestigious, can be terminated at any time by management. You may feel that you have a 'special relationship' with a commissioning editor, and you might have worked for years with a particular paper, magazine or broad-casting station but when it comes to cut-backs in budgets or a change in policy you can be dismissed, sometimes without any notice period or compensation.

Being a freelance isn't easy. It's hard work, the rewards are often little and the problems when they arise often seem large and impossible to solve. But as long as you keep to the basic rules about organising your work you should avoid some of the pitfalls. Here's an advisory checklist.

1 Plan your work carefully.
2 Make sure that you clearly understand what each commission or contract entails.
3 Record the names and positions of people that you deal with – particularly those responsible for payment.
4 Confirm fees and conditions in writing.
5 Follow up where necessary to confirm that material has arrived and is acceptable.
6 Send in an invoice as soon as possible – or confirm that an effective self-billing arrangement operates.
7 Check that payment arrives as promised. If not, start telephoning to find out where it is.
8 Keep records so that you can see who owes you money.

Two final words: Good luck.

NOTES

1 *NUJ Freelance Fees Guide 1997–98*, London: NUJ.

Part V

Read all about it: editorial content in the local press

Chapter 16

Old habits die hard: journalism's changing professional commitments and local newspaper reporting of the 1997 general election

Bob Franklin and Jon Parry

On 21 March 1997 the editor of the *Rotherham Advertiser* declared the newspaper an 'Election Free Zone' for the duration of the campaign. 'With six weeks to go before polling day', he claimed, 'our readers are fed up to the back teeth with electioneering, spin doctors, point scoring and soundbites.' The editor offered a philistine promise that they could 'pick up their *Advertiser* every week ... secure in the knowledge that the pages of their favourite paper will be free from pontificating politicians' (*Rotherham Advertiser*, 21 March 1997, p. 1). By contrast, the editor and eight senior staff at the *Maidenhead Advertiser* resigned, following a management refusal to publish a special supplement planned for the morning after the election. The journalists believed the paper 'had a fundamental duty to its readers to provide the general election results and analysis as a service'; the Board's counter claim was that 'the general election wasn't important enough to justify bringing the supplement out' (Notorantonio, 1997: 1).

These two incidents illustrate the diversity of newspapers' responses to election reporting. They also highlight the growing tension between the market-driven editorial decisions of newspaper managements and journalists' professional commitments to report the election. Old habits die hard even though many journalists concede their readers' lack of interest. Consequently local newspaper coverage of the 1997 election was considerable. But audiences' indifference to electoral news was not confined to local media. During the election 'the newspaper market fell like a stone' (Greenslade, 1997: 9) and ITN and BBC news programmes lost between 16 per cent and 40 per cent of their typical audience share (Methven, 1997: 1).

This chapter examines the coverage of the 1997 general election in twenty-five local newspapers in the West Yorkshire region and draws comparisons with reporting during the 1987 and 1992 elections.[1] The chapter presents a profile of local press election coverage in 1997 which reveals a sharp decline in the number of newspaper reports. Journalists' accounts of the reasons for this decline are examined, but the chapter begins by looking back to the 1987 and 1992 studies to provide some context for the current investigation.

REVISITING OLD HABITS: LOCAL PARTIES, LOCAL JOURNALISM AND THE 1987 AND 1992 GENERAL ELECTIONS

By the late 1980s, academics, journalists, the general public and pundits of every kind seemed increasingly convinced of the significant contribution of media to the electoral fortunes of political parties during general elections. The term 'spin doctor' was beginning to enter the public vocabulary as the 'packaging of politics' became increasingly evident (Franklin, 1994). But little academic or public attention was paid to *local* parties' campaigning and communications strategies in the constituency setting, or to the ways in which *local* media reported these contests. The conventional wisdom was that these local spats were of no substantive consequence for the overall electoral outcome (Butler and Kavanagh 1981: 292).

In 1987, a study of local political communications in ten constituencies (Batley and Spen, Bradford North, Bradford South, Colne Valley, Halifax, Leeds East, Leeds North, Leeds West, Pudsey and Wakefield) challenged this 'wisdom' by posing a number of broad research questions. First, to what extent and with what success were local parties trying to influence local newspapers' coverage of the campaign? Second, how did local journalists respond to these news management initiatives by local parties? Finally, what was local newspapers' campaign coverage like?

Interviews with party election agents, local journalists and newspaper editors during the month after the campaign, in tandem with an analysis of all election related items (editorials, articles and readers' letters) published in the local newspapers circulating in these constituencies during the campaign, provided both quantitative and qualitative answers to these questions (Franklin and Murphy, 1991: 154–90; Franklin, 1989 and 1992). Similar studies were conducted in 1992 and 1997 allowing comparative assessments across three elections.

The intervening decade has witnessed substantive changes in both local media and politics. The number of newspapers has changed radically as a consequence of closures and the launch of new titles; the twenty-one papers in the 1987 study mushroomed to thirty-one in 1992 but had reduced to twenty-five by 1997. Significantly, half the newspapers in 1987 were independently owned by small local companies, whereas by 1997 *all* newspapers had been incorporated into large conglomerates; the circulation of the paid-for weekly and daily newspapers declined dramatically by an average 3 per cent per annum between 1992 and 1997. Political change has also been apparent. In 1987, the ten constituencies were represented by four Conservative, four Labour and two Liberal MPs; the need for political balance was an important criterion informing the selection of constituencies. After the 1997 election, all constituencies had elected a Labour MP.

Party influence?

In 1987, both the Conservative and Labour parties were conscious of local newspapers' campaigning potential, but the Labour Party was by far the greatest enthusiast. Conservative agents remained wedded to the more traditional 'face-to-face' campaigning techniques of public meetings, 'knocking on doors', canvassing and distributing leaflets and posters (Franklin, 1989). By 1992, there had been a decisive shift in local campaigning strategies. Each of the major parties employed a press officer and a systematic media strategy which in some constituencies involved the conduct of detailed market research to identify key local issues of concern to voters for use in subsequent election publicity. Parties targeted the local press. Party press officers held press conferences, issued press releases and placed adverts in the local press (Franklin, 1994: 267). By 1992, local parties were convinced that local newspapers were much more effective in conveying their political messages than public meetings in draughty village halls. Parties also came to understand that local newspapers' extensive penetration of local communities gave them propaganda advantages over the national press. After the 1992 election a regional press officer for the Conservative Party claimed:

> The *Batley News* frankly is more important in Batley and Spen than *The Times*, the *Financial Times* or, dare I say it, the *Telegraph* or even the mass tabloid papers like the *Mirror*. That paper will be lying around for a week, people will be constantly picking it up and reading it and there is this belief that the local paper must be right. The *Mail* and the *Express*, of course, are not actually writing about the local MP. But the *Batley News*, which she has been nurturing for the last five years, will be writing about her . . . It's obvious to me that these local papers have much more influence than the national papers.[2]

Newspapers' influence on readers' attitudes is hotly contested, but the 1992 study certainly provided evidence of local parties' potential for news management. In one constituency a comparison of Labour Party press releases with election coverage in the local newspaper, revealed that twenty-nine press releases triggered twenty-eight stories in the paper. The newspaper published at least one story derived from party sources on each day of the campaign, while on three days *all* of the paper's coverage of the Labour Party emanated from party sources. One-third (31 per cent) of published articles simply replicated the party release verbatim, while a further one-fifth (18 per cent) of articles made little editorial revision to the press release and published between 50 per cent and 75 per cent of the original text without modification (Franklin, 1994: 169).

Journalists' responses?

In interviews following the 1992 election, journalists acknowledged the changed and more pressured circumstances in which their election reporting had to be conducted; they also spoke of the difficulties in reconciling parties' demands for coverage with the professional requirement for journalists to be impartial and balanced in their election coverage. Some journalists conceded their independence and became openly partisan. The *Yorkshire Post*'s support for the Conservative Party was obvious throughout the campaign and culminated in a celebratory editorial headlined 'How Sweet is Victory: Congratulations to John Major' (*Yorkshire Post*, 11 April 1992). Other journalists developed a range of strategies to ensure balanced coverage. Some equated 'balance' rather simplistically with the provision of equal space to politicians from different parties; trainee journalists were duly assigned to measure column inches. Yet further journalists believed that balance was best achieved by offering the various party politicians open access to the newspaper, without the mediation of journalists, so that the paper became a conduit or 'megaphone' for politicians' agendas. One local journalist argued that 'papers have a responsibility to allow MPs and would-be MPs to speak to the electorate directly' (Franklin, 1992: 17).

Local press coverage?

Local press coverage of the general election is typically extensive. In 1987 the twenty-one local papers in the study reported 1,194 items (921 articles, 35 editorials and 238 readers' letters) of election coverage. 1992 witnessed an expansion in coverage with thirty-one newspapers reporting 2,061 items (1,544 articles, 42 editorials and 475 readers' letters) of election news, although the news priority given to election reports varied considerably across different newspapers. The daily papers were the most, the free weekly papers the least, likely to carry election reports.

Coverage was characterised by a 'balance of partisanship'. While there was an overall political balance in local press coverage across the region, this did not reflect any simple aggregation of the balance evident in a number of individual newspapers. Rather it was a balance achieved by the partisan sentiments articulated by one newspaper being offset by the differing political opinions of another. In this balance of partisanship, a range of strident political opinions were expressed in a number of papers.

But local newspapers' reporting of the general election in 1987 and 1992 was impressive and might be judged superior to the coverage in the sister national papers. Reports were extensive, serious and a good deal less partisan than national press coverage. Local newspapers explored an expansive local agenda which identified and reported issues of relevance to their readers and their community. Coverage offered detailed information about policies, politicians and parties. Most significantly, by publishing large numbers of readers' letters, the local press offered a voice to a wide range of people and opinions which the national press could not match. Local papers provided a genuine forum for debate – a truly local public sphere (notwithstanding parties' attempts to hi-jack the letters' page).

INDULGING THE HABIT: LOCAL NEWSPAPERS' COVERAGE OF THE 1997 GENERAL ELECTION

Local newspaper coverage of the 1997 general election was impressive both for its quantity and range of editorial concerns. The twenty-five papers in the 1997 study published 1,248 election-related items (858 (68.8 per cent) articles, 86 (6.9 per cent) editorials and 304 (24.4 per cent) readers' letters) and filled 32,617 square inches of their columns with election news. This coverage was substantially down on 1992 (2,061 items – 45,212 square inches) but slightly higher than election reports in 1987 (1,194 items). While the story count was down in 1997, however, the word count increased; election reports averaged 26.2 square inches in 1997 compared to 21.9 in 1992.

As in previous elections, coverage in 1997 was given a higher news priority in the daily regional and evening papers than the paid-for weekly papers, with reports in the free papers being remarkable largely for their absence (see table 16.1).

Free newspapers' coverage of the 1997 election displayed the same indifference that had characterised reporting in 1987 and 1992; ten free newspapers published only seventy-three items (54 articles, 3 editorials and 16 letters) across the entire campaign. But these data understate the editorial neglect of the election because free press coverage was largely focused in four papers: the *Aire Valley Target*, the *Bradford Star*, the *Leeds Skyrack Express* and the *Wharfe Valley Times* published fifty-six items representing 77 per cent of free press coverage. Consequently, reporting in some free papers was effectively non-existent. The *East Leeds Weekly News*, the *West Leeds Weekly News* and the *North Leeds Weekly News*, with an aggregate circulation of almost 570,000, each published only a single election-related story across the campaign; such editorial neglect risks making the *Calder News'* three items look like overkill!

Free newspapers' unwillingness to publish election news is particularly curious given the findings of a number of studies which suggest that their lack of financial and editorial resources make them particularly receptive to news releases and eager to publish them (Franklin, 1986). At election times, parties' copious press statements would seem to offer free newspapers cheap and ready copy. But this ignores the complexities of news gathering and reporting in the election setting. A local news editor explained:

The problem is you have to make the election a popular story. You have to

Table 16.1 Number of items covering the 1997 general election

Newspaper type	Circulation	Article	Editorial	Letter	Total
Weekly free					
Aire Valley Target	33,280	8	2	4	14
Bradford Star	110,000	10	1	2	13
Weekly Advertiser	56,510	2	–	1	3
East Leeds Weekly	187,500	1	–	–	1
Huddersfield Weekly News	70,000	4	–	2	6
Leeds Skyrack Express	52,415	5	–	2	7
North Leeds Weekly	187,500	1	–	–	1
Weekend Times	37,879	3	–	2	5
West Leeds Weekly	187,500	1	–	–	1
Wharfe Valley Times	45,000	19	–	3	22
Weekly paid-for					
Batley News	9,156	46	5	8	59
Brighouse Echo	6,209	26	2	4	32
Colne Valley Chronicle*	–	6	8	2	16
Dewsbury Reporter	13,508	25	3	9	37
Hebden Bridge Times	3,738	19	–	3	22
Heckmondwike Herald	8,469	55	1	13	69
Holme Valley Express*	–	10	5	4	19
Huddersfield District Chronicle	–	8	1	3	12
Mirfield Reporter	13,470	27	3	7	37
Morley Advertiser	3,538	15	–	5	20
Morley Observer	4,146	20	3	9	32
Spenborough Guardian	8,201	55	1	13	69
Todmorden News	5,129	17	–	3	20
Daily evening					
Halifax Courier	31,937	167	25	164	356
Daily regional					
Yorkshire Post	77,537	308	26	41	375
Total		**858**	**86**	**304**	**1,248**

* Circulation figures not offered

have professional journalists and it takes resources to get it right. It's so easy to be a mouth piece for the political parties, but that would just be boring. The only way to handle the election is to put some editorial resources into it. But free newspapers are looking for easy copy. Easy copy of the election would be boring without the time or resources to make it interesting; they're better off staying clear I think.

By contrast, the paid-for weekly papers offered extensive election coverage, although again, the commitment to coverage was highly variable. The *Spenborough Guardian*, for example, reported sixty-nine election items during the election which, if extrapolated to reflect coverage in a daily paper, would generate 408 reports. At the opposite end of the spectrum of journalists' enthusiasm were the *Huddersfield District Chronicle* (12 items) and the *Colne Valley Chronicle* (16 items) which reported less election news than the most industrious of their free sister papers. The two daily papers, the *Yorkshire Post* (375 items) and the *Halifax Courier* (356) published a substantial number of articles and readers' letters informing and involving readers in the unfolding election story.

Reporting a local agenda

Local journalists believed their editorial priority was to identify, explore and report a local election agenda although many confirmed that the focus on national issues was considerably greater in 1997 than in previous elections. Some national stories were undoubtedly significant; especially visiting political dignitaries 'parachuted' into typically marginal constituencies. A local editor recalled that 'the Prime Minister came to our town. Obviously that's an important story'. Local journalists are intuitively attracted to 'local stories' but there is also a pragmatic reasoning here. A journalist explained:

the news editor's view is very much that if it is not local, it doesn't go in. So far as the election was concerned I was in total agreement with that because I believe that people who read our paper were also watching the *Six O'Clock News* and what they wanted from us, what our angle was, what sold our newspapers was the local issues and that's why we covered it like that.

Table 16.2 reveals the extent of local papers' focus on local stories. At first glance, the aggregate totals suggest a fairly even division between local and national coverage with 620 (49.7 per cent) items focused on 'local' or 'predominantly local' issues and 628 (50.3 per cent) reports targeting 'national' or 'predominantly national' concerns. But different newspapers revealed distinctive preferences for local and national news. These overall totals, moreover, are distorted by the extensive coverage in the *Yorkshire Post* which, as a regional paper, was overwhelmingly oriented towards national news and stories (81.2 per cent of all published items). When the *Yorkshire Post*'s coverage is set aside, the local emphasis becomes apparent; 63 per cent (549 items) of coverage was local or predominantly local, while 37 per cent (322) was national or predominantly national.

The evening *Halifax Courier* also reveals a slight disposition to favour national stories, but each of the thirteen weekly paid-for papers focused overwhelmingly on local issues. The *Brighouse Echo* devoted 88 per cent of its election coverage to local concerns while the *Colne Valley Chronicle* (81 per cent), the *Spenborough Guardian* (74 per cent) and the *Batley News* (73 per cent) offered substantive reports on local issues.

In order to construct the local election agenda, each item of coverage was assigned to one of fifty-two subject topics including taxation, the

Table 16.2 National and local focus in election reporting

Newspaper	Local	National	Pre-dominantly local	Pre-dominantly national	Total
Aire Valley Target	5	5	3	1	14
Bradford Star	6	7	–	–	13
Weekly Advertiser	2	1	–	–	3
East Leeds Weekly	1	–	–	–	1
Huddersfield Weekly News	2	2	2	–	6
Leeds Skyrack Express	3	2	2	–	7
North Leeds Weekly	1	–	–	–	1
Weekend Times	1	2	2	–	5
West Leeds Weekly	1	–	–	–	1
Wharfe Valley Times	18	2	2	–	22
Batley News	27	15	16	1	59
Brighouse Echo	15	4	13	–	32
Colne Valley Chronicle	6	3	7	–	16
Dewsbury Reporter	15	7	9	6	37
Hebden Bridge Times	19	2	1	–	22
Heckmondwike Herald	34	16	17	2	69
Holme Valley Express	7	4	7	1	19
Huddersfield District Chronicle	3	4	4	1	12
Mirfield Reporter	17	5	10	5	37
Morley Advertiser	11	4	4	1	20
Morley Observer	8	13	11	0	32
Spenborough Guardian	34	16	17	2	69
Todmorden News	15	3	2	–	20
Halifax Courier	94	157	75	30	356
Yorkshire Post	38	269	33	37	377
Total	**383** (30.7%)	**541** (43.3%)	**237** (19%)	**87** (7%)	**1,250**

environment, constitutional reform and local government; the fifteen most regularly reported issues are compiled in table 16.3.

Table 16.3 establishes that local newspaper coverage of the election is not simply a poor imitation of national press reports. The high ranking of topics such as Europe, education, health and even 'sleaze' in local newspapers' coverage confirms that some national news stories found a ready hearing at the local level. But local journalists invariably attempt to 'localise', or give a local spin to important national issues such as education and the National Health Service by identifying local examples and concerns to illustrate them. 'There were lots of local examples', a journalist recalled. 'The new hospital, the future of the local grammar schools and the controversy over the Ridings.' Issues such as local government, transport, the environment and

Table 16.3 Issue agenda in local press election coverage

Issue/Topic	Frequency	Percentage
Candidate	132	10.6
Europe	109	8.8
Campaign conduct	73	5.8
Education	68	5.4
Leaders	49	3.9
Polls	40	3.2
Sleaze	37	3.0
Economic management	36	2.9
Health	28	2.2
Local government	28	2.2
Environment	25	2.0
Employment	20	1.6
Transport	19	1.5
Public expenditure	17	1.4
Industry	17	1.4

education enjoyed a higher news priority locally than nationally whereas some issues which enjoyed a considerable airing in the national media – defence (only 4 items in local coverage), Northern Ireland (9) and inflation (4) – found a predictably muted expression in the local press.

Local papers devoted their attentions to more parochial matters. Newspapers' concern to provide their readers with biographies and information about local politicians placed 'candidates' at the head of the local issue agenda accounting for 10.6 per cent (132 items) of all reports. The 'conduct of the Campaign' in local constituencies, which ranked in third place on the local press agenda (73 items, 5.8 per cent), included procedural profiles of local constituencies, details of local meetings and walkabouts, letters from election-weary readers, as well as disputes between parties about the theft or vandalism of posters. The failure of an incumbent Conservative to acknowledge her membership of the party on her election literature was, as a journalist recalled with considerable pleasure, 'an important story for us and it was carried in the *Yorkshire Post* as well, so that was a good story'. Some issues of national significance were excluded from the local agenda while other rather flippant matters enjoyed undue prominence; journalists tend to use these stories to leaven the electoral dough. Elections conducted by children in local schools, for example, were a popular story (13 items) with local papers and were allocated a higher news priority than national issues like Northern Ireland (9), constitutional reform (6), poverty (5), agriculture (4), defence (4), foreign affairs (3) and community care (1). But what ultimately guarantees that local newspapers articulate a local rather than national agenda is the extent to which readers' letters form a substantive (24.4 per cent in 1997) component of election coverage; no national paper provides such a forum for local voices and opinions.

A final point about the local election agenda is noteworthy. In interviews, journalists alleged that the campaign was much more centralised in 1997 and that consequently it was more difficult to address local issues. But the data reveal that if anything coverage was marginally more local in emphasis in 1997 than in previous elections. In 1992, for example, 47.7 per cent of election items focused on local or predominantly local issues with 52.3 per cent being national or predominantly national in emphasis; in 1997 the equivalent figures were 49.7 per cent and 50.3 per cent.

A partisan press?

Party allegations of press bias are routine. An editor claimed 'the Labour Party accuse us of being a Conservative paper and the Tories are convinced we're left wing; so', he concluded erroneously, 'I think we have got it about right.' The issue of bias and partisanship in coverage, however, is not so readily resolved nor easily measured by researchers. Four measures were used to signal partisanship: party prominence in press coverage; the number of published quotations by party spokespeople; the number of published photographs of party members; the number of positive and negative appraisals of the different parties.

First, table 16.4 illustrates that the Conservative Party was prominent in press reports (400 or 32 per cent) more frequently than Labour (269 or 21.6 per cent) or the Liberal Democrats (95 or 7.6 per cent).

The table also reveals the distinctly bi-partisan character of coverage with Labour and Conservatives enjoying prominence in press reports respectively three and four times more frequently than the Liberal Democrats. Each of the two major parties, moreover, enjoyed press prominence on more occasions than the other parties combined. This hierarchy of prominence was sustained across the different editorial formats of articles, editorials and letters and also across the various newspaper types.

Second, Conservative politicians were offered more frequent opportunities

Table 16.4 The predominant party focus of election coverage

Party	Frequency	Percentage
Conservative	400	32.1
Labour	269	21.6
Liberal Democrat	95	7.6
Green	24	1.9
Monster Raving Loony	11	0.9
Referendum Party	37	3.0
Other	41	3.3
No party prominent	371	29.6
Total	**1,248**	**100.0**

to speak directly to readers and voters. Local newspapers published 528 quotations by Conservative politicians compared to 434 by Labour and a mere 224 by Liberal Democrats. The same party ranking was evident for the third measure of partisanship; newspapers published 193 pictures of Conservative politicians but only 153 Labour and 71 Liberal Democrat. But the three quantitative measures outlined so far indicate only the extent but not the political direction of coverage. The Conservatives' prominence in reporting might be because journalists are either praising or denouncing the party's policies in editorials. Consequently the final measure is crucial: the number of negative and positive appraisals of the various political parties.

Table 16.5 shows that the 'balance of partisanship', so evident in the 1987 and 1992 studies, was sustained in 1997. The table reveals an overall proximate balance in coverage across all newspapers. The Conservative Party

Table 16.5 Positive and negative appraisals of political parties in local newspapers

	Conservative		Labour		Liberal Democrat	
	Positive	Negative	Positive	Negative	Positive	Negative
Aire Valley Target	2	4	2	2	1	–
Bradford Star	4	7	2	8	2	2
Weekly Advertiser	–	1	–	1	–	1
East Leeds Weekly	–	–	–	–	–	–
Huddersfield Weekly News	8	6	–	1	–	2
Leeds Skyrack Express	2	1	2	1	1	2
North Leeds Weekly	–	–	–	–	–	–
Weekend Times	–	1	–	2	1	1
West Leeds Weekly	–	–	–	–	–	–
Wharfe Valley Times	–	4	–	1	–	2
Batley News	6	23	7	30	7	5
Brighouse Echo	8	13	7	11	7	5
Colne Valley Chronicle	3	11	11	1	1	2
Dewsbury Reporter	6	5	6	13	1	4
Hebden Bridge Times	7	12	2	7	3	3
Heckmondwike Herald	20	22	14	16	8	4
Holme Valley Express	2	7	7	3	2	3
Huddersfield District Chronicle	2	5	4	4	–	1
Mirfield Reporter	5	11	8	7	1	4
Morley Advertiser	4	6	2	2	2	1
Morley Observer	5	13	5	9	1	2
Spenborough Guardian	20	22	14	16	8	4
Todmorden News	6	10	1	8	2	5
Halifax Courier	72	223	95	125	39	19
Yorkshire Post	126	174	98	234	35	35
Total	**308**	**581**	**287**	**502**	**122**	**107**

received an aggregate 889 press appraisals of which 308 (34.6 per cent) were positive compared to 789 appraisals for Labour of which 287 (36.4 per cent) were positive. A more finely balanced political coverage would be difficult to achieve, but newspapers' partisan sentiments are revealed when individual newspapers are examined. The *Halifax Courier* published 295 appraisals of the Conservative Party, but only 72 (24.4 per cent) were positive whereas 95 (43.2 per cent) of the newspaper's 220 assessments of the Labour Party were positive. The paper also published 20 fewer positive, but 98 more negative, appraisals of the Conservative than the Labour Party. According to this calculus the paper is pro-Labour. A reversed direction for partisanship is signalled by coverage in the *Yorkshire Post*. Described by the editor of a local evening paper as 'the authentic voice of the Conservative Party', the *Yorkshire Post* published 332 appraisals of the Labour Party of which only 98 (29.5 per cent) were positive, but 126 (42 per cent) of the 300 assessments of the Conservative Party were positive. The paper published 28 more positive appraisals of the Conservative than the Labour Party but 60 more negative appraisals of Labour than Conservative; in short, the paper's editorial was distinctly pro-Conservative.

Two other points emerge from table 16.5. First, the deficit of positive comments for both the major political parties (Conservative −273 and Labour −215) reflects the negative character of the campaign. When asked by journalists for comment, spokepeople for the two major parties preferred to attack their opponents rather than promote their own policies. Only two of the twenty-five newspapers (the *Colne Valley Chronicle* and the *Leeds Skyrack Express*) offered more positive than negative appraisals of the parties in their coverage. Interestingly, although journalists repeatedly complained about the increasingly negative character of parties' campaigns in 1997, this was not conveyed in election coverage. In 1987, 62 per cent (839 out of 1,352) of published comments about the Conservative Party were negative and 63 per cent (721 from 1,141) of comments about Labour were similarly negative but these figures had increased only marginally in 1997 to 66 per cent (581 from 881) for Conservatives and 64 per cent (502 from 787) for Labour. This consistency is difficult to explain given journalists' conviction that the 1997 campaign was substantively more negative. Perhaps journalists' initial judgement was incorrect or perhaps journalists' news gathering and reporting regimes, with their emphasis on even-handedness and a requirement for balanced coverage, offset the more negative aspects evident in parties' campaigning styles.

There is a second and related point. As in 1987 and 1992, the Liberal Democrats in 1997 received very few press appraisals but enjoyed a surplus (+15) of positive above negative comments. This seems to reflect little more than the degree to which the party was marginalised in the perceptions of rival parties. In a highly negative campaign, the Liberal Democrats were rarely considered the main opposition by the two major parties and consequently failed to attract their fire; the party was judged unworthy of the effort involved in disdaining.

Election coverage in the *Yorkshire Post* is worthy of closer attention. It is a substantial and serious, daily morning paper with a readership of almost 80,000 and reports the election contest in almost 100 constituencies across the Yorkshire region. The paper's advocacy of Conservative policies, combined with its denunciation of 'new Labour' alongside personal attacks on Tony Blair, made the *Yorkshire Post*'s 1997 election coverage by far the most partisan of any newspaper in the study; this had been the case in 1987 and 1992.

The *Yorkshire Post*'s headlines – as well as the tendency to publish negative commentary noted above – articulated its political beliefs unequivocally. There were nineteen election headlines although three related to the 'sleaze row' involving Martin Bell and Neil Hamilton and made little reference to the main two-party contest. Of the remaining sixteen headlines, ten were unashamedly anti-Labour including 'Roasting from Major on Tax and Scotland: **Blair Gaffe Adds Gloss to Tories Big Rally**' (5 April 1997) and 'Premier Delights Tory Rally with Attack on Labour Leader Who "Cannot Be Trusted with Britain's Future": **Blair Unfit To Be Prime Minister Says Major**' (22 April 1997). By contrast, there were no headlines criticising the Conservative Party. Some headlines, however, were inexplicably optimistic about the Conservatives' prospects given the state of the electoral contest. The paper's headline on 23 April, for example, 'Poll Shows Labour Lead Slashed to 5 Per Cent: **Amazing Turnabout in Tory Fortunes**' is nothing less than misleading and offers a prime example of 'being economical with the truth'. It seems unlikely that the same poll results would have generated such bullish headlines in a less politically committed newspaper. But in a paper supporting the Labour Party, the same story might have been headlined 'Labour 5% Ahead in Final Week' or '5% Labour Lead Promises 100+ Seats Majority'. But even on the eve of poll when few pundits held out any hope of a Conservative victory, with the party facing its worst electoral defeat for decades, the loyal *Yorkshire Post* couched the Conservative's prospects in a heroic and euphuistic prose which announced 'Major's Battle for Britain' (30 April 1997).

A final use of headlines is noteworthy. The *Yorkshire Post* used headlines and the preceding straplines to create political spin. When a particular story reflected badly on the Conservatives but the story was too newsworthy to ignore, the negative story element was captured by the strapline while a more positive headline in bold print was used to ameliorate the worst aspects of the story. The strapline and headline on 18 April offered a classic example of the use of newspaper layout to 'spin' political messages: 'Labour Seize on "Tory Panic" as Clarke and Heseltine not Consulted on Policy Shift over Single Currency: **Major Promises Free Vote**' Similarly, a negative story about Labour was always reported using the bold headline; a positive story relegated the party to the less graphically significant strapline. Hence 'Tories Attack Parcel Force U-Turn: **Labour on Ropes Again over Sell Offs**' (11 April 1997) but 'Poll Shows Labour Lead Slashed to 5 Per Cent: **Amazing Turn Around in Tory Fortunes**' (23 April 1997).

Editorials offered supporting evidence of the *Yorkshire Post*'s partisanship. There were fourteen editorials across the election period. The first (5 April) attacked the Liberal Democrats, a second was neutral and focused on fishing policy (19 April), while a third was highly critical of John Redwood (18 April); the remaining eleven launched a series of diatribes against the Labour Party, Labour policies and Labour politicians – especially Tony Blair. The editorial on 12 April denounced the Labour manifesto as 'old Labour baggage' which left Blair 'shackled to the social chapter, a minimum wage and a pernicious windfall-profits tax' (p. 12). An editorial headed 'Quack Medicine' exposed 'the myth that the NHS would be safer in Labour's hands' (21 April 1997, p. 12), while an editorial devoted to the issue of leadership favourably contrasted John Major's 'experience and wisdom' with Tony Blair's 'callow youthfulness' (22 April 1997, p. 12). In the final week of the campaign, the paper decried Labour's policy on Europe as 'vapid soundbites and empty slogans'. The editorial argued that Blair's commitment to qualified majority voting means 'Europe could impose ... the kind of industrial relations legislation which reduced the country to penury in the 1970s'. That is why the 'union barons' – those much loved Bogeys of the right-wing press – are 'so keen on a Labour victory' (23 April 1997, p. 12). The following day the *Yorkshire Post*, in clairvoyant mode, predicted a Labour government would 'impose tax increases which it would then blame on the outgoing government's mismanagement of the public finances'. Labour, moreover, lacked any original policies. The party's economic plans were barely disguised Conservative ideas which had 'been bought cheaply in a car boot sale of old Tory policies'; Blair was 'running for the final tape bereft of vision for Britain' (25 April 1992, p. 14).

This closely orchestrated anti-Labour editorialising reached a predictable crescendo on the eve of poll when the *Yorkshire Post*'s editorial 'Deserving Better' expressed 'fundamental doubts' about whether 'messianic Blair' was 'fit to govern'. Just in case readers had any remaining doubts by this stage about the paper's political commitments, the *Yorkshire Post* spelt it out: Labour 'should not be given a chance' (30 April 1997, p. 12).

Even the *Yorkshire Post*'s presentation of politicians' photographs articulated the paper's partisanship. By election day the paper had published sixty-eight (2,144 square inches) photographs of Conservative politicians compared to forty-six (1,423) Labour, six (114) Liberal Democrat and ten (177) of politicians from minority parties. Fifteen colour photographs of Conservative politicians were given prominence on the front page compared to four of Labour politicians. Front page pictures of Labour politicians, moreover, were used to illustrate negative stories. On 25 April, for example, a (small) picture of Tony Benn accompanied the headline 'Benn Toes New Labour Line – for Now'; on 10 April a photograph of John Prescott illustrated a story about 'open warfare' in the Labour Party headlined 'Prescott Exposes Cracks'. Photographs of the party leaders enjoyed very different degrees of exposure in the *Yorkshire Post*. Sixteen pictures of John Major, including seven featured on the front page, compared very favourably with the eleven pictures of Tony Blair which included only a single front-page billing. Ashdown was effectively invisible: only two photographs with both consigned to the inner pages. And the most frequently photographed politician, other than the two major party leaders, with eight photographs including two on the front page? That older woman wearing the blue two-piece and blond rinse who could still be heard rehearsing Gordon Reece's soundbites through capped teeth. Margaret Thatcher – who else?

The *Yorkshire Post*'s strident and unrelenting advocacy of the Conservative cause clearly illustrates the strength of some local newspapers' ideological commitments, despite the balance of partisanship which was so evident in coverage across the region. It is difficult to imagine how a local Labour Party's media-based campaigning strategy might overcome such ideological resistance and win favourable coverage in such a committed local newspaper. But the headline 'The Sun Backs Blair' illustrates that the party nationally could reverse such hostile sentiments (*Sun*, 18 March 1997: 1).

KICKING THE HABIT: JOURNALISTS' EXPLANATIONS OF DECLINING ELECTION COVERAGE

In interviews with journalists six reasons emerged to explain the decline in newspapers' election coverage in 1997. First, journalists believed that their readers were not interested in election news; one journalist's observation that the election 'bored people to tears' was widely shared. The long campaign, widespread cynicism about politicians, the allegations of sleaze, the lack of policy differences between the parties and the feeling that a Labour victory was inevitable, left journalists confronting an uphill task to win their readers' interest. It's hard to sell a story about a race when everyone believes they know the result. 'We had Ken Clarke here' an editor recalled 'and it was quite clear he didn't even think it was going to be close, he was just going through the motions. He knew it was all over. I think he knew they were done for.' Another journalist claimed 'They were both safe labour seats here, they were both odds on certs. You'd have put money on them they were so sure of winning.'

Second, journalists' comments signalled a discernible change in their willingness to report certain kinds of stories. Readers' enthusiasm for election news has never matched journalists' commitment to report it, but until recently journalists believed they had a professional duty, a public service obligation, to report the election and guarantee their local community was sufficiently well informed to make considered electoral choices; that commitment is waning. Previously, editors and journalists worked hard to find entertaining formats – perhaps a report on a children's election at a local school – to present election news to a readership which was often assumed to be uninterested. Many continue to do so but others find it easier to declare 'Election Free Zones'.

In 1997 election news was wholly driven by news values. The question journalists asked when selecting stories changed significantly; not 'Is this significant?' but 'Is this interesting?' Election news no longer won editorial space simply by virtue of being *election* news; it had to be a good story. This shift in journalistic commitments prompted changes in the ways which some papers organised election reporting. In previous elections, one local paper offered candidates an editorial quota which guaranteed them an equitable number of articles and photographs to be published each week. In 1997, the quotas were scrapped; candidates had to provide good stories to win coverage. A journalist explained:

> We changed tack this time. During the previous two elections we laid down pretty rigid guidelines about the publishing space we would give to people. Each candidate would be allowed 200 words and two photographs each week and that was it. But this time we said 'It's up to you. Tell us what you are doing and let us know what you want to say but we will decide if that's going to be interesting or not.'

On other papers, journalists have developed strategies which allow them to report the election without alienating uninterested readers. One paper, for example, placed all its election coverage on a single page so that readers would be minimally inconvenienced if they wished to ignore it. The *Guardian*'s daily election supplement offered readers the same prospect of disregarding election news with one deft chuck of the entire supplement into the bin! 'We decided to put all the election news – local and national – on page two' a journalist recalled 'so that if people were interested, it was there. If not, they weren't having to turn every page and find an election story there. . . . We were making it easy for readers to ignore the election reports. It was there if they wanted it, if not . . .'

This shift in journalists' commitments to reporting the election reflects a third and significant factor: the increasingly competitive markets for readers and advertisers in which local papers are obliged to compete. Local papers must minimise the costs of newsgathering and maximise revenues; in corporate ownership they must contribute to group profits. Newspapers' intuitive response has been to go 'downmarket'. Journalists argue this newly competitive market has triggered a preference for 'human interest' stories above 'hard news' such as election coverage. One journalist was explicit. 'The pressures of circulation are on us,' he explained. 'We obviously would love to have human interest stories day after day because we worry about becoming too boring for the public. They're very much keener about what they will buy. Reporting about schools, councils, that sort of thing, you might have got away with that in the past, but now you have to look for good stories and the good stories which sell newspapers are tabloid stories. So for a couple of years now I think there has been a bigger pressure on us to report these tabloid stories'; the paper was bought by the Johnston Press Group in 1994.

Market considerations influence election coverage in more direct ways. Journalists know the social demography of their readerships well; some political views are simply incompatible with the social circumstances of their readerships. A senior news editor argued:

> If we did say we were pro-Labour a large number of our readers would object to that. But on the other hand we have massive housing estates that we're trying to sell on – and we're trying hard to sell on them at the moment – but with the poverty up there it's difficult. So, I mean, it's obvious you're not going to be shouting too many Tory lines at them.

It would be inaccurate to suggest that commercial calculations were 'mugging' editorial judgements here, but they are undoubtedly unduly influential.

Fourth, journalists were very conscious of the rapid development of other local media and the prospect they offered for enhanced competition for audiences and advertisers. The 120 Independent Local Radio (ILR) stations broadcasting during the 1992 election had mushroomed to 180 by 1997; the increased competition and desire for cost cutting obliged the BBC to reduce its local stations from forty-three to thirty-eight. The emergence of local cable television (see chapter 4) is seen as a poisoned chalice which offers short-term support to the local newspaper industry but which is viewed by journalists, even in the medium term, as a potential competitor. Journalists believe these developments in local media have exacerbated the market pressures outlined above and will impact on editorial in predictable and generally deleterious ways.

Fifth, journalists declared local parties, especially local Labour parties, much less committed to the local campaign. In 1987 and 1992, parties made great efforts to provide (inundate?) local papers with press releases and other information about policies and politicians. But in 1997, journalists believed that local Labour candidates were reluctant to discuss policy; the phrase which was repeated in almost mantra fashion was that Labour candidates seemed much more 'controlled from the centre'. One journalist remembered, with a mixture of frustration and farce, that:

> The Labour candidate was unwilling to discuss issues. It wasn't just local issues, it was any issues. . . . He just wouldn't offer any quotes on policy. He was much more controlled from the centre and his difficulty was that he'd never had any involvement in formulating policy, so he was as much in the dark as I was. At one stage he faxed this policy document through

and said well read this for yourself [loud laughter!]. I think that was very much the attitude he was given on policy.

Journalists working in the national press confirmed that Labour had 'with a large degree of success, silenced local elements of the party' (McNamara, 1997: 13). But Millbank's centralised control was not restricted to the nervous hopefuls who should have been more assiduous in maintaining their particular parish pumps; it embraced less timorous political spirits. A news editor recalled how 'the top people came here including Skinner, Benn, Prescott, Frank Dobson – basically the left wing came'. But to his surprise and disappointment, 'they came into this office for interview but they wouldn't be drawn. They were very disciplined.'

Finally, journalists identified two aspects of party campaigning strategies which made the election less relevant or perhaps more unpalatable to a local readership. First, the 1997 campaign was presidential and focused on leaders rather than policies. This was less problematic for national journalists who could access national politicians via press conferences, but local journalists were offered few, if any, opportunities to develop story lines. To be effective, information subsidies for local media must be local in emphasis. A senior political journalist complained that 'we were dominated by what was happening in the morning with the three party leaders and their press conferences. They were faxing stuff up to the regions and local parties were just serving it up to us. But there were very few genuine local stories.' There is evident tension here between the need to service local news media and the desire to centralise media campaigning at Millbank. Second, the campaign was unrelentingly and unprecedentedly negative; this annoyed and dispirited both journalists and readers. One journalist's exasperation is evident:

> Nationally on the news every night, the parties were just slagging each other off. There was very little policy coverage and when the policies did come out, it was difficult to tell the difference between the two main parties. We didn't want to report that. There was so much slagging off going on between the two main parties locally that it was a real effort to drag policies out of them. But to me and the people we talked to, they wanted to know about issues. They certainly weren't interested in people slagging each other off.

MAINTAINING THE HABIT?

Local newspapers' election coverage experienced a dramatic decline in 1997. Reader apathy, increasing competition between newspapers, competition with other local media and the centralising of party campaigns, proved corrosive of journalists' professional and public service commitments to report the election. But old habits die hard. Despite these growing pressures, local press coverage of the 1997 election compared favourably with national reporting. Coverage remained extensive, articulated a local agenda, was less partisan in its commitments than national papers, offered voters detailed accounts of the local political contest to inform their electoral choice and provided a forum in which local voices and opinions could join the political debate. By any standards this is a considerable achievement. But journalists' habits and commitment are changing under new commercial and organisational pressures; and at a pace! It seems unlikely that in future elections the extent and range of coverage will be maintained. But some things never change. In 1997 local newspapers' partisan sentiments seemed as evident as in 1987 and 1992. It is undoubtedly time for some journalists, as well as editors, to concede that some habits are bad habits.

NOTES

1 Thanks are due to the Nuffield Foundation which has awarded grants to finance all three studies.
2 All unattributed quotation material cited is from interviews following the 1987, 1992 and 1997 general elections.

REFERENCES

Butler, D. and Kavanagh, D. (1981) *The British General Election of 1979*, London: Macmillan.
Franklin, B. (1986) 'Public Relations, the Local Press and the Coverage of Local Government', *Local Government Studies*, July/August pp. 25–33.
—— (1989) 'Local Parties, Local Media and the Constituency Campaign' in Crewe, I. and Harrop, M. (eds) *Political Communication: The General Election of 1987*, Cambridge: Cambridge University Press.
—— (1992) 'Local Journalists Hold the Ring', *British Journalism Review*, vol. 3, no. 4, pp. 14–20.
—— (1994) *Packaging Politics: Political Communication in Britain's Media Democracy*, London: Arnold.
Franklin, B. and Murphy, D. (1991) *What News? The Market, Politics and the Local Press*, London: Routledge.
Greenslade, R. (1997) 'How the Broadsheets Stooped to Conquer', *Guardian*, 19 May, p. 9.
McNamara, M. (1997) 'Problems with Localising the National Campaign', *Press Gazette*, 11 April, p. 13
Methven, N. (1997) 'Nine O'Clock News Defends Election Decision to Extend Programme', *Press Gazette*, 18 April, p. 1.
Notorantonio, A. (1997) 'Newspaper Staff Walk Out after Election Supplement is Scrapped', *Press Gazette*, 2 May, p. 1.

Chapter 17

Making race matter: an overview

Karen Ross

> Because mass media reach vast numbers of people at different educational and social levels, their role in encouraging or combating race prejudice can be crucial. Those who work in these media should maintain a positive approach to the promotion of understanding between groups and populations. Representation of people in stereotypes and holding them up to ridicule should be avoided.
>
> UNESCO Declaration, Paris, 1967

As we move towards the new millennium, some commentators would argue, myself included, that some parts of the media are no further forward in achieving UNESCO's goals now than they were thirty years ago when the declaration was first made. While it has become somewhat unfashionable and certainly un-PC to talk about *race* in the rather unconscious way we did in the past – postmodernism has put an end to that kind of homogenising talk – it *is* still possible to talk about rac*ism*. The ways in which media deal with issues of 'race' and racism are important, both in terms of their framing of race-related issues and in their contribution to a discourse in which race is signalled and constructed; nowhere is this more important than in the news arena.

The public rely on the media for information about newsworthy events in the world and mostly regard news media as impartial and value-free. But news is, quite obviously *not* value-free and journalistic routines and practices are determined by a variety of conventions associated with 'newsworthiness'. As numerous commentators have pointed out, real events are subject to processes of selection and are not, in themselves, necessarily newsworthy: they only become news when they are selected for inclusion in news reports (Fowler, 1991; Fiske, 1993, 1996). News thus performs what might be called a 'surveillance' function, 'surveying the trends and events occurring in society and reporting those that seem to be *most* important and consequential to the society's well being' (Wilson and Gutierrez, 1995: 150, emphasis added). Despite the fact that news media regularly transgress the boundaries of 'impartial' reporting, there has been significant resistance on the part of the press, at least in Britain, to have their 'freedom' interfered with by legislative or other pressures, and a concomitant reluctance on the part of successive governments to insist that the press be forced, through legislation, to be more responsible (see chapter 19). Currently, what we have instead of a legal requirement is self-regulation and, for our purposes, this means that reporting on sensitive issues such as 'race' is the subject of guidelines (rather than law) which, by virtue of their non-legal status, are interpreted in a variety of idiosyncratic ways. The National Union of Journalists have drawn up very specific guidelines on the reporting of race issues on a number of occasions and twenty years ago the Royal Commission on the Press advised that

> journalists check sources, bring adequate knowledge to their reporting, and resist the temptation to use over simplified stereotypes. We also believe that in the sensitive and urgent area of race relations, the press can discharge its social responsibilities only if it takes special care and applies exceptional safeguards.
> (Royal Commission on the Press, 1977, 10: 145, cited in MacShane, 1978)

REPORTING RACE IN THE NATIONAL PRESS

The way in which 'race' is reported in the media is, arguably, the result of what Hall calls a kind of racist 'common sense' which has become pervasive in our society and which the media take as their baseline for pursuing a race-related discourse (Hall, 1981). For Hall, what is at issue is the perpetuation of an *ideology* of race/ism and, as such, efforts to subvert the traditional assumptions surrounding race function as strategies to rupture the ideological terrain of race struggles. As Gibbons argues, 'stereotypical images are means of control sometimes exercised by a dominant majority for its own objectives' (Gibbons, 1988: 1) and it is precisely the ways in which those stereotypes take on the mantle of 'fact' that have generated interest (and concern) in mapping the contours of that race/ist discourse. Numerous studies have sought to identify more precisely exactly how ideological racism actually works, at the practical level of constructing race and blackness in news media. All those studies demonstrate unquestionably that something *other* than straightforward factual reporting is going on (if such a thing exists), a something that is often not named specifically as *conscious* racism. But whether this process is consciously understood or not, the result is a distorted and partial coverage of black people and race-related events which promotes and feeds into the original assumptions, creating an endless cycle of assumption-coverage-reinforcement-assumption.

So, what exactly does race-related news coverage look like? Van Dijk is one of the most prolific chroniclers of race reporting in the press and his primary tenet is that a society is as racist as its elites are (van Dijk, 1991). In van Dijk's comprehensive analysis of racial discourse in the press, he argues that while the venality and blatant nature of 'race' reporting diminished during the 1980s, the underlying attitudes, manifesting themselves in preju- dicial and discriminatory assumptions which masquerade as 'neutral' report- ing were (and are still) much in evidence. In particular, the black-as-threat and black-as-problem reporting strategies represent the dominant and exemplary form of racialised/racist subject position. The types of stories in which black people feature are mostly confined to a narrow repertoire of 'problem' categories: immigration, crime, violence and race relations- conflictual (see, for example, Parekh, 1986; Murray, 1986; Pursehouse, 1987; Searle, 1987, 1993). While it would be tempting to suggest that the conven- tions of the news genre demand a necessarily 'negative' slant on *all* stories, black people are involved in all aspects of social, economic, political and cultural life which, in other circumstances (that is, when they are about *white* people), *do* get reported. While the broadsheet press may not be as rabid or overt in its language, there is scant evidence that the underlying sentiment is actually different to that expressed by its less uncompromising tabloid col- leagues. It might provide more background and context and give a column inch or two to the voices of black people themselves, but the hegemony of the master narrative of race or what van Dijk calls the 'ethnic consensus' is scarcely ruptured by those often superficial niceties.

Taking a more historical perspective, Wilson and Gutierrez identify four phases of press reporting of race: (i) exclusionary phase, where minorities were invisible; (ii) threatening-issue where minorities were framed as a threat to the existing social order; (iii) confrontation, where an 'us and them' men- tality prevailed; (iv) stereotypical selection, where reporting confirmed preju- dicial assumptions about black minorites, with the contemporary goal of reporting 'race' as 'multiracial coverage', is seen as the fifth and final phase (Wilson and Gutierrez, 1995: 157–8). The authors identify a number of strategies which would need to be employed if this final phase is to be achieved, including the recruitment of more black journalists and a more general increase in the sensitivity of journalists to attend to stories from a black perspective and to seek actively stories from those sources.

Other research, like Gordon and Rosenberg's news study, concluded that stereotyping black people was a routine and common practice, most usually manifest via the 'black as problem' discourse and found that where more 'positive' stories were reported, these tended to be 'millionaires or sports stars [which] are inaccessible to, and beyond the realm of experience of, most ordinary black people' (Gordon and Rosenberg, 1989: 58). The perpetuation of the *black as criminal* stereotype which posits crime as the employment route of choice, together with the invisibility of 'real' black community life outside the frame of white 'normality', is both mythical and dangerous, contributing to an atmosphere of separation and fear. If a review of race- related reporting in the national press shows that stereotypical reportage is the norm rather than the exception, do local newspapers do things differently?

RACE AND THE LOCAL PRESS

The strength of the provincial newspaper lies in the service that it gives to its own region, a service which cannot be offered by newspapers published elsewhere. While a provincial must aim at being a complete newspaper it must provide its readers with news of their own local and district affairs, in short, become their newspaper. It must mirror the region it serves and while aiming to command its readers' interest, must labour to deserve their trust.

(*Birmingham Post Centenary Edition*, 7 December 1957)

The local press has the opportunity, in principle, to report on 'race-related' news in ways which have a particular local resonance and, therefore, potentially, to influence the ways in which black communities in their particular locale might be viewed or understood by the white majority population. While race-related events or incidents *out there*, that is, 'black as outsider', will be read about in the national press at a general level of interest, events which are reported *in here*, that is, 'black as insider', could be expected to have a greater impact in terms of local community relations. There therefore seems to be a particular responsibility on local newspapers to be sensitive in the ways in which they report 'race' and a need, then, to consider exactly what kinds of discourse are employed by local newspapers. If the local press exists to serve the interests and news appetites of its local population, does it privilege the interests of all members of its local community equally?

The most comprehensive analysis of the local press in Britain was undertaken by Critcher *et al.* in the 1970s when they analysed local newspapers over the period 1963–70 (Critcher *et al.*, 1975). For their sample of evening newspapers, they selected the *Birmingham Evening Mail*, the *Coventry Evening Telegraph* and the *Wolverhampton Express and Star*. The authors claimed that the provincial press in the West Midlands showed characteristics typical of the provincial press in Britain and that the selected newspapers could therefore be seen as 'typical' of the way in which the provincial press 'selects, develops and positions articles with a racial content' (1975: 39). They divided their analysis between 'overseas' news and 'British' news and found that, in aggregate terms, 78 per cent of all 'race-related' news items were British, 13 per cent 'direct' overseas and 9 per cent 'home' overseas – this latter category describing news which made 'explicit the significance of rate related events overseas for British people' (1975: 57). In other words, news which was allegedly about the 'home' countries of British-domiciled non-whites.

The most popular thematic which characterised overseas news was that of conflict, mainly between black and white people (the white colonisers and the oppressed indigenous communities), but also internecine struggles and 'natural' disasters such as famines. The irresistible conclusion from the types of news story reported is that black people, particularly when they are 'given' self-determination, are not civilised enough to take a responsible approach –

power corrupts etc. The authors concluded, from the proportionate decrease in 'overseas' race-related news items over the survey period (and the concomitant increase in 'British' material), that 'race overseas appears in the provincial evening press only as dramatic conflict without history or logic' (1975: 52) and that the complexion of such reporting reinforces and contributes towards the perpetuation of crude racial stereotypes. Galtung and Ruge's comments on foreign news at the time, particularly the almost total lack of historical, social or economic context, seem to have a worrying immediacy and resonance nearly twenty-five years later:

> From such countries, news will have to refer to people, preferably top elites and be preferably negative and unexpected. . . . This will in turn facilitate an image of these countries as dangerous, as ruled by capricious elites, as unchanging in their basic characteristics . . . events occur, they are sudden, like flashes of lightning, with no build-up and no let-down after their occurrence. . . .
>
> (Galtung and Ruge, 1973: 271)

Though the editors of local newspapers might argue that, as their main imperative is to report on *local* issues, they cannot be expected to do considered and in-depth features on international news, the point is less about research and more about presentation and selection. As Critcher *et al.* argued, even when *all* race-related news is taken together, stories demonstrate a consistent lack of contextualisation, a preponderance of 'conflict' themes and a lack of reporting on the everyday, this latter being, arguably, on what a local newspaper specifically charges itself with reporting. The 'home' overseas news items tended to report 'foreign' news through a British lens and, because it is mostly dramatic and extreme events which get covered, the interpretive frame used is necessarily narrow and implicitly colonial.

Turning to British 'race' stories, Critcher *et al.*'s study found that the two most important themes were human interest and crime stories and pointed to the methodological difficulty in conducting content analysis on newspaper reports when trying to disentangle the presentation of individual black actors from their portrayal as 'typical' of black communities more generally. While there were almost equal numbers of 'crime' and 'human interest' stories, Critcher *et al.* argue that these apparently negative and positive stories do not act to balance each other out, since all are endowed with a variety of often *racialised* meanings:

> We would thus emphasise the absolutely vital role of crime *and* [my italics] human interest stories featuring black people as essential, routinised, but far from neutral, components of the representation of race in these evening papers.
>
> (Critcher *et al.*, 1975: 78)

What the analysis of 'British' race news showed over the monitoring period was that the number of race-related stories grew in volume: for example, the percentage rises in column inches for crime and human interest were 20 per cent and 53 per cent respectively between 1963–6 and 1967–70. This change could simply reflect the growing number of black people in the West Midlands but, as the authors suggest, it is more likely to signify the 'increasing visibility and newsworthiness of the "race" situation which is pursued for the most part within pre-existent news categories' (1975: 91). The authors identified three 'levels' of race news:

1 routinised news – crime and human interest 34 per cent;
2 political problem news – race relations, immigration white hostility 22 per cent;
3 social problem news – education, cultural difference 15 per cent.

Together these make 71 per cent of all race-news stories, with the remaining 29 per cent comprising less frequent themes such as discrimination at an individual level, 'immigrant organisations and sport/entertainment stories' (1975: 189).

Across the three evening newspapers, there was a broad consensus on race perspectives and what each considered newsworthy in their specific local context did not seem to be influenced by the racial mix of their actual local populations. Where there were significant distinctions were in the kinds of reference themes employed. The *Birmingham Evening Mail* was most likely to point to cultural difference in negative terms and regard racial integration as being mainly about assimiliation – *you* will become like *us*. The Wolverhampton *Express and Star* also used negative reference themes about cultural difference but with some positive referents and regarded racial integration as being about both assimilation but also accommodation – *we* will tolerate *your* difference – and pluralism. Clement Jones, who was on the staff of the *Express and Star* when Critcher *et al.* completed their study, argued that 'to perpetuate colour prejudice through our papers is anti-social and well-nigh criminal' (Runnymede Trust, 1971: 13), but the findings from Critcher *et al.*'s work suggest that there is a serious credibility gap between the rhetoric of a newspaper's employees and the reality of their output. The *Coventry Evening Telegraph* reported cultural difference in the most diverse ways, referring to differences in language and custom and to the positive effects of cultural diversity: the paper regarded racial integration in terms of accommodation.

THE LOCAL SCENE IN 1997

In an attempt to map the changes which have occurred since Critcher *et al.*'s study was conducted, I revisited the three evening papers which formed the core of that earlier study and monitored the kinds of 'race' and 'race-related' stories which appeared over a one-week period (12–18 May 1997). The picture which emerges from this admittedly very limited monitoring exercise is one which is depressingly familiar in terms of the *types* of story in which black people feature and the orthodox stereotypes of 'black-as-entertainer', 'black-as-athlete' and 'black-as-criminal' are still predominant. Table 17.1 illustrates the major differences (and similarities) in story type between the two studies and demonstrates that there is even less variety in content now than in the past.

Critcher *et al.* tabulated their findings separately in terms of whether stories were about black British individuals and communities or minority ethnic communities and events which happened overseas (international stories). Given the low proportion of international stories in the 1997 study, the first column in table 17.1 based on Critcher *et al.*'s study has been derived

Table 17.1 Comparative table of news content, 1963–70 and 1997

Focus of story	1963–70 (%)	1997 (%)
Crime	311 (22)	11 (9)
Human interest	208 (15)	4 (3)
Race relations	139 (10)	2 (2)
Immigration	116 (8)	2 (2)
White hostility	69 (5)	–
Housing	62 (4.5)	–
Discrimination	62 (4.5)	2 (2)
Education	58 (4.1)	1 (1)
Cultural differences	57 (4.1)	–
Sport and entertainment	48 (3)	*63 (55)
Immigrant organisations	45 (3.2)	–
Racial integration	42 (3)	–
Health	24 (1.7)	–
Employment	23 (1.7)	5 (4)
Numbers	18 (1.3)	–
Celebrities	17 (1.2)	–
Legislation	16 (1.1)	–
Police	13 (0.9)	–
'Inverse' racism (by black people)	3 (0.2)	–
Black hostility	3 (0.2)	–
Other	49 (3)	–
**Background	no category	12 (10)
International news	±	12 (10)
Human rights/asylum	no category	2 (2)
Total items	**1,383**	**116**

* For 1997, entertainment stories accounted for 11 per cent of this figure and sports stories (including photos) accounted for 43 per cent.
** These were stories which were not specifically centred on 'race' themes but which featured black and Asian people as actors in story, mostly as school children in various schools initiatives.
± As this column was derived from Critcher *et al.*'s study of British race-related news, there is no 'international' category; the content of these stories was tabulated separately in Critcher *et al.* (1975).

from their analysis of British news stories only. Bearing that in mind, the earlier study found that the two most popular types of story featuring black and Asian people had 'crime' and 'human interest' themes, but in my study (which bracketed together both 'home' and 'international' news), the major story types were sport (43 per cent), entertainment (11 per cent), international news (10 per cent) and crime (9 per cent). The proportion of international news stories in the 1997 survey is considerably less than that found in Critcher *et al.*'s study (22 per cent of all race-related stories), and the three newspapers in the 1997 study have very little space dedicated to news reporting on non-local issues: the *Birmingham Evening Mail* and the *Coventry Evening Telegraph* both have half-page sections dedicated to 'national and international news', while the Wolverhampton *Express and Star* has no specific section on non-local news. Given the plethora of alternative forms of news information at local, regional and national levels, it may be that the local press has become even more segmented in terms of the type of news it thinks will attract a sustained readership, but this results in a parochial perspective which seems to be alarmingly introspective, providing even less context to broader themes such as 'race relations' which get reported on almost in a vacuum.

The proportion of stories on different themes in the contemporary study is also very different to those in the earlier study, most importantly in the sense that there appears to be an even more restricted repertoire of story types now than in the past and themes which were important in the earlier study are less significant now. For example, the category of 'sport' is the predominant story type featuring black (but not Asian) people, closely followed by 'entertainment', 'crime' and 'international' stories. The focus on sport is not that surprising, given the involvement of black athletes in local as well as national clubs but the prominence of black people in sport stories further reinforces stereotypical notions that this is more or less the only arena in which black people excel: there were only two out of 116 stories which focused on black business success. Some of the more negative story categories such as discrimination and immigration are greatly reduced compared with the earlier study and, again, this is not surprising given that the Race Relations Act became law in the year after Critcher *et al.*'s study was published – 1976.

It could be argued, then, that the reporting of 'race' has become more 'positive' as sport and entertainment categories are now dominant, but that is to underestimate the extent to which the producers of news select items which they feel will appeal to their own particular audience. The Commission for Racial Equality found that the number of racial incidents reported to the police increased from 4,383 in 1988 to 12,222 in 1995–6 and the British Crime Survey carried out in 1988 and 1992 estimated that 130,000 incidents took place in Britain, which the victims believe were racially motivated (CRE, 1996). While this latter figure suggests a significant under-reporting of racially-motivated attacks to the police, even taking the former at face value demonstrates that race relations have hardly become more harmonious over the years.

Although this current monitoring exercise was carried out over a very short time period, it is nonetheless possible to discern trends in journalistic practices which point to a dual process of marginalising black people's involvement in their local communities by selective reporting and of rendering almost invisible the daily fact of racism which is the experience of many black people in Britain, perpetuated by a history of colonialism which is never discussed. During the monitoring period, there were two very interesting reports which illustrate this point well. One story, in the Wolverhampton *Express and Star* was a report on a meeting which was to take place between an Aboriginal leader and the Home Secretary, where the former was requesting the return of the preserved head of a nineteenth-century Aboriginal leader (Yagan) which had been buried in Merseyside. The headline for the story was: 'Aboriginal leader in plea over head' (*WES*, 17 May 1997), immediately placing the leader in the position of asking favours of the British government. More tellingly, the story goes on to report that 'Yagan's head was severed from his body and smoked, to preserve it, and brought to Britain where it fell into the possession of the Liverpool Museum'. It is clear that the original act was one of colonial plunder but the phrasing of the piece, particularly noting that 'it fell into the possession ...', is clearly an attempt to deny that reality and absolve blame.

The second story, in the *Coventry Evening Telegraph* is headlined: '"Outsiders" who made city grow' (12 May 1997) and concerns the curating of a new exhibition spotlighting 'the rich traditions and skills brought to Coventry by immigrants to the city since medieval times'. But the 'immigrants' who apparently made such an important cultural contribution were from 'Ireland, Scotland, Wales and France' and it is only in the last two sentences of the story that reference is made to 'workers from India [and] other immigrants from the West Indies and other Commonwealth countries'. Such a reporting tactic underplays the very important contribution that black migrants have made to many of Britain's cities and although it is laudable, in some ways, to make clear that 'immigrants' to Britain have been white as well as black, the emphasis on white migrants seems odd in terms of reporting on an exhibition which 'traces history of immigration' and uses a photograph of white German entrepreneur – Sir William Lyons – to illustrate the piece. What both these stories do is underplay Britain's colonial role – for example neither make reference to slavery – and the means by which Britain became a multicultural society. They are comfortable stories to tell white readers, encouraging an ahistorical view of Britain as the mother country while at the same time making implicit them/us suggestions – *we* accepted *you*.

BLACK JOURNALISTS

Many commentators suggest improvements could be made in the way in which 'race' and 'race-related' issues get reported by involving more black journalists in the production of news. In the USA, particularly since the LA riots, some local newspapers have attempted to look at their own coverage of 'race' and 'race relations' but what many have found makes depressing reading. In an introspective survey of their own journalists (nine white journalists and eight black) and journalistic practices, the *Akron Beacon Journal* found that although all their journalists worked on the same paper, they saw the issue, and experienced the situation, very differently. The black journalists believe that 'the deck was stacked against them [while] their white colleagues believe that blacks (and black issues) were receiving special treatment' (Cose, 1997: 4). The *Times-Picayune* of New Orleans ran a seven-month series on 'race relations' and concluded that 'we live separately. Worship separately. We stand apart, frozen that way by the mythical but overpowering thing called race' (Cose, 1997: 5). In a text aimed at achieving success for African Americans, Diggs suggests that the first rule is to learn how to get along with white people (Diggs, 1993).

It seems clear that the routine and stereotypical way in which 'race' gets reported could be subverted or at least challenged through the recruitment of more black journalists. Wong argues, in the context of Asian Americans, that hiring more Asian American journalists can help promote a more informed approach to race reporting, although he is keen to point out that the 'right' ethnicity is not enough and that editors should look for journalists 'who bring special language and cultural skills' (Wong, 1997: 52). As the work that some newspapers have carried out on their own workforce demonstrates, however, it is not just a question of numbers, it is as much about attitudes and lived experiences and the ability for 'race' to be reported on sensitively, by both black and white journalists. Hacker argues that although newspapers speak the rhetoric of inclusivity and state that they want to recruit more black journalists, many look for a trait in addition to the usual competences required. 'Frankly stated, what those on board want to know is whether a black candidate will turn out to be hostile, political, resentful and hence likely to be unhappy with his or her assignment and surroundings' (Hacker, 1997: 73).

In 1993 the National Association of Black Journalists Print Task Force in the USA reported that a significant number of African Americans leave the print media within five years of taking up their first posts for a variety of reasons including the lack of commitment among newsroom managers to retain or promote them, that they stay in entry-level positions longer than their white counterparts, and that they are never informed about internal seminars and other opportunities to advance their careers (cited in Corea, 1995: 349). In Ainley's study of black and Asian journalists in British media organisations, she reports that of 4,000 journalists working on national newspapers, a mere twenty are black minority journalists, and in the local press only fifteen of the 8,000 journalists working in that medium are black or Asian (Ainley, 1994). As with other studies of minority journalists' experience of working for the press, Ainley argues that one of the reasons there are so few is that they are doubly disadvantaged: first, by discrimination at the point of entry into the profession via organised journalism training and, second, by discrimination when trying to gain an appointment as a journalist.

White editors are unlikely to increase the number of black journalists unless and until they are convinced that the increase will lead to a better quality of journalism (Campbell, 1995) but those same editors must accept that minority perspectives are not the intrusions of alien values but rather constitute strengths that will enhance newspapers' coverage of any event, not simply race-related ones (Kotz, 1979). Even with an increase in black journalists, how far can their perspectives materially influence the reporting of the social world, not simply issues related to 'race'? Hacker (1997) argues that most black journalists will only be given 'black' or 'race-related' stories to cover and the experience of Emilia Bresciani, a minority journalist working in Australia, seems to bear this out:

> It has been very frustrating for me the past five years to ... convince others that the voice of the Third World is a very important voice. ... I have been restricted culturally, by the mould that exists in this society of which many people are unconscious slaves – and so one of the things that I want to do particularly when I say I'm a development journalist is to promote a different approach to news and current affairs, that departs from everybody's own cultural understanding.
>
> (Bresciani, cited in Jakubowicz et al., 1994: 162)

CONCLUSIONS

While it is not possible, as other scholars in this field can testify, to identify the extent to which British society is (or is not) racist, or the ways in which (if at all) newspapers (both national and local) contribute to a racist ideology through their discourse, it is possible to comment on the journalistic routines of selection and presentation which result in the newsreading public, and in this case, local newspaper consumers, being given a very particular view of their immediate social world. As any hack journalist will readily argue, newspapers thrive on sex, crime and scandal and any 'race' content could therefore be understood as simply incidental. But as Critcher et al. point out, when it comes to local news, where the reporting of even trivial 'offences' is included, possibly as a warning to the local community at large, it is easy to see how sanctions against the deviant behaviour of an individual can be generalised to a larger community, particularly if that community is already regarded as deviant because of its contraventions of the local social norms (Critcher *et al.*, 1975).

The fact that 'crime' stories were amongst the top four categories of story concerning black people in the contemporary study serves to perpetuate the black-as-criminal stereotype. In a story which featured several times during the monitoring period, concerning the gang rape of two teenage girls, although the story itself did not mention the ethnicity of the alleged rapists, each report of the story was accompanied by photographs of the gang members, all of whom were young and black. The concentration of stories on crime, entertainment and sport in local newspapers is extremely partial and cannot be helpful in understanding the complexity of local, national and international relations between black and white people. The three local newspapers which have been scrutinised in this and the earlier study are located in multicultural communities and are presumably aiming to increase their market share by being responsive to local need and reflective of their local community. But where is the 'multi' in multicultural? Over the past two decades since Critcher *et al.*'s study was published, black communities in the West Midlands, as elsewhere, have become much more visible as the children and grandchildren of many settled migrants have grown up in Britain – in 1997, nearly half the members of Britain's black communities are British-born (PSI, 1997). Where is that reality portrayed at local levels?

A chapter as brief as this focusing on a topic as important as this must necessarily be superficial and, to some extent, arbitrary. Analysing local press coverage of 'race' and/or the involvement (and influence) of black journalists on those newspapers, across discrete time spans, can provide *some* insights into the presentation of such reporting, but is only one, albeit significant, domain of a multi-faceted repertoire of cultural domination. 'In one sense news is an integral part of the struggle between dominant and subordinate cultures ... and in this sense it is possible to take news as a particular form of ideological production in a culturally stratified society' (Critcher *et al.*, 1975: 212). Thus, although this chapter has highlighted *some* of the strategies employed by *some* local newspapers in reporting 'race', it is for other researchers to elaborate on these findings and explore other singers and other songs in other contexts.

REFERENCES

Ainley, B. (1994) *Blacks and Asians in the British Media: An Investigation of Discrimination*, London: London School of Economics (published Ph.D. thesis).

Campbell, C. (1995) *Race, Myth and the News*, Thousand Oaks, London and New Delhi: Sage.

Commission for Racial Equality (1996) *Annual Report*, London: CRE.

Corea, A. (1995) 'Racism and the American Way of Media' in Downing, J.,

Mohammadi, A. and Sreberny-Mohammadi, A. (eds) *Questioning the Media* (2nd edn), Thousand Oaks, London, New Delhi: Sage, pp. 345–61.

Cose, E. (1997) 'Seething in Silence – The News in Black and White' in Dennis, E. and Pease, E. (eds) *The Media in Black and White*, New Brunswick: Transaction Publishers, pp. 3–10.

Critcher, C., Parker, M. and Sondhi, R. (1975) *Race in the Provincial Press*, Birmingham: Centre for Contemporary Cultural Studies.

Diggs, A. D. (1993) *Success At Work: A Guide for African Americans*, New York: Barricade Books.

Fiske, J. (1993) *Power Plays Power Works*, London: Verso.

—— (1996) *Media Matters: Everyday Culture and Political Change*, Minneapolis and London: University of Minnesota Press.

Fowler, R. (1991) *Language in the News: Discourse and Ideology in the Press*, London and New York: Routledge.

Galtung, J. and Ruge, M. (1973) 'The Structure of Foreign News' in Cohen, S. and Young, J. (eds) *The Manufacture of News: Deviance, Social Problems and Mass Media*, London: Constable, pp. 250–80.

Gibbons, A. (1988) 'Stereotypes and Black Employment'. in Harte, J. (ed.) *Black People and the Media: Equality in Employment and Training-Policies and Practice*, London: London Borough of Lewisham and the Commission for Racial Equality, pp. 1–10.

Gordon, P. and Rosenberg, D. (1989) *Daily Racism: The Press and Black People in Britain*, London: Runnymede Trust.

Hacker, A. (1997) 'Are the Media Really "White"?' in Dennis, E. and Pease, E. (eds) *The Media in Black and White*, New Brunswick: Transaction Publishers, pp. 71–6.

Hall, S. (1981) 'The Whites of Their Eyes: Racist Ideologies and the Media' in Bridges, G. and Brunt, R. (eds) *Silver Linings: Some Strategies for the Eighties*, London: Lawrence & Wishart, pp. 28–52.

Jakubowicz, A., Hoodall, H., Martin, J., Mitchell, T., Randall, L. and Seneviratne, K. (1994) *Racism, Ethnicity and the Media*, St Leonards, NSW: Allen & Unwin.

Kotz, N. (1979) 'The Minority Struggle for a Place in the Newsroom', *Columbia Journalism Review*, 17 (6), pp. 22–31.

MacShane, D. (1978) *Black and Front: Journalists and Race Reporting*, London: Race Relations Sub-Committee and the National Union of Journalists.

Murray, N. (1986) 'Reporting the "Riots"', *Race and Class*, 27, pp. 86–90.

Nelson, J. (1993) *Volunteer Slavery: My Authentic Negro Experience*, Chicago: Noble Press.

Parekh, B. (1986) 'Prejudice and the Press', *New Society*, 7 Nov. 1986, p. 28.

Policy Studies Institute (1997) *Ethnic Minorities in Britain*, London: PSI.

Pursehouse, M. (1987) *Life's More Fun With Your Number One Sun*, Birmingham: Department of Cultural Studies, University of Birmingham.

Runnymede Trust (1971) *Race and the Press*, London: Runnymede Trust.

Searle, C. (1987) 'Your Daily Dose: Racism and the Sun', *Race and Class*, 29, pp. 55–71.

—— (1993) 'Cricket and the Mirror of Racism', *Race and Class*, 34 (3), pp. 45–54.

van Dijk, T. (1991) *Racism and the Press*, London and New York: Routledge.

Wilson, C. C. and Gutierrez, F. (1995) *Race, Multiculturalism, and the Media: From Mass to Class Communication* (2nd edn), Thousand Oaks, London, New Delhi: Sage.

Wong, W. (1997) 'Covering the Invisible "Model Minority"' in Dennis, E. and Pease, E. (eds) (1997) *The Media in Black and White*, New Brunswick: Transaction Publishers, pp. 45–52.

Chapter 18

Economic news in local newspapers

Andrew Leather

While academic analysis of press content has tended to concentrate on the political or social bias of editorial, new forms of local journalism have developed over recent years which are increasingly aimed at the reader as a consumer rather than as a voter or citizen. In this changed context, categories such as right and left or conservative and liberal are conceptually inadequate since all economic editorial content is pro-business and simply does not address agendas which traditionally would have been seen as litmus tests of political/ideological bias.

An analysis of the economic and business content of the local weekly press makes depressing reading, however, for those who are looking for a local press which at least provides an informative guide to the market in the service of the well-informed consumer, much less has any civic relevance.

The weekly press coverage of local economic news falls into two modes which are almost always mutually exclusive. Some carry business sections filled almost entirely with cheerleader mantras in praise of local manifestations of corporate capitalism. Others concentrate on personal finance sections – set up as if to arm consumers with information necessary to cope with a complex market in services – but whose content is simply an incitement to buy the financial services industry products.

BUSINESS NEWS

These business sections act as 'bulletin boards' where local industry and in particular business support groups 'pin' their locally originated press releases. The personal finance sections are made up of question and answer columns (which provide a platform for a local firm of financial advisers) and news which is almost exclusively verbatim reproductions of national financial services' press releases.

All the newspapers in this sample which had business sections are paid-for. Only one, the *Cumberland News*, depends for its finance on sponsorship. The rest were financed by related advertisements, often supported by 'advertorial'. The lengths of the various local weekly newspaper business columns range from short weekly columns (*Cumberland News, Lynn News, Teignmouth Post*) to longer sections which appear quarterly (*Bucks Herald, Tweedale Press Group*). However, local weekly newspapers' business sections tend to be very short: averaging only a single page each weekly edition.

Articles in the business sections of these local weekly newspapers tend to be very uncritical in emphasis and concentrate almost exclusively upon the activities of their respective local business communities. The non-controversial themes carried by these local weekly newspapers invariably focused on: Awards; Business Support-Meetings; Business Support; New Business; New Jobs; New Premises. The recurrent nature of these topics signals that it is the local business community, rather than journalists, who drive the content of local weekly newspapers' business sections. Traditional notions of news values would be incapable of expanding much of the mind-numbing content which results. Whole articles are published on nothing more gripping than a company moving premises, e.g. Madge Networks (*Bucks Free Press*, 24 November 1995, p. 2) or a local company which had achieved a national standard for their product, e.g. H.O. Short (*Tweedale Press Group*, June 1995, p. 16).

Local weekly newspapers make no attempt to hide their reliance upon local industry press releases: many articles carry no by-lines from journalists whatsoever and the editors of some of the longer business sections actually advertised for such content:

> To book your place in Business '95 ring Joan Berwick . . .
>
> (*Tweedale Press Group*, June 1995)

> If you want your company featured in the Bucks Herald Business Supplement telephone . . .
>
> (*Bucks Herald*, 26 February 1997)

The most persistent contributors to the business sections of local weekly newspapers are local business support agencies such as TECs, Business Forums and Chambers of Commerce. These groups submit press releases to almost all of the newspapers in the sample.

When these support agencies are publicising meetings and workshops their articles tend to conclude with a contact name and a telephone number for readers wanting further information. However, when these business support agencies are launching initiatives and working clubs their articles are usually supplemented with quotes from, and photographs of, their directors or senior managers.

The sycophantic, entirely non-critical, editorial which stems from such a dependence on local press releases is acknowledged in the mottos prominently displayed in a couple of the longer business sections:

> We're in the business of promoting Aylesbury Vale.
>
> (*Bucks Herald*)

Serving businesses throughout the Borders & North Northumberland.

(*Tweedale Press*)

It perhaps reaches its nadir in an article published in the *Mid-Devon Advertiser* (8 December 1995). This feature congratulated South West Water on its recent performance and mentioned increased dividends and earnings to shareholders as a positive thing (at the time South West Water was in the stocks for its water quality and the national media were crucifying the privatised water companies for their vast profits, share option packages and concentration on the interests of shareholders rather than water-users). It concluded with the extraordinary company statement celebrating job losses as an achievement: 'substantial operational savings have been made through the shedding of 449 staff, and the company is "on track" to hit its planned cut of 500 staff through restructuring'.

This illustrates how a notion such as the pursuit of business income leads to support for an ideological postion which, say, two or three decades ago would have been to the right of any of the mainstream political parties in the UK. The reason why press releases, supplemented with pertinent quotes from and promotional photographs of sources in the local business community, are used so frequently in the business sections of local weekly newspapers is that they serve two crucial (market-orientated) roles. First, press releases allow local newspapers to fill the editorial part of their business section without the need to employ many full-time journalists – or any at all. In this way, newspapers minimise costs. Second, advertisers in the respective business section invariably get their press releases published and promotional editorial is therefore an incentive for potential advertisers to swell the section's coffers. By this route, newspapers maximise revenues.

HUMAN INTEREST STORIES

Because local businesses overwhelmingly use local newspapers' business sections either to promote their companies or otherwise to publicise forthcoming business events, there are comparatively few explicitly human-interest stories in these sections. But the *Bucks Free Press* provides two front-page articles which focus on personalities rather than events.

First, they published a profile of two African cleaning ladies who had recently met President F. W. de Clerk when he had visited a local school (*Bucks Free Press*, 24 November 1995). Their second human-interest feature, 'Lloyds can bank on even more babies' (ibid.), described the large number of female employees at the local branch of Lloyds Bank who were either pregnant or who had just had a baby (accompanying the feature with a large picture of staff with their new offspring).

This second feature had been hijacked by Lloyds Bank's publicity machine and turned into yet another business-promotional article: this time for the bank's maternity leave and equal opportunity provisions. Lloyds' senior branch manager was quoted as follows:

all of the twelve mums pictured here have returned to work, mostly on a part-time basis, a policy encouraged by the bank

and

typical of the absence of sex discrimination in Lloyds Bank is the fact that of the twenty new arrivals, ten were girls and ten were boys.

These quotes allowed the Lloyds' manager to explain that occupying very fecund premises was no obstacle to a company being socially responsible and aware of sexual discrimination legislation.

ADVERTISEMENTS

With the exception of the *Cumberland News*, which is sponsored by a combination of Barclays Bank and Cumberland TEC (who have their logos in the top corners of the section) and which carries no business advertisements, the remainder of the business sections normally carry a large number of business adverts per page.

Most significantly, there is a very clear relationship between articles and advertisements in the business sections of local weekly newspapers: as previously stated, those businesses which advertises in the local business section also tend to be featured, in a friendly light, in articles in the section (often on the same page).

For example, the main story in the *Mid-Devon Advertiser*'s business news was actually written and by-lined by Peplows Chartered Accountants, who advertised in the section. This article allowed the company a free rein for

Table 18.1 Advertising in business sections

Paper title	Pages	Adverts
Bucks Free Press	5	24
Bucks Herald (monthly)	2	13*
Bucks Herald (quarterly)	12	33*
Cumberland News	1	2
Lynn News	1	1
Mid-Devon Advertiser/Teignmouth Post/		
Dawlish Post	1	5
Newark/Sleaford/South Notts Advertiser	1.3	10
Tweedale Press Group (Southern Reporter/	June 16	46*
Berwick Advertiser/East Lothian Herald)	October 16	39*

* These figures included the advertisements which accompanied advertorial in these newspapers. These advertisements accounted for between 60 per cent and 70 per cent of the space in these sections.

self-promotion: they publicised their respective qualifications and areas of expertise before concluding with an attempt to attract custom: 'please contact any of Peplow's four offices to discuss ways in which we can be of assistance regarding personal or corporate tax matters'.

Perhaps the most comprehensive example of the close link between a company placing an advert and a favourable article, however, was provided by the content of the *Tweedale Press Group*. An examination of their two quarterly business supplements (June and October 1995) shows that 89 per cent of advertisements were accompanied by favourable editorial material invariably on the same page. Any company which advertised in the *Tweedale Press Group* quarterly business supplement would also get a press release published on the same page if they desired.

Unsurprisingly, this led to a very large amount of non-critical editorial coverage in the Tweedale business supplement which can be illustrated by the extremely supportive tone of the following headlines which accompanied their 'Focus on Kelso' (pages 7–11 of the June business supplement):

Local adviser offers help with your mortgage (Advert, company by-line, photograph)

Kelso Racecourse a runaway success (Advert, by-line, photograph, quotes)

Grandstand job for local builders (Advert, picture)

Keltek at home in the border (Advert)

Duke's course will be the equal of any of Scotland's finest (Advert, picture, quote)

You can bank on a user-friendly office (Advert)

Accounting for local business (Advert, quote)

ADVERTORIAL

Advertorial is a hybrid between editorial and advertisement. For the advertiser it confers on copy the truth claim associated with news. It is clearly meant to deceive the reader. Bearing in mind the generally advertisement-friendly content within the local weekly business section, advertorial needs to be excessively business friendly to be distinguishable from news. But it was a significant part of the make-up of the business sections of the *Bucks Free Press*, the *Bucks Herald* and the *Tweedale Press Group* in this sample of local newspapers.

It was really only the presentation of this advertorial (as opposed to the tone or nature of its editorial content) which marked it out from the press-release driven company profiles which appeared as 'normal' articles within the same columns. Various devices such as miniscule announcements in italics reveal that this apparent editorial is in reality paid for by advertisers.

Bucks Free Press

Advertorial made up some one and a half pages of the five-page *Bucks Free Press* business section (or 30 per cent of total section content). This advertorial came from the following (local) sources:

1 Amersham Business Services (half page)
2 Chiltern Springs (quarter page)
3 Lancasters Chartered Accountants (quarter page)
4 Auditel (half page)

The advertorial from Chiltern Springs, Lancasters Chartered Accountants and Amersham Business Centre each consisted of plain editorial profiling the paying company headed with the phrase '*Bucks Free Press Advertisers' Announcement*' in small italic type. The semantic distinction between an advertisement and advertisers' announcement and a free puff might make an interesting subject for linguistic inquiry.

This advertorial was typically surrounded by between four and six advertisements from associated companies. For example, advertisements stating 'Evans Halshaw of Amersham are proud to provide Amersham Business Supplies with all the vehicles keeping them on the road day after day' or advertisements accompanying the advertorial from various companies who were 'pleased/proud to be associated with Lancasters Chartered Accountants'. The *Bucks Free Press*'s advertorial for Auditel, however, was rather more eye-catching – their whole page, consisting of a half-page advertorial above a half-page Auditel advertisement was produced and by-lined in bright blue ink!

Bucks Herald advertorial

There were three and a quarter pages of advertorial (or just over a quarter of the *Herald*'s total content) in the January 1997 twelve-page *Bucks Herald* quarterly business supplement. This advertorial broke down as follows:

1 Secure Data International Ltd (quarter page)
2 Ancient Order of Foresters Friendly Society (quarter page)
3 Development Associates (quarter page)
4 Sponsors of Business Excellence Awards (six half pages)
5 G.W. Deeley (two pages)

All of the *Bucks Herald*'s quarter-page advertorial features were listed as 'Business Profiles' and consisted of editorial supplemented by a photograph, a by-line and substantial quotes from the respective companies (unlike the *Bucks Free Press* there were no supplementary advertisements). Although these features were not much different in tone or content from the standard editorial in the *Bucks Herald*, (1) their inclusion had been directly paid for and

(2) this was indicated by the phrase 'Advertisement Feature' displayed in tiny script below the name of each advertiser.

However, the two-page advertorial spread in the *Bucks Herald* which celebrated sixty years of a local company, G.W. Deeley Constructions, was rather different in format: this advertorial was headed with 'A Bucks Herald Advertisement Feature' and consisted of editorial describing the history and philosophy of the construction company, accompanied by three historic photographs and nineteen advertisements congratulating the company on reaching their anniversary.

In summary, the extent of advertisements and the sycophantic nature of the editorial in the business sections of local weekly newspapers suggest that such sections are largely justified in terms of their ability to attract a regular income stream rather than in the more traditional terms of empowering the consumers in a market by providing them with the full range of information from which to make their choices.

The editorial content of the business sections in the local weekly press is clearly constructed by means of the publication of press releases contributed by advertisers from the local business community. Such content would suggest a straightforward market-orientated justification for business sections is being employed by the respective local newspapers: with minimal costs (in the form of journalists) combining with maximum revenue (in the form of advertising income) in order to produce maximum profits for the section, and thus the newspaper publishers, as a whole.

PERSONAL FINANCE SECTIONS

An analysis of the personal finance sections reflects a similar positive relationship to the world of business. Of the eight local weekly newspapers which contributed personal finance sections to this analysis, three were free newspapers and five were paid-for. All of these sections, however, share many attributes: they are all extremely short (almost always less than half a page per week) and written by a single person to a similar format (all sections, with the exception of the *Melton/Syston Times*, contained a question-and-answer feature; the *Western Telegraph*, *Essex Chronicle* and *Southport Visitor* also all carried a small amount of editorial).

Significantly, none of the personal finance sections in this sample was written by a staff journalist. All of the sections were written by someone with a professional interest in the financial services industry: four of the columns were directly written by a member of the local financial services community (two by financial advisers, one by a building society and one by a local insurance broker); two of the remaining columns had been written by Tony Hetherington, a freelance personal finance journalist (*Essex Chronicle*, *Western Telegraph*) while the name (and position) of the person who generated articles for the *Waltham Forest Independent* was not given.

Table 18.2 Local weekly newspapers' personal finance sections

Title	Free/Paid	Length	Written by	Q & A
Banbury Citizen	Free	< 0.5 page	Fin. Adviser	Yes
Bracknell & Wokingham News				
Extra	Free	< 0.5 page	Fin. Adviser	Yes
Essex Chronicle	Paid	< 0.5 page	Freelance	Yes
Melton/Syston Times	Paid	1 page	B. Society	No
Southport Visitor	Paid	< 0.5 page	Insurance	Yes
Waltham Forest Independent	Free	< 0.5 page	?	Yes
Western Telegraph	Paid	< 0.5 page	Freelance	Yes

Every personal finance column in this sample carried a rather flattering photograph of the financial 'expert' who was writing the section alongside a disclaimer about the advice which they were offering. In addition, all of the personal finance columns which were written by members of the local financial services community included a large by-line listing the contributor's name, company and address as well as their telephone number for any readers who wanted further advice.

Question-and-answer sections

The Q&A sections in the personal finance sections of local weekly newspapers were very general in nature whether they were written by a freelance journalist (as in the case of the *Western Telegraph* and the *Southport Visitor*), or a member of the local financial services industry (such as Bill Bright from David Roberts & Partners in the *Waltham Forest Independent* or Bill Jenner-Jones from Weston Financial Services in the *Banbury Citizen*).

All of the questions set were answered in a very similar manner: some financial product or service would be explained in a way which presumed little or no financial knowledge on the part of the readership before a short piece of very general advice would be proffered by the 'expert,' sometimes amounting to nothing more specific than recommending that readers should seek independent advice (from a local 'expert') before taking out a financial service product.

A typical example of such a Q&A is given below:

Q. I am in my mid-70s and live on my own. I have been thinking about buying an annuity with some of the capital I have in my building society to boost my income. Is this a good idea?

A. When you purchase an annuity, you give away a sum of money in exchange for an income for the rest of your life or for a fixed period . . . part of this income will be deemed to be a return of capital and so will be tax-free. If you are a non-tax payer, then any tax deducted from the rest of the income can be reclaimed. . . . When it comes to buying an annuity, it is important to shop around to find out who will offer you the best rate. They can vary a lot and the income could be paid for many years to come, meaning that you could lose quite large sums with poor advice. . . . Assuming that you are in good health, a lump sum of £10,000 could provide you with an income before tax of around £100 a month which is equivalent to 12 per cent a year.

('The Citizen Money Desk', *Banbury Citizen*, 7 March 1997)

The general nature of these questions coupled with the fact that neither the questions nor the answers ever mentioned any actual financial service providers or their specific rates of returns (relying instead on industry averages) meant that the respective columns were virtually useless to those readers who wanted a thorough evaluation of the products and providers in a particular financial services sector. Having said this, these Q&A columns were clearly a positive thing for any industry source who wrote them: providing considerable publicity (picture, address, telephone number, company logo, etc.) and 'expert' status for the company in the eyes of the local populace with little real risk, due to the nature of the advice given, of ever recommending the wrong product or provider.

This was particularly the case if, like the financial insurance broker at the *Southport Visitor*, you went further than merely stating that people should take independent advice and actually recommended yourself in response to a reader's query:

you can save money and anxiety by consulting David Roberts & Partners. It costs you nothing to check your cover.

Or, if like Bill Jenner-Jones from Weston Financial Services (*Banbury Citizen*, 7 March 1997) or Peter Sharatt from Berkshire Financial Services (*Bracknell & Wokingham News Extra*, 28 February 1997), you offered your company's Advice Forms as the conclusion to each of your answers!

Editorial sections

The editorial features which accompanied the Q&A columns in the personal finance sections of the *Western Telegraph*, the *Essex Chronicle* and the *Southport Visitor* were both brief in length and general in tone.

The vast majority of these editorial features had clearly been constructed through the substantial reproduction of national press releases from high-street financial services institutions. For example, the article nominally written by the freelance journalist Tony Hetherington in the *Essex Chronicle* (28 February 1997) contained much of a Nationwide press release on their new credit card:

The new credit card currently being launched by Nationwide will definitely protect purchasers against loss, theft and damage . . . cardholders will pay no annual fee. There will be an interest free period of 52 days from the time a purchase is made and interest on outstanding balances will be 16.9 per cent for purchases, or 18.9 per cent for cash withdrawals. . . . Put all the ingredients together and the new Nationwide card does look attractive and with an introductory interest rate of 9.90 per cent for anyone who transfers their existing card debts to Nationwide, there should be no shortage of takers.

Surprisingly, when public relations personnel were asked about their facilitating role in getting their clients' press releases into local newspapers they denied that they fulfilled this function:

We don't send out releases to local weekly newspapers because there are so many of them and they are not very important . . . we would only use local newspapers for local stories.

It may well be true that public relations teams do not *directly* provide press releases to local weekly newspapers (PRs don't usually underplay their contribution to the communications process!). If this is the case then editors/ general reporters involved in the construction of local weekly personal finance sections must routinely access national financial services' press releases *indirectly* in one of the following ways. First, many local papers are part of national publishing groups which receive all financial services' press releases. Although intended for national newspapers they are evidently available for publication by local newspapers. Second, news releases from the national financial services industry appear on-line to subscribers for a host of financial statistics providers including the Press Association and Money£acts (interview with PRO of a major national financial services provider).

The *Western Telegraph* certainly used on-line information, on occasions, to generate comparative articles. For example, their article on children's saving accounts (6 December 1995) mentioned the products and the rates of return offered by a broad range of providers including Midland, Skipton and National Savings. Typically, this article made no direct comparisons and basically recommended all of the products for certain people depending on their individual circumstances.

CONCLUSION

The main characteristics of the economic coverage in local weekly newspaper sections are depressing for professional journalists and academic critics alike. It is written by very few full-time staff journalists and is largely constructed by the reproduction of either local financial services' press releases (business sections) or else national financial services' press releases (personal finance sections). As a result its tone is completely uncritical and non-investigative. And, finally, it is generally surrounded by advertisements which the editorial content supports.

Traditional justifications of journalism, which see the media as serving a democratic function, independently investigating their subject matter so as to provide full information to their audience, are rendered irrelevant in analysing such content. The traditional conflict between the truth claims of the editorial sections of newspapers and the pressure to make money through advertisements is thus eliminated because no concession is made to the need to tell the truth as the journalist sees it. Content becomes a means of earning as much revenue as possible at a minimum cost.

This is achieved by nature of the symbiotic relationship between local business journalists and members of the local business community (perhaps facilitated by public relations personnel): industry sources provide revenue for the section (via advertisements), content to the section (via press releases) and legitimacy to the section (through quotes).

By contributing this content the financial services industry dictates the coverage of the respective business sections and ensures that its own interests are promoted. Such a state of affairs also suits the newspaper proprietor because it means that the section is almost certain to generate a healthy revenue stream (through attracting a large amount of advertising income) without incurring the costs of employing many staff journalists – or any at all in some cases.

This market-orientated model of journalism is becoming ever more prevalent in the modern media and helps us to explain the existence, the content and the tone of ever more supplements in the weekend national press: most obviously their personal finance, gardening, travel, holidays and motoring sections.

In such sections, 'news-values' take on a completely different, quite literal, meaning: space on these newspaper pages must be justified in terms of the market return which they can bring, which puts purely informative news in (unequal) competition with 'business-friendly' news. Stories are ultimately judged in terms of their audience-friendliness and advertiser-attractiveness, rather than on their intrinsic worth for an informed public in a democracy.

Chapter 19

Regulating the local press

Robert Pinker

INTRODUCTION

In this chapter I will review the role of the Press Complaints Commission (PCC) in its administration of the industry's Code of Practice with special reference to the regional and local press. The statistical data which I present cover both types of newspaper but most of the illustrative case material included relates to complaints about the local press. I have served as a member of the Commission since it was established in 1991. I was appointed Privacy Commissioner in 1994 with special responsibility for expediting investigations into complaints that come within this area of the Commission's remit. The responsibility for adjudicating on privacy complaints, however, rests with the full Commission under its Chairman, Lord Wakeham, as is the case with all other complaints received and processed. I have taken this opportunity to express some personal views about the issues of privacy, bias and accuracy in local press reporting. Nevertheless, I have no reason to believe that they differ in any significant degree from those which inform the work of the Commission.

THE PCC: ITS ORIGINS, CONSTITUTION AND REMIT

The Press Complaints Commission was established in 1991 as a successor to the old Press Council which was widely considered to have become ineffective and painstakingly slow in responding to complaints. The industry responded swiftly to Sir David Calcutt's critical report of 1990 in setting up a Press Standards Board of Finance to raise an annual levy with which to establish the new PCC, a Code Committee of industry members to draft a Code of Practice and a committee to appoint the Chairman and the members of the new Commission (Calcutt, 1990). The early days of the PCC were often fraught and difficult. The future of self-regulation was very much in the balance after a series of particularly gross intrusions on the part of some tabloid newspapers into people's privacy (McGregor, 1991 and Newspaper Society, 1992). Nevertheless, we survived and, I would argue, the last few years of the Commission's work mark a record of steady improvement and success.

The Commission currently consists of sixteen members, the majority of them lay members, working under an independent chairman, Lord Wakeham. The PCC is a self-regulatory body entirely independent of both the industry and government. It receives and deals with complaints falling within the remit of the industry's Code of Practice. This Code is kept under continuous review by a committee made up of working editors. The Code of Practice is the bedrock of the Commission's work but its provisions are *not* set in stone. They are responsive to changing practices and technology in the industry, to the concerns of readers and changes in public attitudes and values. Modifications and additions have been made concerning such issues as the use of listening devices and long-lens cameras, the definition of 'private property' and 'public interest', the prevention of jigsaw identification in child sex cases, and the procedures to be followed in dealing with hospital authorities. The Code was most recently revised and strengthened on 26 November 1997.

When a complaint is upheld the offending newspaper or periodical must and does publish the Commission's critical adjudication with due prominence. The Commission also publishes its own adjudications, both the upheld and rejected complaints and also a note of every complaint received. In 1993 the industry agreed that the Commission should have the facility to ask a proprietor/publisher to consider disciplinary action in appropriate circumstances where the breach in question is considered gross or flagrant. To underpin the progress we have made in recent years, more and more publishers are writing a requirement to abide by the Code into their contracts and conditions of employment.

The newspaper industry has given 100 per cent support to the Commission and its administration of the Code. No newspaper or periodical has refused to publish an adverse adjudication. It should also be noted that, during the first five years of the Commission's work, over 70 per cent of all the complaints raising a possible breach of the Code were resolved informally to the satisfaction of the parties involved through the intervention and mediation of the Commission's officers. In 1996 this proportion rose to just over 80 per cent (PCC, 1997a: 6).

PRIVACY AND OTHER COMPLAINTS

The overall number of complaints has increased over the years from 1,520 in 1991 to 2,508 in 1995. In 1996 the number rose to just over 3,000. The greater part of this increase is attributable to the fact that the work of the Commission has become much better known to members of the public. The Commission's information literature has been revised and improved. The key pamphlet, *How to Complain*, has been translated into a range of minority languages and a Text-phone service has been introduced to assist people who are deaf and hard of hearing. The Help-line telephone service received an average of 135 enquiries a week in 1996 (PCC, 1997a: 6).

Almost seven in ten of the complaints received in 1996 were raised under the first three Clauses of the Code which cover matters relating to accuracy (Clause 1), Opportunity to Reply (Clause 2) and Comment, Conjecture and Fact (Clause 3). The proportion of complaints received under Clause 4 of the Code, which deals with privacy, has been rising gradually year by year from about 9 per cent to 13 per cent of the total. In summary the greater part of the Commission's work – over 80 per cent of the all the complaints received – falls within the terms of the first four Clauses of the Code.

In quantitative terms, therefore, cases of unjustified intrusion into people's privacy are not numerous. Nevertheless, invasions of privacy can be deeply hurtful to the individuals affected. Their effects can extend to innocent relatives and friends and they are just as hurtful to ordinary citizens as they are to public figures. Privacy was the issue that caused the government of the day to establish the Calcutt committee of enquiry on the future regulation of the press in 1989 and privacy continues to hold a salient significance in the work of the Commission. These are among the reasons why the Commission appointed one of its members to have a special responsibility for all procedural matters relating to privacy.

THE CODE OF PRACTICE AND THE PUBLIC INTEREST

The recently revised Code contains sixteen Clauses covering a range of ethical practice issues which might give cause for complaint. A newspaper may invoke a public interest defence with reference to Clause 3 (Privacy), Clause 4 (Harassment), Clause 6 (Children), Clause 8 (Listening devices), Clause 9 (Hospitals), Clause 10 (Innocent friends and relatives), Clause 11 (Misrepresentation), Clause 14 (Financial journalism) and Clause 16 which deals with payment for articles. Newspapers may go beyond the requirements of these Clauses if they believe and can subsequently demonstrate that, in doing so, their investigations and reporting served the public interest. The grounds on which editors may invoke a public interest defence are clearly specified; namely, in:

(i)   Detecting or exposing crime or a serious misdemeanour.
(ii) Protecting public health and safety.
(iii) Preventing the public from being misled by some statement or action of an individual or an organisation.

(Code of Practice, 26 November 1987)

The first two exceptions listed above have seldom given rise to difficulties. It is, however subclause (iii) that is most frequently and controversially invoked by editors as providing a prima facie public interest justification for intruding into people's privacy. Editors, for example, will sometimes argue successfully that readers have a right to know when the public statements of politicians are misleading because they can be shown to be seriously inconsistent with aspects of their own private behaviour.

In a recent press release, the Commission's Chairman, Lord Wakeham, warned editors that the Commission would in future 'tighten up on the use of the public interest defence – by making its deployment and the PCC's judgement on it, more transparent to the public and politicians' (PCC, 1996b). He drew particular attention to the need to protect the interests of innocent and vulnerable relatives including children. He stated categorically that the public interest defence ought not and must not be used by editors 'to drive a coach and horses' through the requirements of the Code (PCC, 1995a).

The Code of Practice does not give a definition of privacy which either describes it as an unqualified right or breaks it down into specific sub-categories concerning the public disclosure of embarrassing private facts, or intrusions into a person's physical seclusion or the unauthorised use of someone's image of likeness. There is a long record of failure on the part of many legal authorities and distinguished committees of enquiry in their search for a definition of privacy that might command general agreement and consent. The reason for this lack of agreement is that although privacy is a fundamental human right it is seldom an absolute right. Our claims to privacy must always be set against other rights such as those involving free-dom of expression and the claims of public interest which, though equally important, often conflict with each other. The task of trying to reconcile these competing claims is central to all the adjudications which the Commis-sion makes when dealing with complaints about intrusions into people's privacy.

THE PATTERN OF COMPLAINTS

Since its establishment in 1991, the Commission has published annual breakdowns of investigated complaints by type of publication. It is not possible to give a consistent series of data from 1991 onwards because the method of classification changed in 1994 when Scottish and Northern Ireland titles were desegregated from the English and Welsh titles. With this proviso in mind, there do not appear to be any significant differences in the types of complaint investigated which might distinguish the regional and the local press from the nationals – or for that matter, the broadsheets from the tabloids.

A comparison of the total number of complaints investigated by the Commission throughout 1994, 1995 and 1996 shows that of the 1,162 complaints resolved, withdrawn, or not pursued by the complainant, approximately 49 per cent related to regionals and locals and 44 per cent to national newspapers (see table 19.1). Of the eighty-nine complaints investigated, adjudicated and upheld by the Commission, just under 30 per cent related to regionals and locals and 66 per cent to national newspapers. Of the 144 complaints investigated, adjudicated and not upheld, 35 per cent related to regional and locals and 64 per cent to national newspapers. Table 19.2 shows the distribution of complaints investigated by type of publication for 1994, 1995 and 1996 (Press Complaints Commission, Annual Reports, 1995, 1996, 1996 and 1997).

In 1996 there were 1,206 regional and local newspaper titles with a total combined circulation of 66.3 million (Newspaper Society, 1997: 9). In June 1997 there were eleven national daily titles with a total combined circulation of 13.6 million and nine national Sunday titles with a combined circulation of 14.5 million (*Press Gazette*, 1997: 10). Given the magnitude of these figures in relation to the small number of complaints received and investigated, further comparison between types of newspapers would have little or no statistical significance. When, however, the number of complaints received is set against the thousands of news items published every day and the millions of potential complainants who read them, it becomes evident that the great majority of newspapers are upholding the Code.

Table 19.1 Complaints investigated by type of publication, 1 January 1994 to 31 December 1996

	Complaints resolved, withdrawn or not pursued		Complaints adjudicated by the Commission			
			Upheld		Not upheld	
	No.	%	No.	%	No.	%
National dailies	324		29		49	
National Sundays	191		29		42	
Total	515	44.3	58	65.9	91	63.8
Regional dailies	245		8		28	
Regional weeklies	153		7		12	
Local free newspapers	56		5		–	
Scottish dailies	70		3		7	
Scottish weeklies	30		3		3	
Scottish free newspapers	2		–		–	
Northern Ireland	11					
Total	567	48.8	26	29.4	50	34.7
Magazines	78		5		1	
Agencies	2		–		1	
Total	80	6.9	5	5.7	2	2.0
Total	**1,162**	**100.0**	**89**	**100.0**	**143**	**100.0**

The data presented in tables 19.1 and 19.2 relate to complaints investigated. If, however, the coverage was extended to all complaints received, it is probable that they would reveal more complaints about regional and local newspapers. In every year since 1993, between 900 and 1,000 of the complaints received were 'not pursued' because there were no prima facie grounds for doing so although they came within the remit of the Commission (there is another substantial category of complaints which are not pursued because they fall within the remit of other regulatory bodies like the Advertising Standards Authority). Many of the cases which come within the remit of the Commission but are 'not pursued' involve complaints about court and inquest reporting by regional and local newspapers. With only a few exceptions, which are specified by the courts, these proceedings are deemed to come within the public domain.

Court and inquest reports

Court reports are important and regular features in the news coverage of local newspapers. With certain exceptions, it is an established principle of open justice in the United Kingdom that court cases are heard in public. This principle serves as a safeguard against judicial error and as a deterrent to perjury. Newspapers have a vitally important role to play in reporting court proceedings and what they do in this respect manifestly serves the public interest (PCC, 1994: 5).

The Commission receives a small but steady flow of complaints about the content of court reports. Most of these complaints involve alleged intrusions into privacy but very few of them are taken to formal adjudication. The

Table 19.2 Complaints investigated by type of publication in 1994, 1995 and 1996

	1994		1995		1996	
	No.	%	No.	%	No.	%
National dailies	140	33.1	122	25.6	140	29.5
National Sundays	78	17.5	94	19.8	90	18.9
Regional dailies	95	21.3	88	18.5	98	20.7
Regional weeklies	50	11.2	61	12.8	61	12.9
Local free newspapers	23	5.2	24	5.0	14	3.0
Magazines	28	6.3	32	6.7	24	5.1
Scottish dailies	18	4.0	35	7.4	27	5.7
Scottish weeklies	10	2.2	13	2.7	13	2.7
Scottish free newspapers	1	0.2	1	0.2	0	0
Northern Ireland	1	0.2	6	1.3	4	0.8
Agencies	2	0.4	0	0	2	0.4
Total	**446**	**100**	**476**	**100**	**473**	**100**

Code simply requires newspapers to publish fair, accurate and contemporaneous reports of these proceedings. The Commission will only take up complaints of this kind if the person concerned can show that the report was inaccurate or biased. Allegations of bias occur when a defendant claims that the press have not reported proceedings in a balanced way by giving undue prominence to the prosecution case or inadequate coverage of an acquittal verdict. All of these complaints about inaccuracy received so far have been resolved or disproved and no complaint about bias has ever been deemed of sufficient gravity to warrant investigation.

Numerous complaints are received about the reporting of inquest proceedings by local newspapers. Most of these complaints involve allegations of privacy invasion which are often linked with complaints about intrusion into grief and shock. Inquests, like other court proceedings, are held in public and such reporting serves the public interest. A complainant would have to produce evidence of inaccuracy before the Commission would agree to investigate. Clause 5, which deals with intrusion into grief and shock, covers only the manner in which information is obtained and not with the style and content of the reporting. There have been a few cases in which relatives have complained about insensitive reporting but the Commission does not adjudicate on complaints concerning issues of taste and decency. In practice the great majority of complaints arising from the reporting of inquests result in 'no breach' decisions.

The publication of addresses

Regional and local newspapers frequently publish addresses in their reports on people in the news. This practice is a frequent cause of complaint. National newspapers seldom publish addresses, except in their reporting of court cases which they do in order to ensure accurate investigation. Regional and local newspapers publish addresses in order to emphasise the local relevance of a story but they seldom go beyond naming the street in which the individual lives.

The Commission published an editorial on this matter in 1992 after a number of cases in which local newspapers had failed to exercise common sense and consideration when publishing addresses (PCC, 1992). In one such case a newspaper published the address of a prominent person's weekend house in Wales with the suggestion that 'he had better not tell the Welsh nationalists or they will come and burn it down'. The Commission, unsurprisingly, upheld the complaint under Clause 3 which deals with privacy. The Commission has always taken the view that: 'There is a commonsense obligation on editors to consider responsibly before publishing information which identifies someone's home, when this may put them at increased risk from terrorists or other criminals.' It has also taken the view that, even in cases where the addresses of prominent people are readily available, the Press is not under any obligation to make it easy for cranks and criminals by saving them the bother of researching telephone books and directories. Newspapers should not assist such people in identifying targets for opprobrium and harassment (PCC, 1992).

In matters relating to court reports, however, there is a strong case to be made in defence of the publication of addresses, not only on grounds of public interest, but in order to avoid possible confusions between people with the same name living in the same locality. In a recent case, a complaint about an invasion of privacy was received from a defendant charged with shouting, swearing, fighting and wielding a sledgehammer. The complainant objected that the local newspaper had published his family's full address in its report. The newspaper responded that the address had been freely available on the charge sheet, that no request to withhold the address had been made by the defence, and no such order had been made by the court. The complaint was rejected.

In another complaint under Clause 3, a prison officer found guilty of drinking and driving complained that the publication of his address in the report of a regional newspaper had imperilled the personal security of his family and himself. The Commission found that no formal request for witholding either his identity or address had been made to the court and therefore rejected the complaint.

The public interest defence carries much less authority in cases in which the newspaper has published the address of a victim or a potential victim of crime. In one such case a local newspaper published a story about a widow who received a £240,000 award, following the death of her husband in a car crash. The report stated that the woman was not at the house on the day of its publication and also mentioned that she tended to go away at weekends. The solicitors, acting on the complainant's behalf, argued that this information was entirely gratuitous and of potential use to criminals. The editor apologised and warned his staff to exercise extreme caution if similar circumstances should arise in future. The Commission appreciated this swift response but none the less considered this breach to be a serious one and upheld the complaint.

In another example, a former rape victim and her husband complained under Clause 3 that, in a local newspaper report of a case which the husband had brought to court, reference was made to their home town and to her previous ordeal. As one of her rapists had already been released, the couple feared that the identification of their location had put her at further risk. Although in this instance an actual address had not been published, the editor responded by writing a personal letter of apology to the couple with an assurance that any further reports would not even mention the town.

Innocent relatives and friends

Complaints are also received under Clause 10 from innocent relatives and friends who feel that they have been mentioned in court reports to an excessive degree only because they are well known in the locality. Clause 10 states that, unless it is contrary to the public's right to know, the press should avoid identifying the relatives or friends of persons convicted or accused of crimes.

In one such case a Chief Constable complained under both Clause 3 (privacy) and Clause 10 (innocent relatives and friends) about an article in the *Bristol Evening Post* headlined 'Avon police chief's son on theft charges'. His son had been charged with the theft and handling of stolen motor vehicles and the Chief Constable had personally launched a campaign against vehicle theft during the previous year. The Chief Constable accepted that the newspaper was entitled to refer to his relationship with the accused but objected to the extent to which this relationship was mentioned. In this case the Commission decided that the degree of reference was not excessive and rejected the complaint.

In the case of John Whittingdale, an MP, the Commission received a complaint under Clause 3 (privacy) and Clause 10 (innocent relatives and friends) about a front-page article in a local newspaper which named him in a report on his half-brother who was being sought by police for possible offences involving child pornography. Mr Whittingdale did not object to being identified but he took exception to being cited in the headline and to the undue prominence given to his relationship.

The newspaper editor invoked a public interest defence on the grounds that its readers had a right to know that a member of their local MP's family was being sought by the police. The Commission rejected this defence on the grounds that the newspaper had featured the complainant on the front page and to a degree that constituted an unjustified infringement of privacy. The complaint was upheld.

Jigsaw identification and children in sex cases

The problem of jigsaw identification still arises from time to time in the reporting of sex cases. Jigsaw identification occurs when one item of information which is innocuous on its own when given in a newspaper report results in the identification of a child by neighbours and relatives when it is combined with equally innocuous items from reports in other national, regional and local newspapers.

The commonest cases of jigsaw identification occur when national press, television and radio publish case details without identifying either the child or the relationship between the child and an adult while local newspapers name the defendant. The use of photographs can also increase the risk of identification (PCC, 1993: 5).

The Commission's Code of Practice Committee, under the Chairmanship of Sir David English, has worked hard to reach an agreement within the newspaper industry that there should be only one procedure in the reporting of sex cases involving children. This agreement stipulates that the adult in the case may be identified but the term 'incest' should not be used. The child must not be identified and no relationship between the child and the adult should be implied in the mode of reporting. None the less, the problem persists because it is a media-wide phenomenon.

The Code of Practice lays down stringent requirements concerning the protection of children in sex cases under Clause 7, the protection of adult and child victims of sexual assault under Clause 12, and the rules to be followed when interviewing or photographing children under Clause 6. It should be noted that, under the Code, the press must not identify victims of sexual assault or publish material likely to contribute to such identification, unless, by law, they are free to do so. As for the identification of children under the age of sixteen, the Code goes further than the law and forbids any identification of children involved in cases concerning sexual offences, whether as victims or as witnesses or defendants.

In practice there have been very few such breaches of the Code. Taken together, the complaints that went to adjudication under Clauses 6, 7 and 12 during 1996 accounted for 3 per cent, or thirteen of the 473 complaints investigated in that year. Of the six complaints made about the interviewing or photographing of children under Clause 6, two were upheld. Of the seven complaints made about the protection of children in sex cases under Clause 7, all were upheld. There were no adjudications under Clause 12 regarding the protection of victims of sexual assault. One of the complaints upheld under Clause 6 and two of those upheld under Clause 7 involved local newspapers.

In a recent case an editor of a local newspaper complained that another local newspaper had identified the crime as well as the nature of the relationship between the perpetrator and the victim in a court report of a case involving the sexual abuse of a child, in breach of Clause 7. The complaint was upheld and the offending editor apologised.

In another more complex case, a woman complained under Clause 7 about a newspaper report headlined 'Woman was sexually abused since the age of five'. The report also implied that there was a family relationship between a child and the man convicted of abusing her. The editor claimed that all the information in the report had been given in court, while apologising for any distress that the report had caused the complainant. The Commission noted that this information had been given in court. Nevertheless, it took the view that the newspaper ought not to have implied a family relationship by stating that the victim had been forced to have sex with the defendant before she went to school. The complaint was therefore upheld on the grounds that the newspaper ought to have made sure that nothing in the report made it possible to draw inferences about the relationship between the accused and the child.

In this particular case a second complaint was received from the magistrate's court about a report in another local newspaper. The court authorities alleged that the children involved were placed at risk of jigsaw identification because of the way in which the case was reported. In the course of the Commission's investigation, the editor acknowledged that he had breached the Code and undertook to ensure that no further breaches of this nature would occur. The complaint was upheld.

CONCLUSION

There do not appear to be any significant quantitative differences in the incidence or types of complaints investigated by the Commission that set the regional and local press apart from the nationals. There do, however, seem to be some qualitative differences with regard to privacy and inaccuracy. In general terms, all complaints about privacy intrusions have to be adjudicated in relation to the claims of freedom of expression and the public interest. In the case of local newspapers, the factor of close proximity adds extra dimensions of resentment and concern to such complaints – as it does with regard to complaints about inaccuracy.

Local newspapers serve smaller and more distinct communities than nationals. Consequently, their readers are more likely to know or recognise the individual families reported in their pages. Whether or not this assumption is correct in a verifiably objective sense, there is some circumstantial evidence in the complaints received that many complainants believe this to be the case.

Local newspaper editors argue that publishing names and, at least, partial addresses are essential elements in good local journalism. In their view, it is the quality of localism that sells local papers. They also claim, with some justification, that such attention to detail prevents confusions arising between people who share the same name and live in the same neighbourhood.

Few people object to publicity when the news about them is complimentary or uncontentious. Many of them are, indeed, quick to complain when they spot inaccuracies in reports about everyday social occasions or special events and ceremonies like births, deaths and marriages. When, however, a news item puts someone in a bad light, local reporting may have a more direct and lasting effect on their daily lives than does national exposure. It is possible that local newspapers are held in higher regard by readers than their national counterparts. In a recent survey, 39 per cent of the respondents said that they trusted what they read in their regional and local papers. The comparable figures for the national dailies and Sundays were, respectively, 8 per cent and 2 per cent (Newspaper Society, 1997: 160).

Local newspapers are, perhaps, better placed by virtue of their closer proximity to local events to confirm what some readers may already suspect to be true. Their news reports add a measure of authority or permanence to the transient exchanges of gossip that are always floating across garden walls and the counters of shops and pubs in every neighbourhood.

Privacy is a paradoxical and complex notion. We can only learn the value of privacy by growing up with other people. If, however, we are to enjoy the pleasures and benefits of a social life we must come to terms with the fact that, while society protects our rights to privacy, it also imposes its own limits on those rights. Most of us like to be well regarded by our families, friends and neighbours. We are pleased when our reputations are enhanced and distressed when they are impugned.

The reputations of public figures are intrinsically matters of public interest. Politicians, public servants, sportsmen and women and entertainers become public figures by choice. They need publicity if they are to achieve their public and private purposes. They expect to receive more attention and less consideration than other people from the press when things go wrong. They also expect, although they do not always receive, more attention and approbation when things go right. In general terms, they complain about intrusions into their privacy only when they believe that the information disclosed is inaccurate or has no relevance to their public lives.

As far as most ordinary people are concerned, the boundaries between their private and public worlds are drawn in essentially local terms. They are more likely to be reported in local newspapers than in the regionals and nationals, although a proportion of local stories are taken up by the mass circulation press. Whatever the coverage may be, the aftermath of adverse publicity lasts longer at the local levels of everyday life where the defences of privacy are most vulnerable. As the American poet Robert Frost once wrote – with tongue in cheek – 'good fences make good neighbours' and good neighbours are people who can be turned to when needed but keep their distance at other times. Local newspapers have the power to break down such fences and once they are down it takes a long time to re-erect them. The same might be said of national newspaper intrusions into people's privacy but it is still their local impact that matters most to ordinary people. Looking back over the past six years, I cannot see any evidence in the pattern of complaints received that would justify the creation of a separate system of self-regulation for the regional and local press. There are, however, a number of very sound reasons for keeping the present unitary system.

First, the ethical foundations of journalistic practice are, and ought to remain, the same for all editors and reporters wherever they are employed. This principle is clearly acknowledged and supported by all types of publisher in the support they give to the Commission. Second, ownership networks extend across national, regional and local titles and many staff move, as a matter of course, over this spectrum during their working careers. Third, where different styles of reporting are followed – as occurs in the variations that give rise to jigsaw identification – progress has been made towards greater consistency *because* we have a unitary system of self-regulation. Fourth, in all matters concerning the defence of self regulation, the industry is able to speak with one voice because it subscribes to one Code of Practice. Fifth, the membership of the Commission is drawn from all branches of the industry and this range of cross-representation greatly enhances the quality of its adjudications.

Newspapers vary in their formats, coverage and types of readership but these differences are far less important than the similarities in the kinds of ethical issues that their editors and reporters have to confront in the course of their daily activities. The Code of Practice belongs to the industry as a whole and the authority of the Commission rests on the inequivocal and ubiquitous support which it receives from the industry in its administration of the Code.

REFERENCES

Calcutt, D. (1990) *Report of the Committee on Privacy and Related Matters*, London: Home Office, HMSO, Cm 1102.

McGregor, O. R. (1991) *A Free Press in a Free Society*, Tom Olsen Memorial Lecture, London.

Newspaper Society (1992) *Britain's Press: In Defence of Self-regulation*, London.

—— (1997) *Reaching the Regions: Regional Newspaper Facts and Figures*, London.

Press Complaints Commission (1992) *Report, August*, no. 12, London.

—— (1993) *Report, October/November*, no. 21, p. 5.

—— (1994) *Report, March/April*, no. 2, London.

—— (1995a) *Moving Ahead: The Development of PCC Policy and Practice in 1995*, London.

—— (1995b) *Annual Report, 1994*, London.

—— (1996a) *Annual Report, 1995*, London.

—— (1996b) *Press Release*, 21 November 1996, London.

—— (1997a) *Annual Report, 1996*, London.

—— (1997b) *Code of Practice*, London.

Press Gazette (1997) National Newspaper ABC Circulations, June 1997, 18 July 1997, p. 10.

Index

Making the Local News

Making the Local News is a comprehensive assessment of contemporary local news production. The opening section surveys the current state of local media, including newspapers, radio, and regional and cable television. Subsequent thematic sections cover the economic organisation of the local press, the range of papers available, from free weeklies and paid-for dailies to 'alternative' newspapers, sources for local news, and changing editorial content.

The contributors analyse the distinctive editorial formats of local daily and weekly papers, free and 'alternative' papers, local press regulation, the coverage of political and business news, and the contribution of national and local government agencies to the construction of local news agendas. Taking into account the rapid technological advances of recent years and changing patterns of industrial relations, the book examines training requirements for local journalists, assesses the implications of advances in multimedia technology, such as the Internet, for the production and reporting practices of local newspapers, and considers the future role of local newspapers within the wider setting of national and multinational media and communications.

Bob Franklin is Reader in Media and Communication Studies at Sheffield University. **David Murphy** is Senior Lecturer at the Manchester School of Management at UMIST.